Responsible Finance India Report 2015

Thank you for choosing a SAGE product!
If you have any comment, observation or feedback,
I would like to personally hear from you.
Please write to me at **contactceo@sagepub.in**

Vivek Mehra, Managing Director and CEO,
SAGE Publications India Pvt Ltd, New Delhi

Bulk Sales

SAGE India offers special discounts
for purchase of books in bulk.
We also make available special imprints
and excerpts from our books on demand.

For orders and enquiries, write to us at

Marketing Department
SAGE Publications India Pvt Ltd
B1/I-1, Mohan Cooperative Industrial Area
Mathura Road, Post Bag 7
New Delhi 110044, India

E-mail us at **marketing@sagepub.in**

Get to know more about SAGE

Be invited to SAGE events, get on our mailing list.
Write today to **marketing@sagepub.in**

Responsible Finance India Report 2015
Client First: Tracking Social Performance Practices

Alok Misra

SAGE www.sagepublications.com
Los Angeles • London • New Delhi • Singapore • Washington DC

First published in 2016 by

 SAGE Publications India Pvt Ltd
B1/I-1 Mohan Cooperative Industrial Area
Mathura Road, New Delhi 110 044, India
www.sagepub.in

SAGE Publications Inc
2455 Teller Road
Thousand Oaks, California 91320, USA

SAGE Publications Ltd
1 Oliver's Yard, 55 City Road
London EC1Y 1SP, United Kingdom

SAGE Publications Asia-Pacific Pte Ltd
3 Church Street
#10-04 Samsung Hub
Singapore 049483

ACCESS Development Services
28, Hauz Khas Village
New Delhi 110 016
www.accessdev.org

Published by Vivek Mehra for SAGE Publications India Pvt Ltd, Phototypeset in 10/13 pt Minion Pro by Diligent Typesetter, Delhi and printed at Sourabh Printers Pvt Ltd, New Delhi.

Library of Congress Cataloging-in-Publication Data Available

ISBN: 978-93-515-0867-0 (PB)

SAGE Production Team: Shambhu Sahu, Isha Sachdeva and Rajinder Kaur

Disclaimer: The views expressed in this publication are those of the authors and do not necessarily reflect the views and policies of ACCESS Development Services.

Cover photograph courtesy: ACCESS.

Sponsors & Partners

CORE SPONSOR

OTHER SPONSORS

Contents

List of Tables, Figures, Boxes, Annexures and Abbreviations

Tables

Figures

Boxes

Annexures

Abbreviations

ABF   Axis Bank Foundation
ADB   Asian Development Bank
AFI   Alliance for Financial Inclusion
AMS   Aprajita Mahila Sangh
ANBC   Adjusted Net Bank Credit
APMAS   Andhra Pradesh Mahila Abhivruddhi Society
APY   Atal Pension Yojana
ATM   Automated Teller Machine
BC   Banking Correspondent
BCAs   Business Correspondent Agents
BMZ   German Federal Ministry for Economic Cooperation and Development
BOP   Bottom of the Pyramid
BPL   Below Poverty Line
BPO   Business Process Outsourcing
BRLPS   Bihar Rural Livelihoods Promotion Society
CBNA   Capacity Building Needs Assessment
CBO   Community-based Organisation
CBS   Core Banking System
CCFL   Citi Centre for Financial Literacy
CEGSIL   CSC e-Governance Services India Limited
CEO   Chief Executive Officer
COO   Chief Operation Officer
CFI   Centre for Financial Inclusion
CGAP   Consultative Group to Assist the Poor

CGT	Compulsory Group Trainings
CIBIL	Credit Information Bureau (India) Limited
CIC	Credit Information Company
CoC	Code of Conduct
COCA	Code of Conduct Assessment
CPP	Client Protection Principles
CRISIL	Credit Rating Information Services of India Limited
CSCs	Common Service Centres
CSP	Customer Service Point
CSR	Corporate Social Responsibility
DBT	Direct Benefit Transfer
DFID	Department for International Development
DICGC	Deposit Insurance and Credit Guarantee Corporation
DRDA	District Rural Development Agency
ESG	Environment, Social and Governance
FAO	Food and Agricultural Organization
FAS	Financial Access Survey
FCI	Financial Capability Index
FGD	Focus Group Discussion
FIDWG	Financial Inclusion Data Working Group
FIF	Financial Inclusion Fund
FILC	Financial Inclusion and Literacy Centres
FIP	Financial Inclusion Plan
FITF	Financial Inclusion Technology Fund
FLCs	Financial Literacy Centres
FLCC	Financial Literacy and Counseling Centres
FPC	Fair Practices Code
FSDC	Financial Stability and Development Council
GBA	Gramin Bank of Aryavat
GDP	Gross Domestic Product
GFSPL	Grameen Financial Services Private Limited
GKFSPL	Grameen Koota Financial Services Pvt Ltd.
GNI	Gross National Income
GPFI	Global Partnership for Financial Inclusion
GRT	Group Recognition Test
GTZ	German Technical Cooperation
GVC	Governance and Value Creation
HDI	Human Development Index
HiH	Hand in Hand
IBL	Individual Business Loan
IBZL	Individual Bazaar Loan
IFC	International Finance Corporation
IFMR	Institute for Financial Management and Research
IIM	Indian Institute of Management
IMEF	India Microfinance Equity Fund
IMF	International Monetary Fund
IMFP	India Microfinance Platform
INFE	International Network on Financial Education
IRCS	IFMR Rural Channels and Services

IRDA	Insurance Regulatory and Development Authority
IRDP	Integrated Rural Development Programme
ISMW	Indian School of Microfinance for Women
IVDP	Integrated Village Development Project
JLG	Joint Liability Group
KGFS	Kshetriya Grameen Financial Services
KPI	Key Performance Indicators
KRA	Key Result Area
KYC	Know Your Customer
LAB	Local Area Bank
LDM	Lead District Manager
M-CRIL	Micro-Credit Rating International Limited
MBT	Mutual Benefit Trust
MDBS	Mann Deshi Business School for Rural Women
MDGs	Millennium Development Goals
MEL	Micro Enterprise Loan
MFDEF	Microfinance Development Equity Fund
MEPMA	Mission for Elimination of Poverty in Municipal Areas
MFI	Microfinance Institution
MFIN	Microfinance Institutions Network
MFO	Microfinance Opportunities
MIR	Microfinance Institutional Rating
MIS	Management Information System
MIX	Microfinance Information Exchange
MP	Madhya Pradesh
MPI	Multi-dimensional Poverty Index
MSDF	Michael & Susan Dell Foundation
MUDRA	Micro Units Development and Refinance Agency Ltd.
MYRADA	Mysore Resettlement and Development Agency
NABARD	National Bank for Agriculture and Rural Development
NAFiL	National Alliance for Financial Literacy
NBFC	Non-banking Finance Company
NBFI	Non-bank Financial Institution
NCAER	National Council of Applied Economic Research
NCAF	New Capital Adequacy Framework
NCD	Non-convertible Debenture
NCFE	National Centre for Financial Education
NFLAT	National Financial Literacy Assessment Test
NGO	Non-governmental Organisation
NHG	Neighbourhood Group
NICT	Network for Information and Computer Technology
NISM	National Institute of Securities Markets
NJGB	Narmada Jhabua Gramin Bank
NPA	Non-performing Assets
NPL	National Poverty Line
NPS	National Pension Scheme
NRLM	National Rural Livelihoods Mission
NSFE	National Strategy for Financial Education
OECD	Organisation for Economic Co-operation and Development

OER	Operating Expense Ratio
PACS	Primary Agricultural Credit Societies
PB	Payment Bank
PFRDA	Pension Fund Regulatory and Development Authority
PIIF	Principles for Investors in Inclusive Finance
PMJDY	Prime Minister Jan Dhan Yojana
PMJJBY	Pradhan Mantri Jeevan Jyoti Bima Yojana
PMMY	Prime Minister Mudra Yojana
PMSBY	Pradhan Mantri Suraksha Bima Yojana
POS	Point of Sale
PPI	Progress Out of Poverty Index
PRADAN	Professional Assistance for Development Action
PRSP	Poverty Reduction Strategy Policy
PSIG	Poorest State Inclusive Growth
PSL	Priority Sector Lending
PSMS	Priya Sakhi Mahila Sangh
RBI	Reserve Bank of India
RFF	Responsible Finance Forum
RFIP	Rural Financial Institutions Programme
RGMVP	Rajiv Gandhi Mahila Vikas Pariyojna
RIDF	Rural Infrastructure Development Fund
RoA	Return on Assets
RP	Resource Person
RRB	Regional Rural Bank
RSETI	Rural Self Employment Training Institutes
SAAS	Software As A Service
SAG	Self Affinity Groups
SBLP	SHG-Bank Linkage Programme
SDC	Swiss Agency for Development and Cooperation
SEBI	Securities and Exchange Board of India
SFA	Swadhaar FinAccess
SFB	Small Finance Bank
SFIF	State Financial Inclusion Forums
SGSY	Swarnjayanti Swarojgar Yojana
SHGs	Self-help Groups
SHPA	Self-help Promoting Agency
SIDBI	Small Industries Development Bank of India
SIEFL	School for Investor Education and Financial Literacy
SKDRDP	Sri Kshetra Dharmasthala Rural Development Project
SKS	Swayam Krishi Sangam
SLBC	State Level Bankers' Committee
SM	Sangam Manager
SME	Small and Medium Enterprises
SPM	Social Performance Management
SPTF	Social Performance Task Force
SPV	Special Purpose Vehicle
SRO	Self-regulatory Organisation
TL	Transformation Loan
ToT	Training of Trainers

TSP	Tata Consultancy Services
UBGB	Uttar Bihar Gramin Bank
UCB	Urban Cooperative Bank
UCoC	Unified Code of Conduct
UIDAI	Unique Identification Authority of India
UNPRI	United Nations Principles for Responsible Investment
UNSGSA	United Nations Secretary-General's Special Advocate
UP	Uttar Pradesh
USAID	United States Agency for International Development
USSPM	Universal Standards of Social Performance
VKC	Village Knowledge Centre
VLEs	Village-level Entrepreneurs
WASH	Water Sanitation and Hygiene

Foreword

The financial inclusion space in India is witnessing really exciting and eventful times with the roll-out of several focused programmes and policies, and setting up of new institutions for enhancing delivery of comprehensive financial services to the unbanked and poor. August 2014 was a landmark month with two significant initiatives—announcement of the ambitious Pradhan Mantri Jan Dhan Yojana (PMJDY) by the Government of India for enabling universal access of banking services and the Reserve Bank of India (RBI) seeking inputs on revolutionary policies for setting up two categories of differentiated banks for furthering financial inclusion. Both these initiatives have come a long way in a short time period of 15 months. While the PMJDY claims opening of 180 million new bank accounts along with the implementation of a slew of adjunct schemes covering insurance, pension and credit, the RBI has also kept pace moving from draft guidelines to finalising the in-principle licensees of the new Small Finance Banks (SFBs) and Payments Banks (PBs). Another noteworthy milestone this year was the launch of Bandhan Bank with 500 branches and over 2,000 service centres across 24 states; expectations are high that this would be a universal bank focused on 'small clients'. IDFC Bank also took-off with 65% of its first 23 branches located in rural areas of Madhya Pradesh.

The *Microfinance Social Performance Report* was first published in 2011 as an annual report in view of the need for documenting and showcasing best practices followed by microfinance institutions (MFIs) in social performance management (SPM), covering the areas of client protection, client targeting, human resource management, governance, products and services, and tracking of outcomes; as also the role of other sectoral stakeholders including investors, lenders and technical agencies in promoting greater social performance and responsible lending by MFIs. This was largely in response to a crisis faced by the sector post the Andhra Pradesh Ordinance in 2010 that brought MFI activity practically to a standstill across the country. Over five years since, the MFI sector has exhibited exemplary spirit to revert on a path of growth and stability, learning from the past and rebuilding the basic tenets of microfinance delivery. The social performance reports of the last four years have tracked this rebuilding phase from a lens of client centricity and responsible finance, tracking and reporting social performance data, celebrating good practices, and highlighting gaps and issues in the policy and practice.

Since the MFI model is market based, driven largely by private players, and deals with 'poor and vulnerable' clients, the onus for adherence to principles of 'do no harm' as well as demonstrating evidence of 'doing good' on these institutions has been high. However, it is the same set of clients that other channels of last mile delivery of financial services—SHG-Bank Linkage Programme (SBLP), business correspondent model, cooperative and community-based microfinance and downscaling of direct banking outreach—are catering to. It is, therefore, critical for all such models and channels to adopt and integrate at least the client protection principles, both as mandated by regulation and voluntarily, and work on client financial capability building. While the first report was focused entirely on MFI model, subsequent editions have attempted commentary and analysis on responsible finance aspects of other strands of microfinance and financial inclusion including community-based microfinance, SHG-bank linkage and the agent banking channel.

Since the SPM framework is uniquely and specifically designed around the MFI model, in order to reflect the broadening of its ambit to include diverse channels, the document has been rechristened to *Responsible Finance India Report*. This year's report nevertheless continues to focus on the MFIs in more detail than the other service providers on account of two reasons. First, the MFI sector is again on a surge after overcoming the period of uncertainty and recouping, recording 60% annual growth in the last fiscal year, which necessitated that a stock taking of the progress on social performance standards is undertaken along with a discourse on risks associated with high growth and the role of various actors including MFIs, investors and regulator in managing these. Second, analysis and reporting on the responsible finance pertaining to other formal financial service providers is limited in the absence of granular data on responsible finance indicators and relevant studies and institutional assessments. The report does cover progress on SHG-bank linkage and touches up on the potential of new institutions such as SFBs and Micro Units Development and Refinance Agency Ltd. (MUDRA) to impact financial inclusion with recommendations on integrating responsible finance while these are still taking shape.

With Girija Srinivasan announcing her retirement from the authorship of the *Social Performance Report* after commendably anchoring the first four editions, our quest to identify an appropriate author was tough. The candidature of Dr Alok Misra for leading a document of this nature was irrefutable, and we are glad and grateful that in spite of his tremendously demanding professional commitments, he agreed to author the report. It was great that Veena Yamini Annadanam was able to join to contribute the important chapter on financial literacy. I deeply appreciate and thank all the individuals and institutions that were interviewed and contacted by Alok Misra and Veena Yamini Annadanam for the purpose of data collection for the report. I am thankful to the Board of Directors of ACCESS ASSIST and the Inclusive Finance India Group of Advisors, both led by Mr Y.C. Nanda, for their counsel and guidance on the scope and structuring of the report.

I am glad that this initiative of a 'country SPM report' conceived by Vipin Sharma, Managing Trustee of ASSIST, in 2010 has been able to contribute to the knowledge and deliberation on social performance and responsible finance, and is in some manner regarded as an important and unique reference document both within India and outside. Vipin's spirit and mentoring has continued to guide the evolution of this document over all the five editions. We sincerely thank the sponsors—Standard Chartered Bank, SIDBI and the World Bank Group—for consistently extending financial support to this endeavour for last five years, and their teams for providing technical inputs and guidance. We also thank Dia Vikas Capital for continued interest in supporting our efforts. CRIF High Mark came on board this year as the technical partner for the first time contributing important credit bureau data for analysis. We are happy to re-associate with SAGE Publications as the publishing partner for all the annual documents of ACCESS, and hope that this will help with effective dissemination of the report. I must mention the tireless efforts of my colleague, Anshu Singh, in coordinating the process at ASSIST headquarters and Lalitha for helping with logistics, as also the state teams for their support.

The quest to expand the ambit of the responsible finance lens from MFIs to the more mainstream bank-led models of financial inclusion is a long journey for which the report attempts to make a beginning. There are several questions that the next couple of editions of this document will seek to report on. How will the new Bandhan Bank take the spirit of SPM implemented as an MFI to the universal banking format? Will the MFIs that transition to SFBs continue to demonstrate commitment to SPM as an important operating principle? How will PBs demystify technology to provide effective last mile services to poor clients across the country? Are the financial service providers able to deepen penetration to the remotest geographical areas, and the marginalised and vulnerable communities? We hope that the *Responsible Finance India Report* will pave the way for tracking of appropriate data and studies as also policy advocacy for instilling greater cognizance on the need for financial services being inclusive as well as responsible.

Radhika Agashe
Executive Director, ACCESS ASSIST

Preface

I have been an active participant in the journey of India's financial sector to reach the unbanked. My involvement began in 1992, when the Integrated Rural Development Programme (IRDP) was at its peak, microfinance through SBLP was launched as a pilot and the financial sector policy was being shaped by the recommendations of the Narasimham Committee. Over the past 23 years, momentous changes have taken place and the current phase is ushering in a drastically new paradigm; never has the financial inclusion policy looked so promising and ambitious. The space for financial inclusion of the excluded exhibits interplay of microfinance (both SBLP and MFIs), PMJDY, SFBs, PBs, MUDRA, banking correspondents and the existing commercial banks, regional rural banks (RRBs) and cooperative banks. Much of the initiatives, like SFBs and MUDRA, have taken shape over the last one year or so. Backed by advances in unique identification number (Aadhaar) and technology, the policy objective of reaching the excluded has never looked more achievable. I am thankful that after four years of social performance reports, Vipin Sharma, CEO, Access Development Services, asked me to write a rechristened (*Responsible Finance India Report*) for 2015. I deeply value the trust reposed in me by Vipin, more so because of the fast-paced changes underway in the sector.

Amidst all these changes, the importance of 'Responsible Finance' has only increased, as it is critical that clients' needs and preferences are accorded primacy in delivery of financial services. Dealing with clients belonging to the lower rungs of society makes it more important. At this crucial juncture, all stakeholders need to ensure that mistakes of the past are not repeated; outreach without matching needs of clients is not sustainable. The microfinance sector in India accounts for an outreach of nearly 100 million clients and plays a vital role in financial inclusion of the excluded. MFIs have weathered the 2010 crisis and at present the possibility of transformation as banks have opened new vistas. SBLP after a period of rapid growth has slowed down and is in need of new energy. Post 2010, MFIs have seen a slew of regulatory and industry initiatives to veer them back towards client centricity, and globally there is consensus in the form of Universal Standards of Social Performance (USSPM) on parameters/indicators on which the performance of double bottom-line institutions should be assessed. Considering the distinct space occupied by both forms of microfinance in providing financial services to the excluded, the regulatory focus after 2010 and availability of responsible finance metrics for performance assessment, it is natural that much of the report focuses on microfinance. The coverage of new institutions like SFBs and MUDRA is with a view to ensure that they continue to serve the objectives for which they have been formed. I hope that in coming years, the stakeholders will be able to evolve responsible finance metrics for mainstream financial institutions like banks; this report can serve as defining the broad contours of responsible finance.

A report of this type requires cooperation and sharing of information from several stakeholders. I have a lot of people and organisations to thank for providing data, sparing time for discussions, sharing study findings and reports, and pointing towards useful sources of information.

The starting point for me was the valuable insights provided by Girija Srinivasan who authored the past reports. The chapters on MFIs have benefitted immensely from the insights shared by MFI heads and senior management [Udaya Kumar of Grameen Financial Services Private Limited (GFSPL), Manoj Nambiar of Arohan, P.N. Vasudevan and H.K.N. Raghavan of Equitas, Radhakrishnan of Janalakshmi, Ritesh Chatterjee of SKS, Anup Singh of Sonata, Devesh Sachdev of Fusion, N. Jeyaseelan of Hand in Hand (HiH), Sandhya Suresh of EMFIL and Sakshi Sodhi of Satin], Ratna Vishwanathan, CEO of MFIN, Bankers and Investors (A.K. Samal and Prakash Kumar, SIDBI; Arindom Datta, Rabo Bank; Prashant Thakkar and Balaji Standard Chartered; Srinivas Bonam, IndusInd; Saneesh Singh, Dia Vikas; Arvind Kodikal, Triodos; Absikar Shrestha, MICROVEST; Anya Berezhna, Symbiotics; and Charulata Singal, responsAbility). Equally significant was the contribution of 28 MFIs who responded to the survey questionnaire sent out for collection of data on SPM. It was my good fortune that these senior functionaries spared time to provide valuable insights and data. Girish Bhaskaran Nair from International Finance Corporation (IFC) and Ragini Chaudhary from Department for International Development (DFID) were helpful in listening to my assumptions and ideas, providing feedback as well as data. The data provided by Parijat Garg, CRIF High Mark Credit Information Services, has been valuable in analysing risks. Special thanks are due to Manoj Sharma, Director, Micro-Save, and his team for hosting me and being generous in providing their sector insights and sector-wide reports on responsible business practices of MFIs, Governance and Code of Conduct assessments.

The credit for chapter on SBLP is due to National Bank for Agriculture and Rural Development (NABARD) Chairman Dr H.K. Bhanwala, who not only agreed for an interview but also facilitated discussions with key persons. His passionate exposition of digitisation pilot made me delve deep into this. Subrata Gupta, Chief General Manger (CGM), NABARD, and G.C. Chintala, CGM, NABARD, were gracious in agreeing to long meetings at short notice. Amit Arora from GIZ liberally shared the learnings from SHGs as banking correspondent (BC) project. I am thankful to Dr R. Bhaskaran for providing key insights into SHG data and N.S. Rathore for helping with the documentation of innovative things under SBLP.

I sincerely acknowledge the constant encouragement provided by Professor H.K. Pradhan, XLRI Jamshedpur, during the writing period, and Y.C. Nanda and Brij Mohan for sharing their views. I am thankful to Radhika and Anshu from ACCESS ASSIST for their help throughout the assignment. My colleagues Gaurav Prateek, Shraddha Jha, Shahanur Al Arif and Anindita helped with data and proof of chapters. Finally, I owe thanks to my institution, Micro-Credit Rating International Limited (M-CRIL), for accommodating my writing schedule with work commitments, and also liberally sharing the annual microfinance reviews and social rating reports. The list can go on and on but considering the length limitation, I seek apologies from those whose names I have missed.

The report brings out that despite the enormous ground covered since the Andhra Pradesh crisis by MFIs, there are issues, which require attention, and risks keep emerging. To ensure strong commitment to clients, MFIs aided by stakeholders will need to proactively work on integrating social performance in governance and business planning, product diversity, managing growth in saturated markets and responsibility to staff. Under SBLP, while the digitisation pilot has breathed in a new ray of hope, the lack of synergy with NRLM, deterioration in portfolio quality and stagnation in outreach call for a rethink on both strategy and design. I hope that action on the suggestions in the last chapter will strengthen the cause of responsible finance for the excluded by the existing and emerging institutions.

Alok Misra

Changing discourse: Rural finance to inclusive finance to responsible finance

1.1 RAPIDLY CHANGING LANDSCAPE OF FINANCIAL SERVICES IN INDIA

The past year has been a watershed year for India in enabling access to financial services for all. Building on the work done over last four decades starting with nationalisation of banks in 1969 to designing policies for inclusion and creating specialised institutions, last year (2014–15) witnessed a slew of innovative policies for furthering financial inclusion. Change of guard in both Central Government and the Central Bank has added to the momentum.

It started with the Mor committee[1] report in 2014, which set an ambitious agenda for financial inclusion suggesting that by 1 January 2016, every adult Indian would have an individual, full service, safe and secure electronic bank account, and there will be an access point within walking distance of 15 minutes. Several other milestones pertaining to credit and insurance were also spelt out and backed by enabling policy recommendations. Before the buzz could recede, the RBI released draft guidelines for licensing of small finance banks (SFBs) and payments banks (PBs) in July 2014 and final guidelines in November 2014[2] seeking applications from potential candidates. RBI subsequently declared the list of 11 successful applicants for setting up PBs in end August 2015 and the list of 10 successful applicants for SFBs in mid-September 2015. In between, the new government at the centre came up with an ambitious programme for ensuring universal coverage of bank accounts under Prime Minister Jan Dhan Yojana (PMJDY)[3] in August 2014 on a mission mode. Having achieved opening of 10.32 crore bank accounts by end July[4] 2015, it is now in its second phase which promises universal accident/health insurance and

pension through Pradhan Mantri Suraksha Bima Yojana (PMSBY), Pradhan Mantri Jeevan Jyoti Bima Yojana (PMJJBY) and Atal Pension Yojana (APY). Even as the financial sector was comprehending the implications of these far reaching initiatives, the idea of MUDRA[5] Bank was announced in the budget speech of the Finance Minister for the year 2015–16. In a landscape filled with various types of financial institutions, the underlying rationale offered for MUDRA was the catch phrase 'funding the unfunded'. The pace with which MUDRA was established has taken many industry players by surprise; the institution is, however, a reality now and has started to offer refinance for three types of loan products based on maturity of the micro enterprise being funded.

Though these new initiatives mainly cover the mainstream financial sector but have implications for the microfinance sector. The SFB guidelines made special provisions for MFIs to be considered for SFB license and were seen as providing the MFIs with a framework to graduate to a more formal and tightly regulated legal form of a bank. Not surprisingly, considering the policy tightening post Andhra Pradesh crisis of 2010, 24 MFIs applied for being considered for SFB license, and 8 of the 10 in principle licensees are MFIs. Additionally, the RBI effected two major policy changes for non-banking financial company-microfinance institutions (NBFC-MFIs). First, it conferred self-regulatory organisation (SRO) status to microfinance institutions network (MFIN) in June 2014 and to Sa-Dhan in March 2015. Second, based on consistent advocacy by the industry for relaxing household income norms, the RBI in April 2015[6] raised the annual household income limit of eligible borrowers in rural areas to ₹1 lakh and in urban and peri-urban areas to ₹1.6 lakh as also the maximum permissible individual indebtedness level. These policy relaxations will help the MFIs to move towards the micro-enterprise segment and will serve to increase their client base.

With these new institutions and policy initiatives in the last one year or so, the financial architecture in India has seen changes comparable only to the era of bank nationalisation in 1970s. How do these changes affect the financial inclusion landscape in India and how efficiently and responsibly is this done will be answered in the near future as the initiatives get grounded and scaled up. Meanwhile, the figures show that financial exclusion in India is high and the empirical research shows that costs of exclusion have a direct bearing on India's quest for growth and development. In this scenario of multiple new initiatives, microfinance continues to hold a critical place in financial inclusion with the outreach of both the models [MFIs and SHG-Bank Linkage Programme (SBLP)] together touching nearly 100 million customers.

1.2 DIMENSIONS OF FINANCIAL EXCLUSION AND ITS LINK TO GROWTH AND DEVELOPMENT

1.2.1 Dimensions of financial exclusion

Data on outreach of financial services in India continues to be in silos with RBI reporting figures of scheduled banks, NABARD reporting figures

of cooperative banks and SBLP and industry associations of MFIs reporting their own set of data pertaining to their members. Data pertaining to banking correspondents (BCs) is available with individual banks. Moreover, the data provided by various institutions does not have consistent format and importantly the critical aspect of 'usage' closely associated with the concept of 'responsible finance' is missing. In this backdrop, the data produced by the World Bank in the form of Global FINDEX[7] database provides a comprehensive picture covering all channels and also significantly captures demand-side indicators to track the financial lives of individuals over time. The recent dataset released in 2015 is the second round of data under Global FINDEX initiative and captures progress over 2011 data set. India has shown significant improvement under key indicators (Table 1.1) but the problem of exclusion continues to be huge and becomes more challenging if access data is juxtaposed.

While effect of new initiatives described in section 1.1 especially PMJDY has not been captured in the 2014 data, the significant jump in percentage of adults having a savings account is directly attributable to the earlier version of PMJDY like mass enrolment programme called financial inclusion plan (FIP), which focused on opening of basic services banking account. When the numbers of PMJDY are taken into account in the next round, it is envisaged that figures will indicate near universal coverage. While this is a laudable achievement, close review

Table 1.1 Global FINDEX database for India

Population, age 15+ (million) 887.9 gross national income per capita ($) 1,570		
S. No. Particulars	Country data (2011)	Country data (2014)
1. **Account (% age 15+)**		
All adults	35.2	53.1
Women	26.5	43.1
Adults belonging to the poorest 40%	27.1	43.9
2. **Mobile Account (% age 15+)**		
All adults	2.2	2.4
3. **Savings in the Past Year (% age 15+)**		
Saved at a financial institution	22.4	14.4
4. **Credit in the Past Year (% age 15+)**		
Borrowed from a financial institution	7.7	6.4
Borrowed from family or friends	19.7	32.3
Borrowed from a private informal lender	6.6	12.6

Source: http://www.worldbank.org/en/programs/globalfindex

of the data points to the agenda for future work. The mass opening of accounts akin to 'quantitative easing' has not translated to usage with only 14.4% saving any amount in the last year. Similarly, as the focus till now has been on deposits, the credit side is lagging behind with only 7.7% borrowing from a financial institution in the last year. Figures for other much needed financial services like pension, remittance and insurance also remain much below the desired level.

The real hard part of financial inclusion begins now, which will require work on the demand side. Opening of savings accounts does not entail much decision on the part of the excluded but continuous usage and expanding the coverage to credit, insurance, remittances and pension will require extensive financial literacy training to change attitudes and mind set. The other critical part relates to ensuring that institutions provide these services transparently and in a cost-effective manner. Exclusion is more pronounced in the lower-income segment and considering their vulnerability, the inclusion approach also needs to be 'responsible'.

1.2.2 Link of financial inclusion to development

As India moves towards expanding financial inclusion, it is worthwhile to emphasise that various research studies have shown a clear link between financial inclusion and growth. The international monetary fund (IMF) recently released the 2013 data of their financial access survey (FAS).[8] The FAS aims to map financial inclusion with the help of some basic indicators (e.g., number of deposits per 1,000 people). The 2013 data for the first time included two indicators on mobile money. The FAS provides geographic and demographic data worldwide, offering a strong quantitative underpinning to the theoretical literature linking financial inclusion with economic growth. The positive correlation between increase in the use of commercial banks services (a measure of financial inclusion) and increase in gross domestic product (GDP) per capita (a measure of economic growth) is especially noteworthy when comparing financial inclusion trends. Among African countries reporting data on commercial bank depositors, for instance, depositors per 1,000 adults experienced a fivefold increase from 2004 to 2013, while simultaneously achieving a 40% growth in real GDP per capita.

Similarly a comparative analysis of the growth rates of various countries over three decades by Honohan and Beck, 2007[9] (Figure 1.1) has brought out evidence regarding the correlation between deeper financial system and economic growth. At the given level of national income, the incidence of poverty is also less in nations having deep financial system.

The World Bank Group's *Global Financial Development Report 2014*[10] provides strong evidence to the link between inclusion and development. The report highlights new evidence that people, especially the poor, benefit greatly from using basic payments, savings and insurance services. It concludes that financial inclusion can be a powerful accelerator of economic growth and help achieve the goals of eliminating extreme poverty and building shared prosperity.

The report also stresses that achieving those benefits requires addressing market and government failures. It suggests that policymakers need to provide an enabling environment of strong laws and regulations, good information and healthy competition among financial service providers. By doing this, the private sector is encouraged to embrace new technologies, such as mobile banking and biometric borrower identification, and also create new and innovative products, such as commitment savings accounts or index insurance.

In the wake of overwhelming evidence, the thrust on financial inclusion has to be the key strategy of public policy in India aiming to achieve growth with equality and inclusiveness. However, as the title of this report suggests, the global discourse has moved beyond inclusive finance to responsible finance. The following sections delineate the movement of global thought from inclusive finance to responsible finance and its comparison with changes in India's approach to inclusion.

1.3 GLOBAL FOCUS ON INCLUSIVE FINANCE

In most developing countries, the earlier financial sector policy focused on rural finance and mostly pursued providing subsidised credit through state controlled or directed institutions to rural segments of population. This approach was based on the premise that rural micro-entrepreneurs are unable to organise themselves; they need subsidised credit for increasing their income and are too poor to

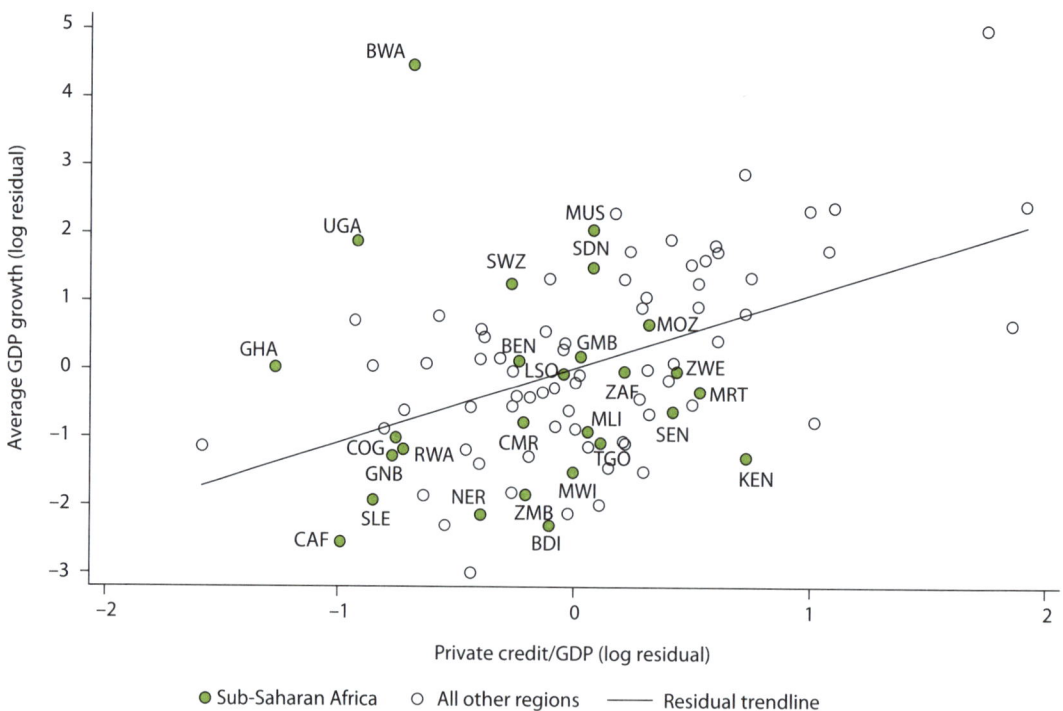

Figure 1.1 Gross domestic product (GDP) growth rates and financial depth, 1980–2003

Source: Based on data beck 2006.
Notes: This figure plots for 99 countries the relationship between private credit from the banking system, expressed as percentage of GDP, and average annual growth in GDP per capita, controlling for the effect of initial (1980) GDP per capita, inflation, trade openness, government consumption, average years of schooling and black-market premium.

save. Under this approach, the distortions and imperfections in rural credit markets were addressed through government interventions, and while the degree of interventions varied across countries, most of developing countries pursued these policies from 1950 to 1980. This approach was critiqued initially by the economists at the Ohio State University[11] and later in the United States Agency for International Development (USAID) spring review (1972/73) of Small Farmer Credit covering 60 reports on specific farm credit programmes in developing countries and by a World Conference on Credit for Farmers in Developing Countries in 1975 organised by Food and Agricultural Organization (FAO). The ineffectiveness of the approach was argued as interest rate subsidies, administrative loan allocations and targeted credit programmes that failed to reach the intended beneficiaries as also displaced informal sources of credit. It was also pointed out that these interventions led to a heavy economic cost in the form of weak financial structure. Exclusive focus on agriculture finance

in place of rural finance promoted unbalanced overall development. These developments coupled with the emergence of microfinance demonstrating sustainable private sector approach to providing financial services to the poor, shifted the focus from rural finance to inclusive finance in 1990s.

The term 'financial exclusion' was first coined in 1993 by geographers concerned about bank branch closures and the resulting limited physical access to banking services. This idea gained momentum but it was not until around 1998 that the term was first used in a broader sense to describe people who have limited access to mainstream financial services.[12] This was followed by countries and global institutions like the World Bank focusing on financial inclusion and microfinance. In 1998, HM Treasury created the Credit Union Taskforce, and 14 policy action teams were established in the United Kingdom. One of these teams had the specific task of developing a strategy to increase access to financial services for people living in deprived neighbourhoods. The World Bank mainstreamed microfinance as part of its poverty reduction strategy policy (PRSP), and Asian Development Bank (ADB) came up with a microfinance development strategy in 1999. Though financial inclusion was not a direct goal under millennium development goals (MDGs), James Wolfenshon, former World Bank President, acknowledged the role of microfinance in reducing poverty and a critical condition for achievement of MDGs.

While the decade of 1990 and 2000 saw the focus shift to emphasis on sustainability, role of private sector, microfinance and financial inclusion backed by numerous efforts worldwide at both institutional and country level, Maya declaration in 2011[13] by Alliance for Financial Inclusion (AFI) members can be considered as the first large scale global commitment to financial inclusion. Established in 2008 with support from Bill & Melinda Gates Foundation and AusAid, the AFI is the world's largest network of financial inclusion policymakers from developing and emerging economies who use a poly-lateral development approach that encourages peer to peer learning and sharing of best practices in order to improve access to and quality of financial services available in their countries. In 2011, the members ratified the Maya Declaration,[14] which has since then become a crucial international framework for catalysing financial inclusion through bottom-up initiatives by the participating countries. Though, several countries used the forum to announce new initiatives to expand their population's access to financial services, the declaration remained more at the level of stating commitment and broad principles for financial inclusion. The declaration recognised the critical importance of financial inclusion for empowering and transforming the lives of people, especially the poor, its role in improving national and global financial stability and integrity, and its essential contribution to strong and inclusive growth in developing and emerging market countries. It committed the financial regulators and policymakers of member states to:

a. putting in place a financial inclusion policy that creates an enabling environment for cost-effective access to financial services that makes full use of appropriate innovative technology and substantially lowers the unit cost of financial services;

b. implementing a sound and proportional regulatory framework that achieves the complementary goals of financial inclusion, financial stability and financial integrity;

c. recognising consumer protection and empowerment as key pillars of financial inclusion efforts to ensure that all people are included in their country's financial sector; and

d. making evidence-based financial inclusion policy a priority by collecting and analysing comprehensive data, tracking the changing profile of financial inclusion and producing comparable indicators in the network.

The Maya Declaration was followed by the Sasana Accord which was signed by the members of the AFI network in 2013 in order to strengthen the effectiveness of the Maya Declaration (see Box 1.1). The Sasana accord recognises the wide-ranging impacts of the institutional commitments to galvanise national financial inclusion initiatives, outlines concrete actions to further strengthen their effectiveness, primarily through setting quantifiable national goals, as well as measuring and reporting progress based on the core set of indicators identified by AFI's Financial Inclusion Data Working Group (FIDWG). As per the last report of 2014,[15] the accord has been able to have 47 institutional commitments on quantitative targets, which is 50% of the total AFI membership of 95 countries.

Box 1.1 Sasana accord

In September 2013, we, the members of AFI on the occasion of the AFI Global Policy Forum held at Sasana Kijang in Kuala Lumpur, following the wide ranging impact and contributions to financial inclusion made in the Maya Declaration and the commitments it has inspired, hereby agree to strengthen the effectiveness of the members' commitments by undertaking the following actions:

• We will strive to achieve our commitments to financial inclusion through a set of measurable national goals.

• We will measure our progress in financial inclusion based on common indicators as identified and quantified in the core set of AFI Financial

Inclusion Data and will publicly release this information annually.

- We will continue to work in a cooperative and cohesive manner to integrate the financial inclusion agenda into our countries' policies and programmes, and ensure that the implementation of financial inclusion at the national level will contribute towards improvement of the underserved in the global community.
- We will reinforce our institutional capacity and talent for formulation and implementation of effective financial inclusion policies that will deliver the optimal impact.

Source: http://www.bnm.gov.my/documents/2013/Sasana_Accord_AFI2013.pdf

In November 2010, the G20 leaders concretised their commitment to financial inclusion by approving a Financial Inclusion Action Plan, and creating the G20 Global Partnership for Financial Inclusion (GPFI), a body to oversee its implementation. Since its launch in late 2010, the GPFI has emerged as an important global force for financial inclusion, with its recommendations endorsed at every subsequent G20 summit. At their Brisbane Summit in November 2014, the G20 Leaders reaffirmed financial inclusion as a key element in the body's broader development agenda, approving a revised Financial Inclusion Action Plan that retains a strong focus on regulation and standard-setting. Queen Máxima of the Netherlands is the United Nations Secretary-General's Special Advocate for Inclusive Finance for Development (UNSGSA). Since June 2011, she has also been Honorary Patron of the GPFI in her capacity as UNSGSA, and her main function in the two capacities is to strengthen the synergy between the UN and the G20 nations on promoting universal access to financial services.[16] Consultative Group to Assist the Poor (CGAP) plays an active part in these initiatives being involved in all the sub-groups of GPFI and supports the work of UNSGSA through its global policy architecture work.

It is evident that financial inclusion has occupied centre stage in global development discourse and is one of the key focus areas. Based on experience, it is being realised that while there has been a major progress from state owned and supply driven rural

finance paradigm to broader financial inclusion involving both public and private players, to achieve the desired results of inclusive growth it also needs to be responsible.

1.4 FINANCIAL INCLUSION IS NOT ENOUGH; IT NEEDS TO BE 'RESPONSIBLE FINANCE'

The above initiatives aimed at increasing financial inclusion coincidentally happened at a time when the world was trying to recover from the global financial crisis of 2008. The global financial crisis highlighted the need for going beyond financial inclusion to responsible delivery of financial services. Driving home the point of responsible finance and its difference with inclusive finance, CGAP in its note on responsible finance asks:

Is it responsible when a financial co-operative tells its clients that their loan's interest rate is "only 3%" (without mentioning that this price is per month, is calculated on a flat basis, and excludes the fees and a premium for high-priced credit life insurance)? How about when "dormancy fees" erode a depositor's account balance every month?[17]

Responsible finance has emerged as a critical issue related to the financial sector, especially during the last few years, as the global financial and economic crisis aggravated by commodity, fuel, and energy crises highlighted the importance of transparent, inclusive, sustainable and equitable financial practices. The consultation draft paper prepared by the Responsible Finance Forum (RFF) reports:

With the recent failures of regulatory regimes to fully address the imbalances in financial markets and concerns of rising indebtedness in various countries, policy makers, practitioners, donors and investors have started paying greater attention to the issue of responsible finance. The situation in India's federal state of Andhra Pradesh has further increased global attention to this issue, demonstrating the urgency of advancing the responsible finance discussion across all financial sectors, including microfinance.[18]

While it is difficult to ascertain who/which agency first started using the phrase 'responsible finance', governments, global financial regulatory bodies, non-governmental organisations (NGOs) and the private sector worldwide are now emphasising it. The discourse has now shifted to 'responsible finance', with both the World Bank[19] and the CGAP using the term. Similarly, there are various definitions of responsible finance, but one can identify the key themes running across all the definitions. International Finance Corporation (IFC) defines responsible finance as 'coordinated public and private sector interventions that encourage and assist financial services providers and their clients in improving understanding and approaches, practices, and behaviors to create more transparent, inclusive, and equitable financial markets balanced in favor of all income groups.'[20] The CGAP gives a very practical insight on understanding responsible finance: 'responsible finance is a way of doing business—a never-ending process of adapting products, processes and policies, while keeping clients at the center.'[21]

RFF founded in 2010 as a global initiative by the German Federal Ministry for Economic Cooperation and Development (BMZ), the Ministry of Foreign Affairs of the Netherlands, the CGAP and the IFC is the first joint platform to support the efforts of participating institutions in the development community. RFF also partners with the World Bank Group on responsible finance as well as the United Nations Capital Development Fund. As it reflects the global consensus on responsible finance,

it is prudent to use the framework it provides for defining and understanding the subject. In its consultation report referred to above, the RFF defines responsible finance as:

> In its broadest meaning, it can be understood as a guiding principle for how financial services should be delivered to live up to the challenge of promoting sustainable development; therefore the work must incorporate social, developmental, and environmental dimensions and have support from governments, investors, consumer organizations, educators, and other stakeholders. One of the critical dimensions of financial sector responsibility is fair treatment of clients and acting in ways that protect clients' social and economic welfare.

Going beyond defining responsible finance, the consultation draft also clearly illustrates the framework through a diagram showing key stakeholders and areas of action (Figure 1.2).

The Principles for Investors in Inclusive Finance (PIIF) is an initiative launched under the umbrella of the United Nations Principles for Responsible Investment (UNPRI) in 2011 in order to create the right incentives for investees to treat clients appropriately (Box 1.2). PRI also endorses the client protection principles (CPP) developed by the SMART campaign, the social performance task force (SPTF)[22] standards as well as the environment, social and governance (ESG) criteria into investment

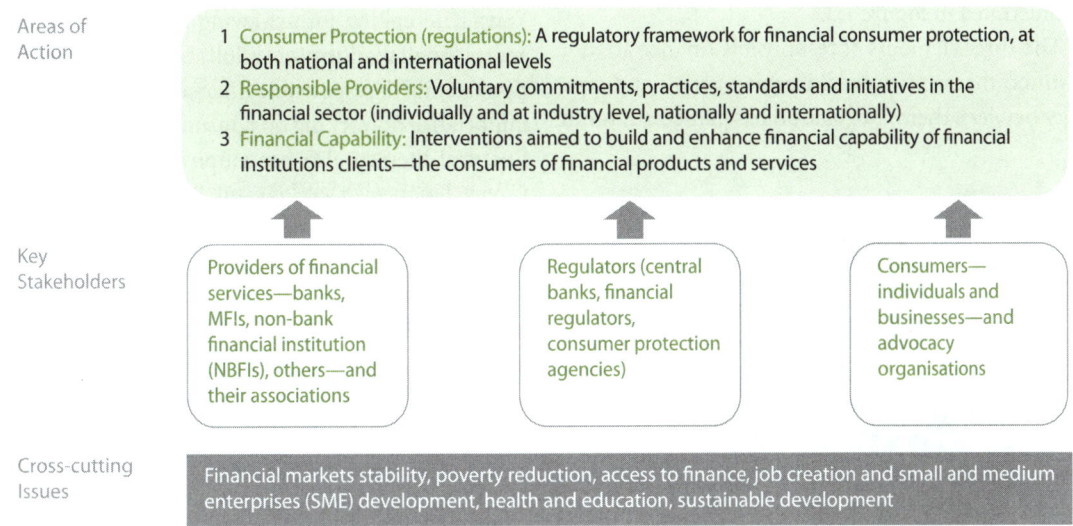

Figure 1.2 Responsible finance: A multi-stakeholder (three-pillar) approach

Source: Adapted from Responsible Finance Forum. 2011. *Advancing Responsible Finance for Greater Development Impact.* Consultation Draft.

> **Box 1.2 Principles for investors in inclusive finance**
>
> - Expanding the range of financial services available to low-income people;
> - integrating client protection into all policies and practices;
> - treating investees fairly, with clear and balanced contracts, and dispute resolution procedures;
> - integrating ESG factors into policies and reporting;
> - promoting transparency in all operations;
> - pursuing balanced long-term returns that reflect the interests of clients, retail providers and end investors; and
> - working together to develop common investor standards on inclusive finance.

Source: http://www.unpri.org/areas-of-work/implementation-support/piif/

decisions and reporting. Each PRI principle is accompanied by a set of possible actions, from which the indicators in the inclusive finance modules in the PRI reporting framework are derived.

With the review of various literature on the subject of responsible finance, it is evident that pinned to a single phrase, it has to be 'client-centric' approach to financial inclusion. The client centricity has to be achieved through the three pillars of regulation, consumer protection and financial education as illustrated in Figure 1.3.

The three elements of responsible finance are not distinct; there exists considerable overlap and synergy between them. Regulation has gained attention in the wake of global crisis. Regulation has to ensure that increase in access to finance occurs in a manner that preserves systemic stability and at the same time ensures that consumers are made aware of financial access conditionalities and protects them against unscrupulous practices of financial intermediaries. The main principle is that access to financial services should balance stability with consumer protection, and policy has to place customer at the centre. Financial service providers can adhere to this framework by incorporating responsible finance practices in everything the organisation does commencing from defining its mission, strategy and governance, customer acquisition and relationship management, employee relations, product design and delivery channels, processes and risk management, and financial education.[24]

The point about synergy among the three pillars is self-evident. For instance, effective financial education of customers makes them capable of making right choices, differentiate between various service providers, avoid over borrowing and thereby help maintain the stability of the financial sector. The customer centricity approach recognises the information asymmetry, power and resources between service providers and customers, and thereby focuses on clients' vulnerability, regardless of whether the consumers are from low-income segment or high-income segment.

At a time when A2F has become the guiding force of policy, with World Bank Group President Jim Yong Kim calling for achieving universal financial access for all working-age adults by 2020, the time is ripe to embed 'responsible finance' in practices. The importance of working on consumer protection and financial literacy also has empirical evidence. The *Global Financial Development Report 2014*[25] of the World Bank team undertook a global survey (Financial Barometer) to track the views on financial sector development among financial sector practitioners (such as central bankers, finance ministry officials, market participants and representatives of NGOs) around the world. One of the survey questions related to finding views on the most effective policy to improve access to finance, and though the responses were split across six policy actions, 32% ranked financial education as the most preferred policy choice followed by 27% choosing better legal framework and credit information (Figure 1.4).

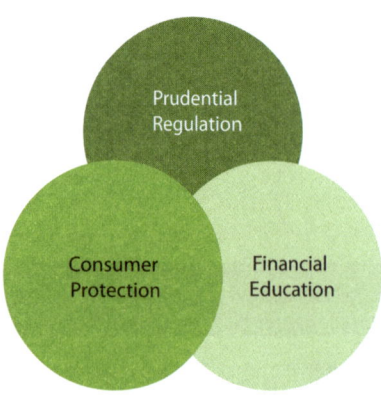

Figure 1.3 Three pillars of responsible finance[23]

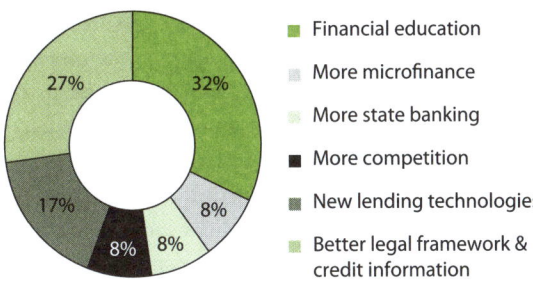

Figure 1.4 Policy choices to increase financial inclusion
Source: Global Financial Development Report 2014.

The two most preferred choices are closely aligned with the three pillars of responsible finance, financial education, consumer protection and regulation. Being a global survey, it brings to focus that the global consensus is fully aligned to placing customer protection and education at the core of financial inclusion initiatives. It makes the job of regulation and policy more complex as it has to balance systemic and macro-economic stability with interest of customers. In other words, focus has to be judiciously balanced between supply- and demand-side factors.

1.5 MICROFINANCE AND RESPONSIBLE FINANCE

While the discourse on mainstreaming of responsible finance elements in the broader financial sector has only begun, it is to the credit of microfinance sector that it has been quite early off the blocks in this sphere. Though a major contributing factor has been the drift of microfinance service providers from their developmental mission to chasing profitability, it gained urgency in the wake of Andhra Pradesh crisis in India and various other parts of the world like Bosnia, Nicaragua, Morocco and Pakistan. The focus on responsible finance is also natural for a sector founded on the idea of providing access to financial services to the unserved or underserved clients in a financially sustainable manner. As most of these clients belong to low-income segment and are vulnerable, it is particularly critical for the sector to pay particular attention to its responsibilities to clients.

The responsible finance movement in the microfinance sector consists of several initiatives to enhance client protection, define standards of social performance management, and ensure that MFIs remain committed to the concept of double bottom line. Globally, SPTF[26] was set up in 2005 to develop social performance framework for microfinance, and over the years it has not only developed the social performance framework but also the standards of social performance. Its global and consensual approach is evident from the fact that it has around 2,500 members and the development of standards involved extensive contributions from all over the globe and reflect industry consensus on the issue. The other major global initiative was the development and launch of CPP by the SMART Campaign.[27] The current version of CPP standards was released in January 2013 and focus exclusively on client protection. Though the microfinance rating agencies have been working on social performance assessment through social ratings since 2006, in recent years they have embedded these initiatives in their rating/assessment framework. As mentioned earlier, the responsible finance matrix has not remained limited to financial service providers but extended to investors in MFIs. More than 50 investors have signed the PIIF to express their commitment to follow responsible finance practices while extending support to their investees. Considering the important role investors play in creating incentives for responsible practice by MFIs, this initiative ensures that responsible finance considerations are streamlined across the value chain. The global initiatives have been backed by national level initiatives by either the regulator or industry associations. Globally in the last five years, microfinance is moving towards regulated responsible finance as against earlier situation of largely unregulated and profitability driven operations. India has been no exception with a host of national and global initiatives of responsible finance shaping the course of microfinance. The report in the subsequent chapter details these measures and analyses the progress of Indian MFIs on responsible finance framework.

These efforts to refocus the orientation of microfinance providers and other industry stakeholders has led to increased emphasis on delivering services that are safe, offer competitive pricing to ensure good value for money, and at the same time aims to generate benefits for poor clients. MFIs being not only a pure financial intermediary but also having a development mission need to play special emphasis on client protection and social performance management. More importantly, the sector has progressed beyond broad principles and established well-defined and measurable metrics of responsible finance.

It is worthwhile to address the issue of social performance versus responsible finance. While responsible finance is a new and broader term and its usage is across all types of financial institutions, the term social performance is used mainly for microfinance. However, the term social performance not only covers responsible finance areas but also goes beyond to cover additional areas in line with the double bottom line objective of microfinance; this is elaborated further in the following chapter.

1.6 REPORT STRUCTURE

After four years of publishing the social performance report, the rechristening of the report is to reflect the change in global discourse from inclusive finance to responsible finance. Social performance is a term commonly used with microfinance as it deals with the poor and balancing financial and social performance has to be the key for players in this space. However, social performance as defined for microfinance is in complete sync with the essential pillars of responsible finance; it rather extends to cover areas like responsibility to staff and poverty outreach. Moreover, as the concept of social performance for microfinance emerged in mid-2000, it has seen concrete initiatives in terms of global initiatives like the SPTF defining social performance dimensions and specific tools like Social rating and CPP for measuring social performance. As such, it is logical that much of the focus in this report continues to be on microfinance.

Having defined how the discourse has moved to responsible finance and illustrated the key elements of responsible finance, Chapter 2 is focused on applying the responsible finance lens on Indian MFIs. It presents the various initiatives at both national and global level, which drive MFIs towards responsible finance and uses the analytical frame of Universal Standards of Social Performance (USSPM) to analyse the performance of Indian MFIs on responsible finance. The USSPM framework encompasses the guidelines/covenants of various other initiatives like CPP and code of conduct (CoC), covers essential pillars of responsible finance and is globally accepted in microfinance as the benchmark for best practices in social performance. The journey of the Indian MFIs has gone through various phases and

the recent period is shaped by the lessons learnt from the crisis of 2010. The chapter attempts to present all initiatives undertaken by the industry since 2010 including regulator and stakeholders, towards mainstreaming responsible finance.

It is a cliché to state that institutional sustainability is the bedrock on which other aspects like social performance and responsible finance are built, and hence the subject of Chapter 3 is on emerging risks in the microfinance sector. Though at a time, when the industry is in a buoyant mood with Bandhan's commencing operations as a universal bank in August 2015 and receipt of in-principle licenses for setting up SFBs by eight other MFIs, the discussion on risks may seem out of place. But the industry needs to be ever vigilant as the model of unsecured lending to the poor will always be subject to greater scrutiny, and episodic events of client distress can swiftly turn into a pan India phenomena.

In the past years, the social performance report did bring in the other major player in microfinance, i.e., SBLP and attempted to flag the gaps in the programme from responsible finance angle. As both MFIs and SBLP work with the same set of customers in similar geographies, it is imperative that both adhere to best practices and work in synergy. Chapter 4 is focused on the SBLP and analyses the progress from clients' perspective, lists the various initiatives taken during the past year to address gaps in responsible finance and innovations to make the programme more client-centric.

As discussed, financial literacy is a key component of the responsible finance framework and it becomes more critical for a sector, which works with vulnerable people having little or no knowledge of financial products. Considering the importance of financial literacy in a supply-driven market, Chapter 5 examines the progress in financial literacy across channels. The focus of analysis is to see whether financial literacy is being mainstreamed as part of normal business activity or remains as an isolated activity divorced from main business.

The concluding Chapter 6 starts with analysing the new initiatives of SFBs and MUDRA and their possible impact on the national agenda of meeting the financial needs of the excluded poor. Even though both of these are still in infancy, it is imperative that they strengthen the cause of responsible finance for the excluded and do not drift. Experience shows that changing the operational mind set after maturity of an institution or channel is difficult and in this spirit suggestions are made for making SFB and MUDRA more effective in their roles.

In the last section, building on the previous chapters relating to microfinance, areas requiring action on part of policy as well as MFIs are suggested to strengthen the responsible finance agenda of microfinance. The impact of regulation and other stakeholders in guiding the microfinance sector towards responsible finance has been significant, but still a few areas need fine tuning to enable MFIs to have the flexibility to innovate, follow a tempered growth path and be more responsive to the customers. Similarly, MFIs need to take steps to integrate social performance in their business model and go beyond the dominant trend of being limited by compliance to external guidelines.

Hopefully in coming years, the financial sector stakeholders will be able to evolve standards of responsible finance for the mainstream financial sector and those can be used to analyse the performance of banks and NBFCs.

NOTES AND REFERENCES

1. Committee on Comprehensive Financial Services for Small Businesses and Low Income Households released on 7 January 2014. https://rbi.org.in/scripts/BS_PressReleaseDisplay.aspx?prid=30353 (accessed on 29 September 2015).
2. https://rbi.org.in/scripts/BS_PressReleaseDisplay.aspx?prid=32614 (accessed on 29 September 2015).
3. http://www.pmjdy.gov.in/Circular/English/Pradhan%20Mantri%20Jan%20Dhan%20Yojana%20(PMJDY).pdf (accessed on 30 September 2015).
4. http://www.pmjdy.gov.in/account-statistics-country.aspx (accessed on 30 September 2015).
5. Micro Units Development & Refinance Agency Limited.
6. RBI Circular no. DNBR.CC.PD.No.027/03.10.01/2014–15, dated 8 April 2015.
7. http://datatopics.worldbank.org/financialinclusion/country/india (accessed on 1 October 2015).
8. http://www.imf.org/external/np/sec/pr/2014/pr14425.htm (accessed on 29 September 2015).
9. Honohan, P., and T. Beck. 2007. *Making Finance Work for Africa*. Washington, DC: The International Bank for Reconstruction and Development/The World Bank.
10. http://www.cgap.org/news/world-bank-group-report-lays-out-road-map-financial-inclusion (accessed on 30 September 2015).
11. Dale Adams, Carlos Cuevas, Gordon Donald, Claudio Gonzalez-Vega and J.D. von Pischke are the best known members of 'Ohio School'.
12. Aynsley, Helen. *Financial Inclusion and Financial Capability: What's in a Name?* http://www.toynbee-hall.org.uk/data/files/Services/Financial_Inclusion/Financial_Inlcusion_and_Capability_-_Whats_In_A_Name.pdf (accessed on 29 September 2015).
13. Drafted and ratified by Alliance for Financial Inclusion (AFI) members in Riviera Maya, Mexico.
14. http://www.afi-global.org/sites/default/files/publications/Maya%20Declaration_2011.pdf (accessed on 3 October 2015).
15. AFI. *The 2014 Maya Declaration Progress Report: Measurable Goals with Optimal Impact.* http://www.afi-global.org/library/publications/2014-maya-declaration-progress-report-measurable-goals-optimal-impact (accessed on 2 October 2015).
16. http://www.cgap.org/topics/global-bodies-and-financial-inclusion (accessed on 4 October 2015).
17. http://www.cgap.org/topics/responsible-finance (accessed on 2 October 2015).
18. Responsible Finance Forum. January 2011. *Advancing Responsible Finance for Greater Development Impact, Consultation Draft.* https://www.responsible-financeforum.org/wp-content/uploads/Responsible-FinanceReport.pdf (accessed on 30 September 2015).
19. http://responsiblefinance.worldbank.org (accessed on 30 September 2015).
20. https://responsiblefinanceforum.org/about/the-three-pillars/ (accessed on 28 September 2015).
21. http://www.cgap.org/blog/responsible-finance-your-dna (accessed on 30 September 2015).
22. CPP and SPTF relate to microfinance and are discussed in detail in Chapter 2.
23. https://responsiblefinanceforum.org/about/the-three-pillars/ (accessed on 30 September 2015).
24. http://www.ifc.org/wps/wcm/connect/19ed8f804295a2cb8740af0dc33b630b/RFF+Report+final+low+res.pdf?MOD=AJPERES (accessed on 30 September 2015).
25. http://econ.worldbank.org/WBSITE/EXTERNAL/EXTDEC/EXTGLOBALFINREPORT/0,,contentMDK:23267383~pagePK:64168182~piPK:64168060~theSitePK:8816097,00.html (accessed on 30 September 2015).
26. http://sptf.info/sp-task-force (accessed on 1 October 2015).
27. http://www.smartcampaign.org (accessed on 1 October 2015).

The journey of Indian MFIs towards responsible finance: Factors and progress

2.1 ROOTS IN CLIENT-CENTRICITY AND RESPONSIBLE FINANCE

Responsible finance has come to occupy the centre stage in financial inclusion, which to a large extent is focused on keeping clients at the centre. In this context, it is pertinent to remind ourselves that the raison d'être for the emergence of MFIs lay in the inadequacies of the mainstream lenders to deliver services to low-income clients in a client-centric manner. While the impetus for kick-start of microfinance intervention in India in the early 1990s can be attributed to multiple factors, the main reasons were realisation of the inability of the formal banking system to reach the poor sustainably coupled with demonstrated experience of successful microfinance interventions across the world. By 1990, it was realised that even after sweeping credit market interventions through bank nationalisation and other means like directed credit and subsidised interest rates, the share of formal sector in rural household debt was a meagre 30%.[1] Despite impressive macro figures of outreach especially in terms of average population served by bank branches and increase in loan volume over the years, banks failed to meet the consumption and varied needs of the poor in the absence of customised products. Insistence on physical collateral in lending further limited the outreach. While on one hand the needs of the excluded and the poor could not be met adequately, the fallacy of basing the supply on subsidised rates without factoring the last mile delivery costs led to unviable operations.

In this background of inability of the formal structure to do last mile inclusion viably and emergence of successful microfinance interventions across the world, both SBLP and MFI model of microfinance took shape in India. Both models were and are strategically based on the concept of working with homogenous groups, social collateral in place of physical collateral and flexibility to accommodate needs of clients. The difference lies in operational model of financial intermediation as SBLP links these groups to banks, while MFI model does financial intermediation through an intermediate agency leveraging funds from the investors and banks. It is well accepted that as both models work with building social capital in the form of groups and then using social structures to undertake financial intermediation, it takes time and intensive work with the clients to scale. In addition, design of products to suit the varied needs of clients and frequent doorstep contact add to the complexity of being client centric while serving the excluded market.

Times have changed and the ambit of services has broadened to individual loan products, coverage of urban areas, adoption of technology in the form of POS and biometric cards but the basics remain the same. The responsible finance framework discussed in Chapter 1 shows that if financial service providers adhere to the basic tenets of their genesis in letter and spirit, they will automatically be responsible. It is easy to be dismissive about these facts by terming them as clichéd and cite major technological and architecture changes since then to argue that the industry has changed. However, parts of this chapter and the next chapter clearly show that ignoring the basic building blocks brought about the crisis in the past and can also wipe out the gains in future.

2.2 HOW DID THE DRIFT HAPPEN?

The social capital-based approach adopted under the MFI model lasted till about 2004/2005 and the sector was dominated by the NGO-MFIs who had transformed their developmental mandate to include financial intermediation. Slow progress is reflected by a combined outreach of 1.76 million customers by 2005.[2] Success had been demonstrated in reaching the Bottom of the Pyramid (BOP) market in a viable manner and banks started wholesale lending to MFIs based on third-party assessments of their performance. In a country where fast growth is justified in the context of vast numbers, the only impediment to growth at that point seemed to come from banks insistence on prudential norms like debt to equity ratio. MFIs registered as societies and trusts were finding it difficult to raise capital from external sources, triggering the transformation phase with MFIs reconfiguring institutional structure and form into NBFCs—the legal form acceptable to equity investors. By 2008, all major MFIs had transformed as NBFCs and dominated the sector accounting for 90% of the market share by 2010. Issues involved with the transformation process like use of mutual benefit trusts (MBTs) as a route to reckon client savings as part of equity by some of the leading MFIs were the earliest pointers of the sector drifting from client focus and have been well captured in the paper by Professor M.S. Sriram.[3]

With suitable legal form under the belt, success factors of the model were showcased in the form of high recovery rates and massive jump in outreach, peppered with an occasional anecdotal story of a smiling client. The story was too good for the investors to resist and equity investors of all sizes and shapes ranging from multilaterals like IFC to venture capital funds like Sequoia capital to private equity flocked in. The equity deals reached a peak in 2009–10 with equity valuation touching a high price/book value of 7 to 10.[4] With equity in place, bank funding to MFIs also touched a high of ~₹17,000 crore by March 2010 excluding portfolio sales and securitisations. Growth became the mantra, and it was achieved by cutting corners on client acquisition process, improving efficiency and thereby profitability, ignoring investments in control systems and Management Information System (MIS), and competing in similar areas. Plain vanilla loan product (50/52-week loan) obviated the necessity of higher investment in staff training and changes in operational systems. The client focus was

effectively lost and the prevailing scenario has been well captured by Srinivasan in his State of the Sector report, 2009.

> Many MFIs started financing the poor but somewhere they lost the customer focus and along with that mission too…. It is no more about improving income generation in the hands of the customers. Book value multiples, price to earning ratios and enterprise valuations dominate the discussion.

As stakeholders kept pointing to the loss of customer focus at the altar of growth, growing incidents from the field of reported over-indebtedness and inappropriate collection practices in pursuit of zero delinquency, leading to client unrest added to the evidence. Crisis in Krishna district of Andhra Pradesh in 2006 and Kolar in Karnataka in 2009 were two big events, which showed the vulnerability of the sector to political interference, and it was clear that the only way MFIs could ring fence themselves from external interferences was by being client centric.

While the focus was rapidly shifting from the clients, the industry was largely free of any regulation focusing on responsible finance even though NBFCs were registered with the RBI. The Task Force constituted by NABARD deliberated the first attempt at regulation way back in 1997 and chose self-regulation arguing that regulation could stifle growth and rob the sector of informality and flexibility. The recommendations did not attract much traction. The industry association (Sa-Dhan) did not follow up the recommendations proactively. Post the Krishna crisis of 2006, Sa-Dhan came up with a voluntary CoC in March 2006. The CoC included elements of responsible finance like client-centric practices, transparency, integrity and non-discrimination but being voluntary its effect was limited. The RBI on its part also issued guidelines on fair practices code (FPC), which also had aspects related to responsible finance, but its utility was limited by the absence of any checks on adherence as well as being limited in its applicability to NBFCs. The government was also not far behind and introduced a bill in 2007 in the Lok Sabha named as 'Micro Financial Sector (Development & Regulation) Bill', 2007. The bill was hotly contested as it seemed to be raising more issues than resolving the existing gaps and its life ended with the dissolution of the 14th Lok Sabha in 2009. While the details of what happened to this bill are not relevant here and have been discussed at length in various State of Sector reports in the past as well as the policy paper on microfinance regulation, it is pertinent to mention that it contained provisions relating to information dissemination, transparency, consumer education and institutional development.

In short, despite some attempts, the sector continued its drift from its original social mission and it was the Andhra Pradesh crisis of 2010, which changed things drastically. Many reasons have been offered as the trigger points leading to the harsh and sweeping ordinance by the state government, but linking it solely to government's genuine concern for microfinance borrowers is not fair as there were a host of factors triggering the government ordinance. Industry observers and borrowers have pointed to variety of reasons like overlap with the SHG programme, multiple borrowings, rising default rate under SHG programme as also intense media scrutiny of Swayam Krishi Sangam (SKS) IPO and possible envy/concern with profitability of MFIs, of which not all could be attributed solely to the MFIs. However, the underlying learning for the MFIs was that the industry by its practices focusing on increasing outreach at the expense of client welfare coupled with incidents of client distress provided fodder to the sledge-hammer policy response of the state government. The major reasons offered by the Andhra Pradesh government focused on coercive recovery practices, indiscriminate lending leading to over-indebtedness and usurious interest rates all of which are connected with the responsible finance framework. It however jolted the industry badly with ~95% of MFI loans in Andhra Pradesh becoming non-performing followed by drying of funding support from banks.

The effect of the crisis on financial health of the MFIs was disastrous, especially on those having a larger portfolio concentration in Andhra Pradesh, but as all adversities have a silver lining, this mega crisis brought the essential theme of being client centric and responsible finance back to the centre stage. The problem was immense with potential to flare up at pan India level and thereby needed swift action. It was beyond MFIs at that stage to salvage the situation and appropriately RBI stepped in followed by other industry initiatives. The architecture for responsible finance put in place for Indian MFIs since 2010 has been contributed by various national and international initiatives and the following section

details the current situation relating to each initiative and then uses the framework of USSPM to capture the current state of practice among MFIs.

2.3 2010 TO 2015: INITIATIVES SHAPING RESPONSIBLE FINANCE PRACTICES IN MICROFINANCE

2.3.1 National initiatives

Two things have majorly shaped the operations of MFIs post 2010—RBI regulations and CoC adopted by the industry. Despite being more of an external push to ensure that MFIs stick to client centricity, adopt ethical practices, have effective governance and sound financial health, the impact has been significant in as much as the RBI regulations being mandatory and the CoC adopted by the industry being subject to external checks.

2.3.1.1 Role of RBI regulations in promoting responsible finance

The positive fall out of the Andhra Pradesh crisis of 2010 was that it changed the earlier stand of RBI from benign negligence of the credit only MFIs to a more proactive stand. RBI's earlier stance seemed predicated on the premise that only deposit-based institutions need tighter oversight. It also seems plausible that MFIs were considered as being a small segment of the financial sector and thereby not posing any significant threat to the stability of the financial sector. Andhra Pradesh crisis changed the perception for good and RBI appointed a committee of the board in October 2010 chaired by Y.H. Malegam to look into the entire spectrum of MFI operations. The committee investigated the events leading to the crisis and other sectoral issues and came up with a set of recommendations in January 2011, the most important of which being the creation of a separate class of NBFCs for MFIs. It also suggested a host of operational rules pertaining to customer selection based on household income ceilings, guidelines to prevent the risk of multiple loans and over-indebtedness, caps on interest rate and maximum margin. RBI reviewed the recommendations and held further consultations with the industry stakeholders before releasing the policy circular on regulations applicable to NBFC-MFIs in May 2011. It took mere six months since the crisis for the regulation to take a 360 degree change going from passive stance to micro management. Crafting a uniform policy for a sector, which has so many nuances in terms of lending methodology and geographical diversity, is not an easy task and that is reflected in the number of changes that have taken place in the regulations since 2011.

The regulations prescribed by RBI are specific to the NBFC-MFIs and need to be adhered if the lending by banks to MFIs is to be reckoned under priority sector guidelines. However, its applicability has extended to all types of MFIs including societies, trusts and section-25 companies as banks demand adherence to these guidelines for their lending decisions. The last modification to the guidelines was effected in April 2015,[5] which addressed the long-standing demand of the sector to raise the

annual household income ceiling as well as permissible loan purposes.

Another important guideline from RBI for NBFC-MFIs that shapes the responsible finance agenda of the MFIs is FPC. The FPC is applicable to all NBFCs including NBFC-MFIs. First issued in September 2006,[6] it has subsequently been revised to incorporate specific aspects relating to NBFC-MFIs.

A comparative of key RBI guidelines including the FPC code with the three-dimensional responsible finance framework discussed in Chapter 1 indicates coverage of all aspects in the guidelines (Table 2.1).

Table 2.1   RBI guidelines mapped to responsible finance matrix

Responsible finance	RBI guidelines
Regulation and systemic stability	• Guidelines pertaining to minimum net owned funds, capital adequacy, asset classification and provisioning norms
	• NBFC-MFI to be member of the credit bureau
	• Constitution of board committees on audit, nomination and risk management by systemically important NBFCs[7]
Consumer protection	• To lend to rural households with annual income less than ₹1 lakh and urban-semi urban households with annual income less than ₹1.6 lakh
	• Loan amount capped at ₹60,000 in first cycle and ₹100,000 in subsequent cycles
	• Total indebtedness of an individual borrower excluding medical and education expenses not to exceed ₹1 lakh
	• Loan tenure not less than 24 months for loan amounts in excess of ₹15,000
	• Loans given for income generation should constitute at least 50% of the total loans of the NBFC-MFI
	• Pricing: The average base rate of five largest commercial banks multiplied by 2.75 per annum or cost of funds plus margin cap of 10% for MFIs having loan portfolio above ₹100 crore and 12% for those with loan portfolio less than 100 crore
	• Only three components in pricing: (i) interest rate, (ii) 1% processing fee and (iii) actual cost of insurance
	• Not more than two NBFC-MFIs to lend to the same borrower
	• Loan card in vernacular to disclose effective interest rate, terms and conditions, grievance redressal system and name of nodal officer
	• Loan recovery should normally be made only at a centrally designated place
	• No penalty on prepayment or delayed payment
	• Board of Directors should lay down the appropriate grievance redressal mechanism as also periodically review adherence to FPC
	• The effective rate of interest and grievance redressal system to be prominently displayed in all the offices
	• Training of field staff to inculcate appropriate behaviour towards borrowers without adopting coercive or abusive debt collection practices
Financial education	• Training, if any, offered to the borrowers shall be free of cost. Field staff to be trained to offer such training and make borrowers fully aware of the procedure and systems.

Source: Created by the author mapping key microfinance regulations to responsible finance matrix.

Coming in the wake of Andhra Pradesh crisis where the main issues related to interest rates, excessive credit leading to debt distress and inappropriate and sometimes coercive collection practices, it is self-explanatory that bulk of the focus has been on customer protection. The impact of recent changes (April 2015) in household income level, indebtedness level and reduction in loans for productive purposes to 50% will have their impact on MFI operations in near future. For the major part of last year, the annual household income limit for rural areas and urban areas was ₹60,000 and ₹120,000, respectively and the indebtedness level was capped at ₹50,000. Quite a few of the regulations go beyond promoting responsible finance and stifle operational flexibility of the MFIs and these aspects are discussed in section 2.4.

The onus of verifying compliance has been placed on NBFC-MFIs and the guidelines require them to submit statutory auditors certificate at the end of each financial year indicating that the company meets all stipulated conditions. Leaving the compliance on customer protection issues to statutory auditors is debatable; microfinance being a field based activity, checking adherence to these guidelines in operations calls for a competency different than an auditor. However, in addition to this, RBI conducts annual inspection of systematically important NBFC-MFIs and others once in two years, and it is expected that adherence to these guidelines is examined at the time of inspection. As the inspection reports are not available in public domain, it is not possible to comment on the adequacy of checks.

2.3.1.2 Industry code of conduct

The crisis also gave wake up call to the industry associations Sa-Dhan and MFIN to move beyond advocacy and play a more active role in guiding the sector towards responsible business practices. IFC and Michael & Susan Dell Foundation (MSDF) took a initiative of bringing the two industry bodies together for working on a common CoC guiding the business practices of their respective member MFIs. The objective was realised with the release of Unified Code of Conduct (UCoC) in December 2011. The UCoC comprises of (i) core values of microfinance, (ii) CoC, (iii) guidelines on client protection and (iv) guidelines for institutional conduct. The UCoC combines elements from earlier voluntary CoC, CPP developed by the SMART campaign, RBI guidelines for NBFC-MFIs as well as FPC. It also has a few points

like recruitment of staff, which are not covered by other initiatives. The main significance of the UCoC related to being compulsory for member MFIs to adhere to it rather than leaving it in voluntary mode.

Being mandatory, UCoC has significantly impacted the practices of Indian MFIs since 2011. Its usefulness in promoting responsible finance can be seen from Table 2.2 which maps its essential covenants with the responsible finance framework.

Additionally, UCoC also covers aspects related to staff recruitment by prescribing mandatory checks from the previous employer, time bound reply to such queries by the previous employer and honouring of the notice period. Though these additions do not strictly fit in with the responsible finance framework but are a key part of social performance as detailed later in section 2.4.

Being mandatory, MFIN, the industry association of NBFC-MFIs, monitors compliance to it through self-reported data from member MFIs on a quarterly basis. MFIN has developed a quantitative responsible business index comprising of 90 indicators from the UCoC and FPC organised under four broad heads (disclosure, customer engagement,

Table 2.2 UCoC mapped to responsible finance matrix

Responsible finance	RBI guidelines
Regulation and systemic stability	• MFIs to observe high governance standards
	• One-third of the board to be independent directors
	• Audit committee to be headed by independent director
	• Board to approve debt restructuring policy
	• MFIs to follow accounting standards set by the Institute of Chartered Accountants of India
	• Board to monitor compliance with UCoC
Consumer protection	• Broadly reiterates RBI guidelines and FPC on (i) transparency in dealing with clients, (ii) interest rates, (iii) indebtedness, (iv) grievance redressal and (v) appropriate collection practices
	• MFIs to keep personal client information confidential and such information can be disclosed to third party under specific conditions
	• UCoC to be prominently displayed in all the offices
Financial education	• MFIs to have dedicated process to raise client's awareness of the options, choices and responsibilities about offered services
	• MFIs to ensure regular checks on client awareness and understanding of the key terms and conditions

Source: Created by the author mapping key microfinance regulations to responsible finance matrix.

institutional process and transparency). Based on the self-reported data, member MFIs are scored on their compliance level and the same is overseen by the enforcement committee of MFIN. A big limitation of this approach relates to it being based on self-reported data and being not available in public domain for other stakeholders to monitor. It is believed that MFIN realising this inadequacy is now moving towards a system of independent verification of compliance. For this, MFIN will empanel external agencies to conduct annual verification of each member's compliance, and to ensure reporting consistency, a reporting template will also be developed as part of the process. To begin with, MFIN plans to get 15 verifications done by the empanelled agencies during 2015–16. In parallel, work on revision of the UCoC to account for changes in the sector is in progress.

Apart from MFIN's compliance mechanism based on self-reported data, Small Industries Development Bank of India (SIDBI) has taken a leadership role since 2010 in getting compliance with UCoC checked by external agencies. Till date, 80 CoC assessments including repeat assessments have been funded by SIDBI. SIDBI funding was supposed to be a market making exercise but it has so turned out that even after five years, no banks or investors or MFIs have commissioned a CoC assessment without availability of SIDBI funding. The issues connected with CoC assessments being done by different agencies were detailed in the Social Performance Report, 2012[8] and have also been recently elaborated in a study by MicroSave for SIDBI.[9] Despite the limitations of subjectivity and different reporting templates, the redeeming feature of these external assessments has been that most agencies also included compliance with FPC and RBI guidelines in their assessment framework.

2.3.1.3 Push for responsible finance beyond guidelines

Though mandatory guidelines in the form of RBI guidelines and UCoC define the contours of responsible finance, other stakeholders have been doing their bit for ensuring that these practices are mainstreamed and MFIs go beyond regulation-induced responsible finance. SIDBI as the major guiding force in shaping the course of microfinance industry in India not only continued its work on providing debt and equity funding to MFIs

but also took several steps to promote responsible finance practices during the past year. Major initiatives relate to pilot project on financial literacy continued support to CoC assessments as well as loan portfolio audits and social assessments to boost confidence in the sector and capacity building of MFIs on gender. Much of its work in the area of responsible finance has been under the World Bank project and poorest state inclusive growth (PSIG) programme funded by the Department for International Development (DFID). It also continued to influence policy through its work with RFF, lenders forum as well as national level think tank established as part of PSIG programme. Key details of SIDBI's initiative and support during 2014–15 are given in Annexure 2.1.

IFC on its part has continued the drive towards responsible finance beyond UCoC by forming an RFF in 2011. RFF is a voluntary platform for microfinance sector participants—lenders, investors, donors, industry associations and experts chosen by IFC with the objective of facilitating adoption, adherence and strengthening of responsible finance.

The forum with representation from important sectoral stakeholders aims to catalyse, mobilise and mainstream the responsible finance policies and practices in the country. In its quarterly meetings during 2014–15, quite a few key initiatives were taken: (i) advocacy with RBI on raising the income limit of MFI clients, (ii) working with DFID to commission a study on indebtedness in four states with data from High Mark credit bureau, (iii) study on status of governance in MFIs done by DFID in association with MicroSave and (iv) revision of CoC. RFF is also working towards commissioning a study on compensation and performance management systems as well as a human resource certification course including responsible finance component as a mandatory criteria for MFI field staff.

The primary objective of all these key national initiatives is to ensure that the MFIs have sound financials, robust governance, provide services in an efficient, transparent and responsible manner, and avoid mistreating clients and over-indebting them. The range of guidelines and the accompanying compliance mechanism put in place post 2011 are unparalleled across the world. Indian MFIs as of now have the most stringent and comprehensive guidelines in place.

2.3.2 International initiatives in responsible finance

As discussed in Chapter 1, there have been several global efforts in promoting consumer protection and responsible finance in microfinance. A matrix showing such global initiatives in self-assessment, reporting and external checks/audits is given in Annexure 2.2. Of these, the one, which had the most impact on Indian MFIs, is CPP assessment and certification. Few other initiatives like Truelift promoted by the Microcredit Summit and Progress out of Poverty (PPI) certification initiated by Grameen Foundation aimed at measuring pro-poor intent and practices have not made much headway.

2.3.2.1 Client protection and SMART campaign

Smart campaign is a global effort to unite microfinance leaders around the common goal of keeping clients as the driving force of the industry and is housed at Accion's Centre for Financial Inclusion (CFI). SMART campaign worked with a task force of over 30 experts representing various stakeholders to develop and vet the standards of client protection. The first set of seven standards was released in 2013 containing seven principles and 95 indicators (Box 2.1).

Parallel to release of first set of principles, SMART campaign set in motion a process of CPP assessments and certifications. While CPP assessments are aimed towards helping the MFI identify gaps and provide recommendations to meet those gaps, CPP certification is an examination of MFIs adherence to these principles and indicators and on meeting all indicators, the CPP certificate is awarded by the SMART campaign and the certification agency.[10] The wide appeal of CPP is reflected in having 4,530

Box 2.1 Seven principles of client protection (number of indicators)

- Appropriate product design and delivery (5)
- Prevention of over-indebtedness (24)
- Transparency (15)
- Responsible pricing (3)
- Fair and respectful treatment of clients (21)
- Privacy of client data (16)
- Mechanisms for complaint resolution (11)

Source: http://www.smartcampaign.org/about/smart-microfinance-and-the-client-protection-principles

---

global endorsements.[11] Considering its global appeal especially among investors, Indian MFIs have been involved in the process since 2013. It is heartening that out of 40 institutions certified globally, 10 are from India.[12] In addition to CPP certification, which can be considered as the gold standard, nine MFIs have undergone SMART assessment and are on their way towards certification.

As the industry moves with adoption of new services and delivery mechanisms, the CPP also need to adjust. SMART campaign is at present working on developing indicators for savings and insurance as well as piloting assessments to develop indicators for digital finance and hopes to roll out V.2 of the CPP by June 2016. Though the standards will be frozen by end of 2015, it will allow time for consultation with stakeholders and for institutions to prepare for changes.

2.4 WHY USE USSPM FOR ANALYSING RESPONSIBLE FINANCE PRACTICES?

At a time when MFIs are already subject to such a vast array of mandatory national and international guidelines, it is logical to ask as to why an additional lens is needed to analyse their performance. Responsible finance is a generic concept applicable to the entire financial sector not just microfinance. And three main strategies can help advance responsible finance. Consumer protection is the foremost of these strategies and can be achieved by regulation and supervision, whereby mandatory rules can be put in place to ensure that services are offered transparently and efficiently and customers are protected from risks such as over-indebtedness through excessive supply of credit. This has been done in India with RBI putting in place a detailed regulatory regime. The regulatory efforts can be supplemented by industry initiatives and this has also been done in India with mandatory adoption of UCoC. The second strategy relates to ensuring that financial institutions are financially sound and the third strategy relates to building clients' awareness and strengthening their financial capability. Financial soundness is also in place in India thanks to prudential regulation by the RBI, and both RBI guidelines and UCoC also touch upon financial education.

The moot point is that the steps taken by the regulator and industry association are more attuned to ensuring that financial institutions 'do no harm', to clients and focus on protecting clients. This is logical as the regulatory architecture for NBFC-MFIs put in place after 2010 has been influenced to a large extent by the factors which caused the Andhra Pradesh crisis.

However, microfinance and MFIs cannot be equated with mainstream financial institutions as they deal with the poor and excluded and also have a social mission focused on financial inclusion. MFIs are not purely profit-motivated providers. They are also committed to a double or triple bottom line and thereby need to go beyond 'do no harm' to 'doing good'. The point of MFIs being required to go beyond 'do no harm' is also enunciated in the UCoC. In the section on core values in microfinance, it says 'to provide low-income clients—women and men—and their families, with access to financial services that are client focused and designed to enhance their well being...' and goes on to say 'to monitor and report social as well as financial data'. Though there exists a contrarian view which considers microfinance to be like any other financial market albeit with a different market segment and 'doing good' as a mandate belonging to welfare programmes and government, it is not in line with the majority consensus on what defines responsible microfinance. There is a global consensus that microfinance providers in line with their double bottom line commitment and mission need to move to social performance management and USSPM framework defines the metrics of social performance.

Social performance goes beyond responsible finance and is related with double bottom line institutions understanding how their practices and services affect clients and how to provide products and services that clients' value. Social Performance Management aims at enabling the institution to take its social goals into account in concrete ways, and integrate financial decisions with social consequences. This balanced approach to management benefits both the institution (e.g., client loyalty/retention) and the client (e.g., appropriate products). Management of social goals also allows the institution to demonstrate client-level results to both internal and external stakeholders using real social data rather than anecdotes.[13] CGAP in its brief on SPM[14] succinctly captures the essence of SPM by saying

SPM is a management style that puts customers at the center of all strategic and operational decisions. SPM begins with a clear social strategy, which is then carried out by the board, management, and employees. Providers with strong SPM design products that help clients cope with emergencies, invest in economic opportunities, build assets, and manage their daily and life cycle financial needs. Such FSPs also treat employees responsibly and carefully balance the institution's financial and social goals.

It goes on to say that focusing on social performance is not antithetical to financial performance rather it provides sustainability to it.

The SPTF is a global non-profit organisation consisting of over 1,700 members from every region and multiple microfinance stakeholder groups. It worked painstakingly for several years to evolve consensus on a set of core management practices that constitute USSPM which were released in 2013. The Universal Standards are organised into six dimensions and each dimension contains multiple standards. A standard is a simple statement of what the institution should do to manage social performance. For each of these standards, there are several 'Essential Practices,' which detail how to achieve the standard.

The suitability of the USSPM framework to analyse MFIs stems not only from its being more suitable for MFIs committed to social mission but also from the fact that it includes elements from regulation, CoC and CPP applicable to Indian MFIs. Table 2.3 shows the mapping of RBI regulation, UCoC guidelines and CPP with dimensions and standards of USSPM to illustrate the point.

Table 2.3 shows that the initiatives influencing the sector are clustered around client-protection dimension and also have some commonality with other dimensions of USSPM. For example, while both RBI guidelines and UCoC cover governance in terms of having subcommittees of the board, minimum number of independent board members and review of compliance with CoC and FPC, they do not go further to cover social performance monitoring. In addition to partial overlap, there are few aspects which are not covered by the USSPM but are part of the existing guidelines. UCoC specifically talks about staff recruitment mandating that recruiting organisations must seek reference letter from the previous employer, honour notice period while processing resignation and not assigning the

Table 2.3 Universal standards of social performance mapped with regulatory and industry guidelines

	USSPM	CPP	UCoC	RBI guidelines	RBI FPC
Dimension	**DEFINE AND MONITOR SOCIAL GOALS**				
Standards	The institution has a strategy to achieve social goals				
	The institution collects, reports and ensures the accuracy of client-level data that are specific to the social goals				
Dimension	**ENSURE BOARD MANAGEMENT AND EMPLOYEE COMMITMENT TO SOCIAL GOALS**				
Standards	Members of the Board of Directors should hold the institution accountable to its mission and social goals	Partial			Partial
	Senior management oversees implementation of the institution's strategy for achieving its social goals				
	Employees are recruited, evaluated and recognised based on both social and financial performance criteria	Full			Full
Dimension	**DESIGN PRODUCTS, SERVICES, DELIVERY MODELS AND CHANNELS THAT MEET CLIENT'S NEEDS AND PREFERENCES**				
Standards	The institution understands the needs and preferences of different types of clients	Full			
	The institution's products, services, delivery models and channels are designed to benefit clients in line with the institution's social goals	Full			Partial
Dimension	**TREAT CLIENTS RESPONSIBLY**				
Standards	Prevention of over-indebtedness	Full	Full	Full	Full
	Transparency	Full	Full	Full	Full
	Fair and respectful treatment of clients	Full	Full	Full	Full
	Privacy of client data	Full	Full	Full	Partial
	Mechanism for complaint resolution	Full	Full	Full	Full
Dimension	**TREAT EMPLOYEES RESPONSIBLY**				
Standards	The institution follows a written human resources policy that protects employees and creates a supportive working environment	Partial	Partial		Partial
	The institution communicates to all employees the terms of their employment and provides training for essential job functions	Partial			Partial
	The institution monitors employee satisfaction and turnover				
Dimension	**BALANCE FINANCIAL AND SOCIAL PERFORMANCE**				
Standards	The institution sets and monitors growth rates that promote both financial sustainability and client well-being	Partial			
	Equity investors, lenders, board and management are aligned on the institution's double bottom line and implement an appropriate financial structure in its mix of sources, terms and desired returns				
	Pursuit of profits does not undermine the long-term sustainability of the institution or client well-being	Full		Partial	Full
	The institution offers compensation to senior managers that is appropriate to a double bottom line institution				

Partial overlap

Full overlap

Source: Mapped by Author.

recruited staff in the area where he/she had worked for the previous employer. These are specific to Indian conditions and were made part of the guidelines to deter poaching of staff and clients. The focus of both RBI guidelines and UCoC is on customer protection, which is an integral part of social performance but do not cover the full spectrum of social performance.

Before delving into analysis, it is pertinent to discuss the data availability on social performance indicators as the subsequent analysis is based on available data. It was mentioned earlier that RBI inspection reports are not public documents and so is the case with MFIN's responsible business index constructed from MFI's self-reported data on UCoC. Microfinance Information Exchange (MIX) does collect social performance data but it is very minimal and moreover the data for the last financial year 2014–15 was not available at the time of writing—September 2015. Social rating covers all dimensions of USSPM in depth but unfortunately social rating is not much in vogue in Indian market dominated by banks. As per Micro-Credit Rating International Limited (M-CRIL), during the year 2014–15 only eight social ratings were conducted and the demand came from socially oriented MFIs as well as through the funding made available under the PSIG programme of DFID being implemented by SIDBI. SIDBI has not only made the CoC assessment reports public but also commissioned a comparative study by MicroSave of first 50 CoC assessments. In addition, SIDBI also commissioned two studies of relevance to the topic of responsible finance.[15] Besides these, to delve further, a questionnaire was designed for MFIs and sent to 55 MFIs, of which only 28 responded. To get practical insights, personal interviews were conducted with nine MFI CEOs, five bankers, key industry experts and investors.

2.4.1 Social goals and governance (Dimensions 1 and 2): Need to go beyond Corporate Social Responsibility (CSR) and compliance mode

The USSPM dimensions of having social goals aligned to the mission, clear strategy to achive social goals and board's involvement in setting and monitoring of social goals, are intended to ensure that MFIs have a double bottom line performance metrics.

As mission is the foundation for monitoring performance, it should be specific and clear and should allow the institution to answer three key questions:

- Whom does it want to reach (target population)?
- How does it intend to serve them?
- What changes does it hope to influence?

It is desirable that the social goals should be SMART that is specific, measurable, achievable, relevant and time bound. Once the goals have been articulated and defined, these should be monitored, disseminated across the organisation and be integrated in business planning.

While Indian MFIs do well on first two questions—whom do they want to reach and how, the experience on the third is mixed. Box 2.2 shows mission statements of a few prominent MFIs and it is seen that the two questions of 'whom' and 'how' are addressed in the mission statement.

Box 2.2 Select mission statements of MFIs

'Our mission is to identify below poverty line (BPL) women in rural areas and to provide financial and other vital credit plus services in an honest, timely and efficient manner'.

'Our mission is to provide financial services to the economically weaker sections'.

'Provide full range of financial services to the economically active poor to build better lives'.

'New-age financial institution for the urban underserved while simultaneously being a profitable company with established controls, and high standards of ethics and corporate governance'.

'Provide financial assistance to a large number of households which are excluded from the ambit of mainstream financial service providers so as to enhance their livelihood and promote a productive environment'.

'To transform and uplift the lives of poor and low-income families with microfinance and other development services'.

'And to be a sustainable, friendly and trusted provider of affordable and need-based services'.

Source: Websites of MFIs.

Most have also broken it down into specifics. For example, Ujjivan targets clients below $2.5 poverty line, CASHPOR uses its housing index and poverty line of $1.5 to screen clients as per its mission. Though client targeting is influenced by area of operation, most of the MFIs have also specifically defined their target segment. Ujjivan being primarily an urban MFI has a higher poverty line targeting as compared to CASHPOR which is predominantly rural and operates in poorer areas of eastern Uttar Pradesh (UP) and Bihar.

MIX social performance data available for 2014 does not give a full picture—out of the 40 reporting NBFCs, only six are shown as using any type of poverty screening tool. Data received from 28 MFIs in response to the questionnaire shows that a vast majority (22) use either household index or PPI as targeting tool. The other dimension of targeted outreach pertains to gender. Historically, Indian MFIs have focused on women and it continues even today. As per MIX data, all 32 reporting NBFCs and 21 NGOs mentioned women as their primary target clientele.

Box 2.2 shows that most MFIs have the words excluded, poor and disadvantaged as their target population, and thereby they do focus on poverty outreach. Though some of the MFIs are urban focused or use terms like 'unserved' and 'excluded', it is common knowledge that it is the poor who are normally excluded. Analysing the poverty outreach of MFIs can show whether the targeted clientele is being reached. Data on poverty outreach of various MFIs is difficult to get and MIX data is not only self-reported but also incomplete. Last year, Grameen foundation undertook a study of the poverty outreach of MFIs in the states of UP, Odisha and Madhya Pradesh under the PSIG programme. The study findings provide significant indicators on the poverty outreach of MFIs as the study collected data for first-cycle loan clients and extrapolated it to entire portfolio. This approach is more robust than seeing poverty outreach across a cross-segment of clients as the first-cycle clients poverty status is without any microfinance impact.

The sample clients included in the study by the Grameen foundation covered 10 MFIs in UP spread across 41 districts, five MFIs spread over 22 districts in Odisha and 10 MFIs spread across 36 districts in Madhya Pradesh. The sample included both rural and urban clients and its representativeness is seen

from the fact that MFIs covered in UP accounted for 81% share of the microfinance market.

The study results were analysed using four poverty lines—National Poverty Line (NPL) (Tendulkar), <$1.25 per day, <$1.88 per day and <$2.5 per day adjusted to account for state-specific differences. The study defined people living below NPL as very poor, <$1.25 as poor, <$1.88 as borderline poor and <$2.5 as vulnerable poor. Figures 2.1, 2.2 and 2.3 show the results for UP, Odisha and MP, respectively.

The results are mixed; while in UP, MFIs poverty outreach mirrors state poverty incidence, in Odisha and MP, MFIs outreach across all four measures is lower than the state poverty incidence. Even in UP, the MFI outreach is slightly lower than the state poverty incidence across first three measures covering

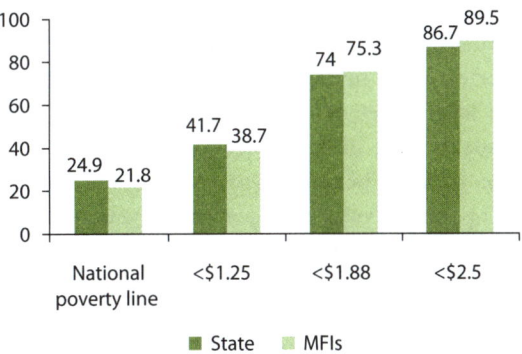

Figure 2.1 State poverty incidence and MFIs outreach in UP

Source: Poverty Outreach Report, Grameen Foundation 2015, under aegis of Poorest State Inclusive Growth Programme supported by UK's Department of International Development and SIDBI.

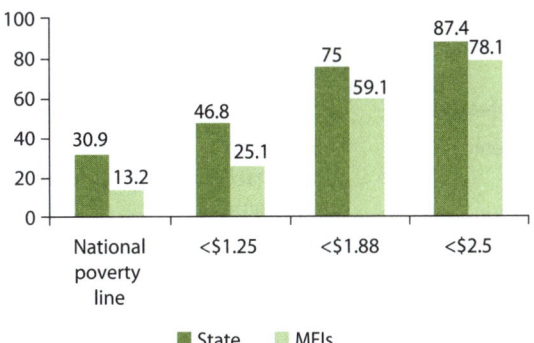

Figure 2.2 State poverty incidence and MFIs outreach in Odisha

Source: Poverty Outreach Report, Grameen Foundation 2015, under aegis of Poorest State Inclusive Growth Programme supported by UK's Department of International Development and SIDBI.

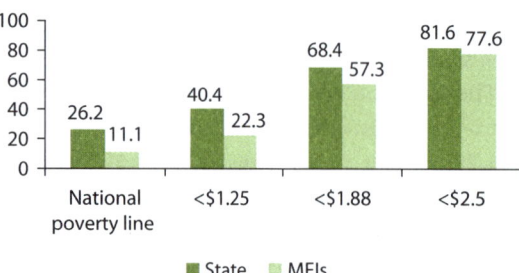

Figure 2.3 State poverty incidence and MFIs outreach in MP

Source: Poverty Outreach Report, Grameen Foundation 2015, under aegis of Poorest State Inclusive Growth Programme supported by UK's Department of International Development and SIDBI.

very poor, poor and borderline poor. Going away from the self-reported data by MFIs, this study shows that the outreach of MFIs is more towards borderline poor rather than very poor and poor categories. It has been argued that core poor are not the ideal target of commercial microfinance; the model is more suited for economically active poor who typically belong to the categories of borderline poor and vulnerable poor and the data clearly shows that. However, it will be a worthwhile study to compare the stated poverty outreach of major MFIs and actual outreach to see if the outreach is in line with stated outreach.

Though there is no similar study to show whether the poverty outreach of MFIs has improved or drifted over the years, some inferences can be drawn from the study conducted by National Council of Applied Economic Research (NCAER) in 2011.[16] The study covered five clusters across India and included 10,188

households. It found that the mean monthly income in case of microfinance borrowers was lowest in case of MFIs, followed by SHG borrower, informal sector borrower and bank borrowers. As per the report, the mean monthly income of MFI borrowers was ₹1,448. Even after accounting for inflation, the reported income level of MFI borrowers corresponds to below $1.25 measure. Thus despite difference in area and time, it throws some pointers to a shift in the microfinance sector towards less poor clients.

The third aspect of having a social mission relates to having measurable social goals in alignment with the mission. While almost all MFIs have social goals and undertake various initiatives, there are only a few examples of having social goals aligned to mission and also integrated with business planning. Grameen Financial Services Private Limited (GFSPL) is poverty focused MFI and has set specific social goals for the next five years. Its mission statement states transforming lives of clients through financial and developmental initiatives. To achieve it, GFSPL has set specific targets for coverage of its clients in next five years through healthcare insurance coverage, pension coverage, training on sanitation, safe drinking water training and financial literacy coverage (Annexure 2.3). Hand in Hand (HiH) has disaggregated its mission objectives of social and economic empowerment into specific granular objectives. HiH has identified literacy, creation of social capital, access to sanitation, creating linkages and participation in decision making at village level as the objectives under social empowerment. The objectives have been further disaggregated on log frame matrix across activities, output, outcome and impact. Table 2.4 shows some of these

Table 2.4 HiH social goals impact matrix

Objectives	Activities	Output	Outcome	Impact
Literacy	Conducting functional literacy programmes	No. of women members trained	No. of literate members	Increased awareness
Sanitation	Providing water and sanitation loans	No. of loans given	Improved access to sanitation	Health improvement and reduction in water-borne diseases
Decision making at village level	Sensitising them to attend Gram Sabha meetings	No. of members attending Gram Sabha meetings	Increased leadership qualities	Recognition in family and society
Livelihood strengthening	Loans and enterprise training	No. of loans and trainings provided	Enterprise, income and job	Resilient livelihoods

Source: Information provided by HiH.

key objectives under social and economic empowerment set by HiH.

Equitas has a mission statement of 'improving quality of life' and 'asset value' of those not effectively serviced by the formal sector. To operationalise the ecosystem for achieving the mission, it uses both parent NBFC as well as the trust (Equitas Development Initiatives Trust) and allocates 5% of the NBFC profit each year for the trust. The following services are offered through the NBFC with the objective of raising the quality of life and value of assets.

- Every branch is mandated to conduct one health camp a month and a budget of ₹2,000 per branch per month is provided. On an average 70,000 people are covered in a month.
- Each branch is mandated to skill train at least 20 women a month. The CSR team has a set of skill trainers empanelled who conduct the week-long skill training.
- It has partnered with Microcredit Summit Campaign and Freedom From Hunger for imparting health education to women 'Healthy Habits for Life', which is delivered over five lessons, each of a duration of 30 minutes. The skill trainers providing vocational training to clients are trained to deliver health education.

Equitas also goes beyond social goals related to its mission statement and clients in doing various other socially useful activities like rehabilitation of pavement dwellers and conducting job fairs for unemployed youth among the low-income households. It has also specified numbers to be achieved under each social activity and these activities have 20% weight in the KRAs of the branches. Similarly, GFSPL also does other developmental and welfare activities. It is working on a programme called Sugrama with the objective of transforming selected villages by making them open defecation free, adoption of rain water harvesting and improved solid and liquid waste management through its NGO arm.

While these are a few examples of identifying social goals, setting targets and integrating them into business planning, overall there is a tendency to correlate social goals with CSR and the same is typically exhibited in terms of number of health camps or awareness raising campaigns with various levels of outreach. It is nobody's contention that these are not important activities but these can be additional activities and certainly not be a substitute for setting

social goals aligned to mission, setting measurable targets and integrating it in business planning. A typical case to stress the point can be seen with reference to one of the leading North India based MFI. As part of its social initiatives, it lists free medical camps, eye health check-up, awareness camp on 'No Tobacco day', disaster relief and cancer awareness camps. Most of the MFIs have a similar story to tell under social goals, which by no means is not useful but is not in line with creating optimal social value for the clients. The report of evaluation of CoC assessments[17] reinforces this point by saying that 62% of MFIs have approved policies for offering credit plus services like financial literacy, environmental awareness camps, health camps and children education. These activities belong to the domain of CSR, and while the intent is positive, there is a need to do it systematically to 'do good' to the clients. Another related point on social goals relates to the scale of outreach. While ideally, the social goals should be embedded in service delivery and all clients availing financial services should be covered, the problem with having broader social initiatives in place of well-defined social goals is that outreach numbers under them are far below the client base. There is a general tendency to state outreach targets in terms of percentage of poor clients and women clients in place of well-defined goals related to making positive changes in lives of clients.

When social goals are not well-defined and embedded in service delivery, it is natural that monitoring mechanisms to capture progress on mission achievement takes a backseat. The questionnaire sent to MFIs in connection with this report had a specific question on whether the MFI carried out any impact assessment of its clients in the last one year—only five answered in affirmative. It is proven that those who define social goals clearly also measure the impact periodically. While in-house assessment is always open to questions of rigour and sample bias, the social performance literature shows that institutions with clearly defined social goals integrate the information required to capture change in the MIS obviating the need for additional evaluations. CASHPOR, for example, uses PPI scores over loan cycles to capture progress in achievement of its mission of poverty alleviation and also backs it up with an annual survey of clients to know their perception on change. But even amongst those who use targeting tools, the practice of measuring progress is rarely seen. Data from 13 social ratings done in last two years by M-CRIL shows that out of six MFIs using PPI as a targeting tool, only two used it to track progress.

Another example of measuring change/impact related to its mission comes from Equitas. It captures household assets details prior to first loan disbursement and the same are recaptured in subsequent loan cycles and changes in assets is seen as a surrogate measure of improvement in quality of life. As per data shared by Equitas, 94% of fourth-cycle clients reported increase in household assets as against 85% third-cycle clients and 67% second loan cycle clients.

The other side of measuring change comes from SKS, which does not have any defined social goals related to change but still as an MFI weeded to impacting lives of its clients, it conducted an impact study covering 500 client households through M-CRIL during 2014–15. The study covered third-cycle onwards clients and measured change through recall in the absence of baseline. Detailed infographic showing the findings is given as Annexure 2.4, while some of the findings are in Box 2.3. Though a broad-based impact assessment from external agency is a good practice, its limitations arise from being generic assessment of change rather than being related to specific goals related to mission as well as being limited in coverage.

The other proxy of a strong focus on measuring change and social outcomes is emphasis placed on social performance in performance evaluation of the CEO and senior management team as well as

---

Box 2.3 Key findings of SKS impact assessment

- Eight per cent clients were able to diversify their livelihood.
- Farm activities based clients recorded annual increase in income by 19%; 20.6% in case of non-farm.
- 9.2% increase in savings with formal sector.
- ~20% decrease in the proportion of working children in IGAs.
- Proportion of school going girls significantly increased from the 76.7% at the baseline to 91.9% at the end line.

Source: M-CRIL. 2015. SKS Quick Impact Study: Impact of SKS's Efforts in Delivering 'High Value' to the Customers through Credit Service.

---

field-level staff. MicroSave's governance study covering 42 MFIs shows minimal progress on it. It says that most MFIs do not have a formal documented framework for evaluating the performance of the CEO and senior management team on social performance indicators and the common metrics of performance evaluation continue to be operational and financial performance. The report gives only one example of an MFI in North India having social performance as part of the evaluation. The rating reports publicly available confirm this finding and also find similar paradigm in case of field-level staff.

While much is being done by MFIs to further social goals and positively impact client lives, it is not being done in an integrated manner. The practice can be improved if MFIs define the outcome/impact they want to achieve, break it down into SMART targets, integrate data related to these indicators in the MIS and periodically review it to track progress. The CoC assessment report by MicroSave covered 50 assessments including 32 NBFC-MFIs and found that only 37% MFIs have a documented SPM policy in place, which is the first step. In the absence of this, much of what is being done by MFIs remains unappreciated and gives rise to the charges of mission drift. Industry associations can also collate the data and put it in public domain to positively influence public perception of MFIs.

2.4.1.1 Governance: Needs to go beyond corporate governance

Most present day MFIs can be closely associated with one charismatic promoter/leader who established the institution and nurtured it. The exuberance of growth and the trend of chasing valuations seen before the crisis of 2010 were to a large extent the result of weak governance structures. The weaknesses in governance structures were exhibited through non-independence of the board from the executive, limited involvement in decision making and less representation of independent members of the board. Logically, the regulations put in place after the Andhra Pradesh crisis including tenets of UCoC lay greater emphasis on adopting corporate governance practices. RBI guidelines on corporate governance reinforce the best practices like having independent directors, subcommittees of the board and clear separation of powers between the governance and executive structures. The assumption behind these initiatives is that effective governance structures can ensure sustainability of operations as well as keep the operations weeded to the organisational mission.

The last two years' SPM report show that governance practices among Indian MFIs has improved considerably. The study on governance practices done by MicroSave last year provided evidence to this and key findings of the study were captured in last year's SPM report. The governance study report was formally released in June 2015 with detailed findings. The analysis in this section uses the detailed findings of the report in a two-dimensional manner—from the angle of the corporate governance and social performance. MIX data as well as rating reports made available by M-CRIL and the two other studies on responsible business practices and CoC done by MicroSave have also been made use of. Considering the sample size of 42 MFIs, the governance study remains the best possible source of information on sector-wide practices. Major aspects analysed in the report pertaining to good corporate governance practices relate to board composition, board administration and commitment to roles and responsibilities. Each of these broad criteria has been analysed in the governance study through various sub-parameters and the performance of MFIs has been presented across each sub-parameter on a three-point scale—low, average and high.

Board composition and structure have been analysed through 10 parameters and the scores on a few key aspects mandated by guidelines are presented in Figure 2.4. It is seen that almost 75% of MFIs in the sample score either average or high across the four parameters. Considering that NBFC-MFIs accounted for 71% of the sample and the fact that RBI's corporate governance guidelines apply to them, the results reflect the effect. The findings show that nearly two-thirds of the microfinance sector is doing average or exceeding the requirements in having independent directors, separating the roles between governance and executive and constitution of required subcommittees. The noteworthy feature is that across the four parameters, nearly one-third of the institutions are doing even better than what is required by the regulations/guidelines.

Ujjivan has put in place a sound corporate governance system. As per RBI guidelines on corporate governance and provisions of the companies act 2013, it has not only put in place ALCO, audit, governance, nomination and remuneration and CSR subcommittees of the board but also gone beyond by having three other board committees on risk management, human resources and SFB transition committee. Ujjivan has also developed its corporate governance code highlighting the terms of reference for its board and board committees, defining the role and responsibilities of its directors and key management personnel, framed and adopted new policies and procedures, established vigilance mechanism amongst other as a measure towards best corporate practices. Equitas on its part got its governance practices rated by Credit Rating Information Services of India Limited (CRISIL) through its 'Governance and Value Creation' (GVC) rating in 2013 and got GVC Level 2 grade. The practice of having requisite (one-third) number of independent members is now seen almost across all NBFC-MFIs and most NGO-MFIs, but the practice of board subcommittees on key areas like ALCO, audit and nominations is more prevalent across NBFC-MFIs.

Despite overall good performance under board composition and structure, a few grey areas have been identified in the report that find resonance in publicly available rating reports. Nearly 48% of MFIs continue to have the practice of promoter-cum-managing director/CEO acting as the board chair and nearly 39% of the MFIs had less than the prescribed number of independent members on the board. The author conducted interactions with CEOs of nine MFIs and this question of not having the required number of independent directors was probed. The common constraint cited was difficulty in getting qualified independent members, and it

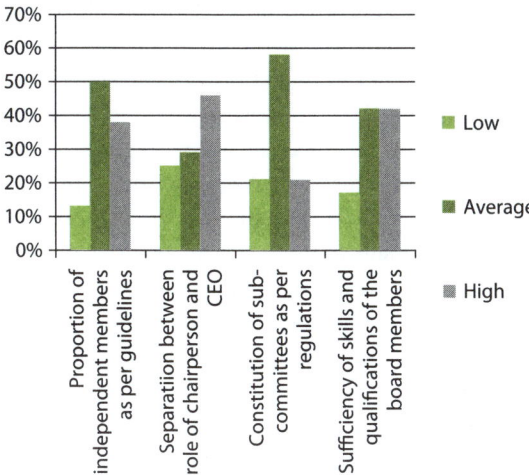

Figure 2.4 Board composition and structure

Source: MicroSave. June 2015. Governance Practices among Microfinance Institutions in India.

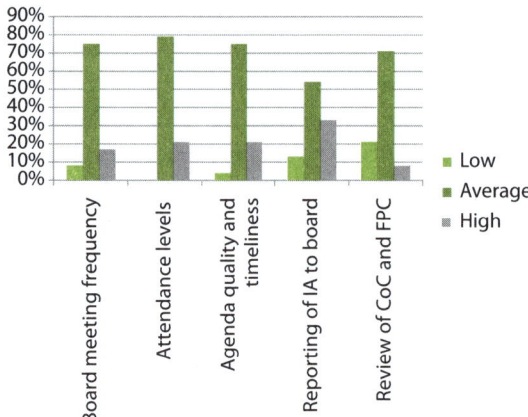

Figure 2.5 Process and functions of the board

Source: MicroSave. June 2015. Governance Practices among Microfinance Institutions in India.

was pointed out that to overcome this constraint many MFIs appoint retired bureaucrats and bankers as independent members. The challenge becomes more acute for smaller MFIs headquartered in non-metro locations.

Related to the aspect of board composition are the processes and functions associated with it. The findings of the governance study show that lot of progress has been made and the industry stands on a firm footing in these areas (Figure 2.5). It is seen that nearly 75% of MFIs had acceptable scores on frequency of board meetings, attendance levels, quality of agenda and review of CoC and FPC compliance. Noteworthy is the fact that only a very small fraction of MFIs had low score across all five parameters. Almost all MFIs hold at least one board meeting every quarter, 93% of MFIs had more than 75% attendance levels in board meetings, most NBFC-MFIs have a system wherein the internal auditor reports directly to the board through the audit subcommittee and 95% of the MFIs reported compliance on CoC and FPC to the board.

These key findings show that post Andhra Pradesh crisis, the sector has moved quite a bit towards good corporate governance practices. Evidence for this also comes from the comparative study of CoC assessments. MFIs assessed by M-CRIL in the last three years scored in the range of 66 to 97% under governance parameter. Acknowledging this fact, Microfinance Banana Skins report, 2014[18] did not identify governance in the list of top 10 risks faced by the microfinance sector in India, while globally governance remains a top risk area at number five.

The aspects discussed here look at the board's role primarily focusing on corporate oversight and fiduciary responsibilities. SPM for double bottom line institutions requires that governance structures go beyond corporate governance and also hold the institution responsible for its social goals. It requires that the board should be oriented on the institutions' social mission and goals, should review the social performance data connected with set social goals and use this data to provide strategic direction to the institution. Double bottom line institutions are also expected to integrate social performance metrics in performance evaluation of CEO and senior managers. As discussed under the section on social goals, the first step emanates from having SMART social goals and typically institutions having robust SPM practices report following data to the board.

- Outreach to target clients
- Social indicators that measure progress toward social targets
- Client retention/feedback data or satisfaction surveys/exit survey data
- Client protection risks and practices
- Employee retention and satisfaction
- Profit allocation and data/discussion on 'responsible prices and profits'.

As most MFIs in India do not have well-defined social goals and the focus on governance has been on traditional areas, lot of work is required to mainstream social performance in governance. Few critical findings from the governance study point to this. While most of the MFIs have the regulation required committees of the board, only 17% of the MFIs have SPM subcommittee and the performance of MFIs on key aspects of social performance related governance falls much short of what is required (Figure 2.6). However, the MIX data on social performance for 2014 shows that out of 63 reporting MFIs, 29 have either an SPM champion in the organisation or have SPM subcommittee of the board. Comparing the performance on social governance with the results presented in Figures 2.4 and 2.5 brings home the point that the sector has accorded higher focus on compliance-related governance, while social performance still remains in the relegated zone.

Absence of clearly defined social goals not only results in deficient reporting of social performance data but also weaknesses in integrating social metrics in performance evaluation of the CEO/senior

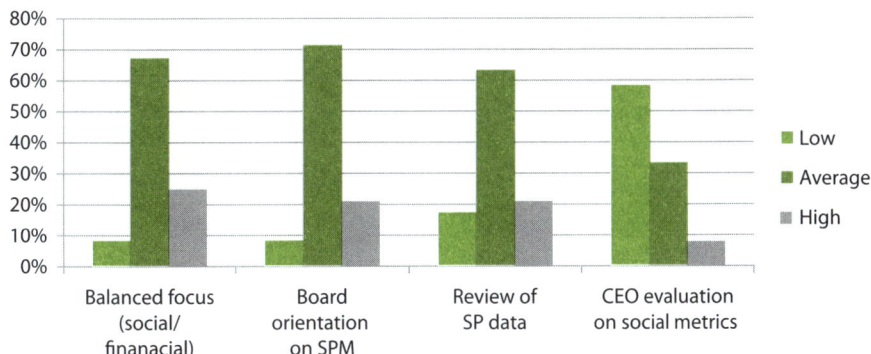

Figure 2.6 Board and social performance

Source: MicroSave. June 2015. Governance Practices among Microfinance Institutions in India.

management. A search through the rating reports of 18 MFIs on most common metrics in performance evaluation came up with profitability, outreach, revenue diversification, corporate governance and funds mobilisation as the most common performance evaluation metrics. The data points in Figure 2.6 do not reflect the entire picture. While the score on orientation of board members on social mission shows that 71% MFIs were in average category and 21% had a high score but the narrative mentions that most MFIs do not orient the board members on social mission. The obvious discrepancy is resolved by the explanation that as many board members have background in microfinance, the need for SPM orientation is obviated. This is a weak argument and the report also indicates that several board members equate SPM with CSR. Similarly, the focus of the board to adopt SPM revolves mainly around compliance, and the impetus to adopt global best practices in SPM is missing. The data in Figure 2.6 also shows that very few MFIs go beyond the compliance mode and majority fall under acceptable range.

Few MFIs have however gone the extra mile in this regard. CASHPOR's performance appraisal system for the MD includes social parameters like outreach of clients with PPI score of less than 25. Also the board is regularly provided reports on results of change survey, client grievances and outreach of non-financial services. Similarly, GFSPL's performance appraisal of CEO includes social aspects like uptake of social development loans [Water Sanitation and Hygiene (WASH) loans], outreach of activities related to social goals and client retention rate. At the industry level, the primary focus under governance remains on being compliant with the existing regulations, whether it is income ceiling prescribed by the RBI or governance standards set by the CoC and corporate governance guidelines of RBI. For 'doing good', industry needs to move from what is mandatory to what is desirable and this cannot be done by regulation and industry organisations (MFIN and Sa-Dhan)—it has to be done by the MFIs.

2.4.2 Client protection (USSPM dimensions 3 and 4): Good progress aided by regulation

The area of client protection has seen maximum action post 2010 crisis. As shown in Table 2.3, the focus of the national microfinance framework through regulatory guidelines and industry guidelines has been in this area and the global campaign on client protection is also focused on this area. This was natural as the major causative factors of the Andhra Pradesh crisis namely inappropriate collection practices, high interest rates, non-disclosure of full terms and conditions and absence of product diversity fall under CPP as defined by the SMART campaign. However, aspects like understanding the needs of clients and offering services in line with them go beyond client protection to mainstreaming client-centric practices. USSPM rightly categorises it as a separate dimension 3 under SPM while keeping all other aspects under dimension 4 terming it 'treat clients responsibly'. Lot of progress has been achieved by Indian MFIs under these dimensions since 2010 and it is no mean achievement that till data 10 MFIs have been CPP certified. This demonstrates that they meet the certification standards of care in implementing all of the CPP through their operations, product offerings and treatment of clients.

2.4.2.1 Product diversity and suitability to clients: Hemmed in by regulation or growth considerations?

Prior to 2010, the sector saw little product innovation as during the earlier phase, time was spent in stabilising the model of group loans and later during the expansion phase innovation took a backseat. It was easier to scale up with a plain vanilla one-year loan product as it obviated the necessity of investing in staff training and changes in operational systems. The regulatory structure in place since 2010 not only continues with the earlier policy of not allowing MFIs of any legal form to accept deposits, or offer insurance and pension products except as an agent but also prescribes loan sizes, its uses as well as the repayment period. Before the recent relaxations in April 2015 in loan size, the regulations prescribed that maximum loan amount in the first cycle and subsequent cycles should not exceed ₹35,000 and ₹50,000, respectively, loans above ₹15,000 to be repayable in not less than 24 months and 70% of loans to be provided for income generation purposes. The impact of the recent revision making the maximum loan size ₹60,000 and ₹1 lakh, respectively as well as lowering the percentage of income generating loans to 50% is yet to be seen on the ground. These micro-operational rules coupled with the prescribed household income ceiling for clients have considerably affected the room for innovation on credit products.

However, despite the regulatory limitations, MFIs had room to innovate and design new products by utilising the scope available on 15% of net assets,[19] which do not need to meet these requirements as well as the flexibility to offer 30% loans for non-income generating activities. Further, even within the category of qualifying assets, MFIs have the opportunity to diversify from the traditional group loan product to livelihood and microenterprise based loans matching the loan repayment with client's cash flow.

There is no comprehensive sector wide data on share of diversity of loan products and its relative share in loan portfolio. Industry associations do not collect data on product diversity. In the absence of this information, the CoC assessment review done by MicroSave provides a good pointer to product diversification. As per the study, which covered CoC assessment reports of 50 MFIs, the main product

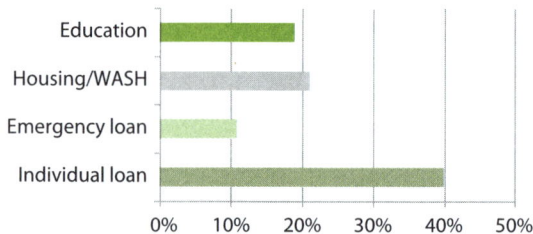

Figure 2.7 Diversified loan products offered by MFIs (n=50)

Source: MicroSave. November 2014. Code of Conduct Assessment for the Microfinance Sector: A Macro and Micro View of MFIs Compliance to the Code of Conduct.

diversification areas have been individual loans, emergency loans, micro-housing, WASH and education loans (Figure 2.7).

Individual loans have been introduced by many MFIs (40% as per CoC study sample) to meet the higher loan size requirement of mature clients. However, even though it the most prevalent loan product other than typical group loan, its share in the loan portfolio remains low on account of two reasons. First, being of higher size than allowable under RBI guidelines for qualifying assets, it cannot be more than 15% of net assets. Further, as higher size individual loans are often backed by collateral, they do not qualify to be reckoned as eligible to be classified as microfinance loans under RBI guidelines. Utkarsh, a Varanasi based MFI has been offering micro enterprise loans (MEL) for last three years. The loan amount under MEL ranges from ₹50,000 to ₹3 lakh with loans up to ₹1 lakh being unsecured and higher than ₹1 Lakh loans backed by security. As these loans cater to better off clients, the repayment is done either through post-dated cheques or electronic clearing. However, as per the data reported by Utkarsh, MEL loans along with house improvement loans, which are the two individual loan products it has, account for mere 5% of portfolio.

Ujjivan also offers individual business loan (IBL) catering to the needs of individual microentrepreneurs from its existing borrowers, who have a running business and require funds for working capital or fixed assets. A variant of this product, called individual bazaar loan (IBZL), is also offered to micro-entrepreneurs who do not have a repayment track record with Ujjivan. The loan size ranges from ₹41,000 to ₹150,000. However, similar to Utkarsh, individual business loans account for ~5% of loan portfolio. Janalakshmi is another prominent lender in Individual business loans category. Its nano business loans range from ₹60,000 to ₹2 lakh and have a maximum repayment period of 36 months. Janalakshmi's outreach under nano loans is also small—10,927 customers with a portfolio share of 2.13%.

Micro-housing and home improvement loans is another area, which has seen some action. Quite a few leading MFIs offer such loans; however, considering the size and collateral requirement, these also have limited share in portfolio. GFSPL has been very active in this area offering both home construction and improvement loans (Table 2.5). Home improvement loans include sanitation purposes such as availing water connections and construction of toilets and for improvement as well as extension of existing houses, i.e., repair or replace a roof, wall, floor or door, monsoon proofing, adding a room or kitchen.

Despite being an early mover in this space, home construction loans have a total outstanding portfolio of ₹2.6 crore and home improvement loans have a total outstanding of ₹137.55 crores. As against this, the total loan portfolio of GFSPL is in the range of ₹1,500 crore. To its credit, despite low portfolio share, home improvement loans have an impressive outreach of 215,882 borrowers. This is more credible as its home improvement loans include WASH loans, which require higher end-use monitoring and push up the operational cost.

Equitas has adopted another model for its micro-housing foray. As this product is fully secured and is of higher loan size, these loans though sourced by microfinance staff, are booked under Equitas

Table 2.5 Features of GFSPL home construction and improvement loans

	Home construction loan	Home improvement loan
Loan amount	₹25,000 to ₹200,000	₹5,000 to ₹25,000
Tenure	104 weeks to 260 weeks	52 weeks to 104 weeks
Rate of interest	22% per annum	22% per annum

Source: Grameen Financial Services.

Housing Finance (a separate Asset Finance NBFC) due to norms laid by RBI on 'Qualifying Assets'. So far, about 2,000 clients have availed micro-housing loan from Equitas to the tune of about ₹55 crores with an average loan size of around 1.80 lakhs for converting their *kutcha* houses to *pucca*, completing unfinished construction and for replacing their thatched roof. This model will allow scaling operations unfettered by regulatory restrictions.

Two points emerge—first, despite some movement in offering different loan products, such loans continue to constitute a very small percentage of total microfinance loans and the sector continues to be dominated by old style Joint Liability Group (JLG) loans. The examples given above pertain to MFIs, which are in top 10 list by asset size and if all MFIs are analysed, the diversification beyond group loans is even lower. Second, as RBI has recently relaxed the guidelines on loan sizes and allowed for higher percentage of non-income generating loans, it is time for the sector to scale up such loan products. Many sector experts however view the increased offering of higher sized individual business loans as a strategy to lower operational costs. There is some merit in this argument as there is a practice among some MFIs to have different types of loans like business loans, enterprise loans and housing loans which gives an impression of product diversity but a closer look reveals that the only significant distinguishing feature amongst these loans is the name.

Going beyond the broad typology of business loans, home improvement loans and WASH loans, the sector has seen little progress in product diversity.

While the regulatory limitations on loan size potentially constrained scale up of higher-sized business loans and insistence on income generating activities affected WASH and emergency loans, innovations related to offering small size cash flow linked livelihood loans could have been done within the regulatory boundary. Small shopkeepers, vendors and small landholding cultivators have different cash flow cycles; and either weekly or fortnightly loan repayments of one/two year do not match their cash flows. Sector scan shows negligible progress on this leaving aside a few examples like Ujjivan's agriculture loan product (Box 2.4). A similar agriculture loan product had been introduced by ESAF Microfin way back in 2004 with bullet repayment at the end

---

Box 2.4 Ujjivan's agriculture loan

Agriculture loan offers credit support to tenant, marginal and small farmers with land holding 0–2 acres and cultivating at least 0.5 acre of irrigated land and having an alternative source of income in the family. Loan size ranges from ₹31,000 to ₹80,000 and repayment period ranges from 4 to 12 months.

Individual agriculture loan product was launched in June 2015 in Satara and Karad. Loan is provided for crop cultivation expenses like:

- Purchase of agriculture inputs (seeds, fertilisers, agrochemicals, etc.).
- Paying for labour cost.
- Paying for irrigation.
- Buying small agricultural tools.

Multiple repayment options (bullet type and EMI) are provided to the farmers on the basis of their convenience. Loan amount and repayment is linked to crop and duration of cultivation.

Agriculture loan was expanded in other branches of East and South region. Presently 30 branches of Ujjivan offer this product.

Source: Material for Responsible Finance Report sent by Ujjivan.

of nine months but it has not been scaled up. It is offered only in one branch (Pakhanjore) and had 379 clients as on 31 July 2015.

Technology-based product and process improvement in loan products have seen an increase beyond point of sale (POS) machines and mobile-based transactions. Janalakshmi's JanaCash Wallet is mobile payments platform targeted towards existing loan customers as well as open market customers. The holder of the Jana Cash Wallet can opt for a LINKED Jana Cash Card and can seamlessly transfer money between the two instruments. Customers can load money into the wallet by visiting a nearby Jana Mitra outlet or from debit card, net banking or credit card accounts. JanaCash Wallet holders can undertake wide variety of transactions including mobile recharge, bill payment, peer-to-peer transfer, remittances, online payments, etc. Several other services are likely to be enabled in the future. Ujjivan has implemented a process change of cashless disbursements and repayments which not only provides

operational ease to the customer and Ujjivan but also ensures financial inclusion through a bank account. During the year 2014–15, it managed to disburse 9.76 lakh loans out of the 1.73 lakh loans processed during the year through bank account.

SKS also initiated a project with Airtel's M-Pesa during last year involving mobile wallets to be serviced by M-Pesa agents for repayments. Under this project, client loads e-money from the agent and adds SKS as a beneficiary to make repayment from her mobile phone. Both SKS field staff and client get instant messages confirming the transaction. At present, the project is in a pilot stage in two branches of Rajasthan—Sikar and Bassi.

Retailing of pension product is another area, which has seen lot of activity in recent years. While few MFIs had become aggregators of the Pension Fund Regulatory and Development Authority (PFRDA) for enrolling its members under NPS-Swavalamban now redesigned at Atal Pension Yojana (APY), quite a few act as sub-aggregators. The sector has seen quite a bit of traction under this with MFIN members recording 1.9 million pension accounts, which forms around 7% of total client base of 30 million. As more and more institutions were getting involved in this, the government reformulated it as APY which has a defined benefit component as against the earlier scheme based on defined contribution. This change would have been seamless as per the provisions enabling transfer of existing contributors to the new scheme but for the rule which stipulates that only banks can become aggregators for APY. The change adversely affects MFIs acting as aggregators as not only their commission gets halved but also on account of the fact that availability of bank branches in many rural areas is limited. A representation has been made to PFRDA by some MFIs and hopefully the issue will be resolved allowing MFIs to increase the pension outreach.

As against traction under pension schemes, the mobilisation of deposits as banking correspondent by NBFC-MFIs has not picked up. RBI allowed NBFC-MFIs to act as BC after a lot of representations by the industry asking for it, but since the issue of revised guidelines in July 2014, none of the big MFIs have taken it up. Quite a few MFIs have the opinion that with around ₹1 commission[20] per transaction, the activity is not viable as they need to hire a new staff to avoid co-mingling concerns. On the other hand, few MFIs indicated that banks are not willing to engage MFIs preferring conventional BCs over them. Offering of savings service would complete the circle of financial services and may be MFIs need to think of partly cross subsidising costs of deposit mobilisation. Absence of savings products is going to be a major competitive disadvantage in future as SFBs will offer both savings and loans.

2.4.2.2 Transparency, grievance redressal and collection practices: Good progress

Considering the focus of RBI guidelines and CoC on these aspects, it is logical that the practices have improved considerably in these areas. For increasing transparency, most MFIs have continued the practice of conducting compulsory group trainings (CGT) for all new clients during which the features and terms and conditions are communicated in vernacular to the clients. Going further, the sector has also seen innovative practices. SKS uses interactive tools such as cooperation games to explain the concept of joint liability and physical money to explain the concept of declining interest rate. Swadhar, based in western India, has introduced a flipchart type booklet for staff to help them communicate and to ensure that all the terms are also visually communicated for ease of clients. Utkarsh offers a product brochure with a summary of product details and the terms and conditions to its clients at the time of application. Sonata in order to ensure that clients make an informed choice includes comparative rate of interest from other sources like rural banks, SHG programme and banks in the loan application form.

The practice of transparency in pricing has been well grounded in operations of all MFIs. Almost all MFIs follow the norm of stating the interest rate in declining terms and the processing fee as mandated by regulation in the loan card. As a best practice, many MFIs in addition to mentioning all charges on the loan card/passbook also provide clients with a copy of the loan contract—all 10 CPP certified MFIs do offer copy of loan contract to the clients. Post 2010, another significant change has been use of vernacular in documents related to the client. To increase transparency, all MFI branches display the CoC guidelines as well as product terms and conditions. All receipts are acknowledged by various means—sign of the loan officer, written receipts, thermal receipts, etc. The minimum average time taken between loan application and disbursement (for new clients) in

---

Box 2.5 Aspects covered in internal audit by Sonata Finance

- Group formation, CGT and group recognition test (GRT) processes.
- Client's awareness regarding grievance mechanism and RBI guidelines.
- Verification of cases of pre-closure, advance payments and dropouts.
- Staff conduct during centre meetings, whether staff has any personal relations with any clients.
- Issuance and updating of loan cards.
- Verification of Insurance claim settlement.

Source: Discussions with Anoop Singh, MD, Sonata Finance.

---

the sector has reduced to around seven days during which the clients can reconsider their decision of availing the loan. The efforts in communicating with clients have been backed up by including these aspects in monitoring system to ensure that the policies are being followed in the field. Most MFIs have incorporated aspects related to awareness and complaints in their internal audit process.

These efforts have had a significant impact on the awareness levels of clients as evidenced by data collated from 12 social ratings conducted by M-CRIL in last two years. The results are based on interaction of the rating team with the clients through surveys and focus group discussions (FGDs). The results show that nearly 70% clients are aware of the loan product and credit life insurance terms and conditions (Figure 2.8). These results become more noteworthy considering that most MFI clients do

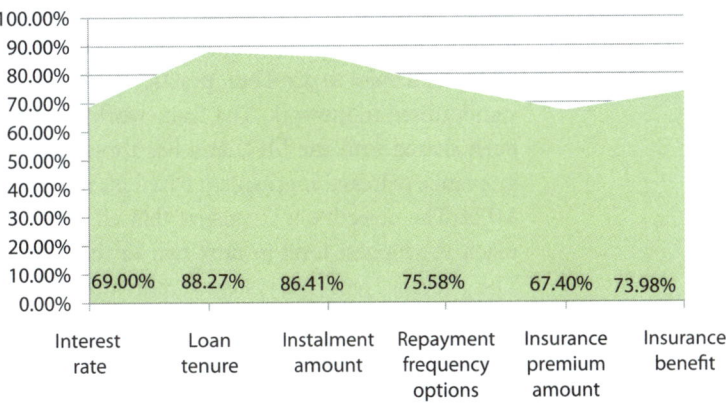

Figure 2.8 Clients awareness level in 12 MFIs

Source: Social rating reports of M-CRIL.

not have functional literacy at the time of associating with MFIs. The range of MFIs in the sample include three MFIs with operations in poorer parts of eastern UP and Bihar and it can be safely deduced that the awareness levels would be even higher in southern and eastern parts of the country.

Total 94 Indian MFIs provided data to microfinance transparency, which further reinforces transparency in operations of Indian MFIs,[21] and the comforting state of practice is reflected in Indian MFIs scoring 'Good' under its pricing transparency index. Regulatory guidelines on fixing processing fee at 1% of the loan amount, no extra charges on insurance premium and declaration of effective interest rate have immensely contributed to this improvement.

2.4.2.3 Grievance redressal: Movement towards multi-channel approach

Effective grievance redressal is a key principle of client protection architecture; it ensures that the client voices are heard and resolved for effective service delivery. Grievance redressal systems act as early warning systems for problems in the field. Pre-2010 growth phase saw weakening of this system as the focus was mainly on building loan book and ensuring timely repayments, which resulted in field officers reducing client relationship to transaction-based meetings. In hindsight, it can be postulated that a stronger relationship with clients could have enabled better handling of the defaults in 2010. The FPC of RBI keeps this as a strong focus area making board of directors responsible for ensuring an effective grievance redressal policy.

While MFIs have strengthened their grievance redressal systems, MFIN as industry association has also placed importance on it. MFIN has a two-tiered approach to resolving customer grievances. MFIN collected grievance redressal policies of its members and shared it with the SMART campaign and tasked them to distil best practices and evolve a standardised framework. The framework has since been shared with the MFIs and has three levels of grievance redressal mechanism based on the size of MFIs. The objective is to ensure that all members reach the highest level in next two to three years. The grievance redressal system at individual MFIs is monitored by MFIN on a monthly basis. MFIN has prescribed a template for reporting, which has details of complaint, client details, timelines and action taken. Further, as an appellate, it has set up an IVR helpline. Calls are routed based on geography to its head office or its regional offices. MFIN follows up the complaints with the member MFIs and action taken report is shared with enforcement committee. It has set a turnaround time of 15 days to resolve the complaints received. In order to popularise the IVR helpline number, MFIN has circulated sample stickers to all members to be pasted on each loan card/pass book. The helpline started in June 2015 and by end July around 150 calls were received.[22]

Typically MFIs are adopting multiple channels to ensure that client grievances are heard and the most common practices are toll free number/customer care number, phone number of branch, branch manager and area head printed on loan cards and complaint boxes at branches. Clients are made aware of these channels during group training as well as through mentioning it on the loan card. Information gleaned through data provided by MFIs, CPP certifications and social ratings done by M-CRIL shows that this is followed by putting in place a mechanism to consolidate complaints, policies related to escalation matrix and resolution time. Larger MFIs operating in multiple states across the country have multi-lingual teams to handle customer calls.

Few MFIs have also gone beyond these measures. SKS has put in place a robust client grievance redressal policy and also appointed an external person as an ombudsman to oversee the grievance architecture. The grievance redressal is a three-step process in SKS. As a first step, the member addresses the issue to the Sangam Manager (SM).[23] The SM registers the complaint in the centre register and resolves the issue within the prescribed resolution time and if the member is not satisfied with the resolution provided by the SM, as a second step she can call the 1–800 member helpline and register the complaint. Member helpline executive registers the complaint and a ticket number is generated while resolution is done within the TAT (members can also trace the complaint with their customer id. The helpline is operational for 14 hours in a day and is manned by executives who can handle calls in seven languages. All calls are recorded and based on the geographical origin are automatically routed to the relevant language team. The final step relates to calling the ombudsman team. It is backed up by an elaborate escalation matrix (Figure 2.9). SKS has trained its key process team members on lean and six sigma to work on continuous improvement of key business processes and ensure satisfaction of customers.

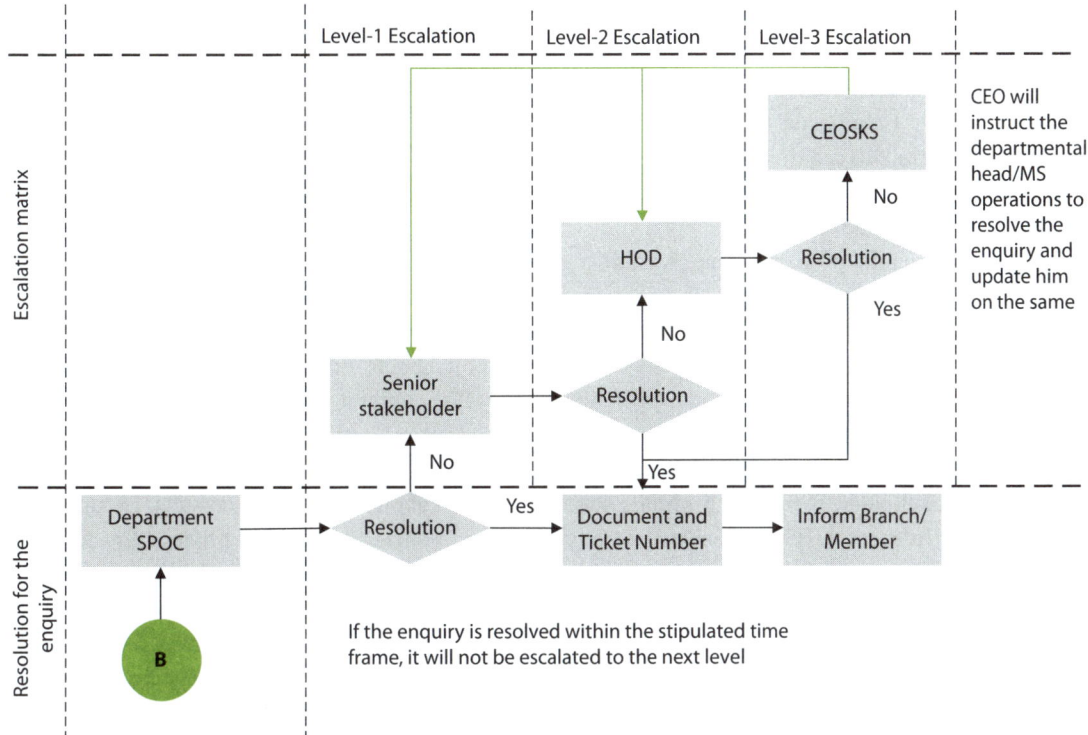

Figure 2.9 SKS complaint escalation matrix

Source: SKS Microfinance.

Another example of best practice comes from Ujjivan. Its service quality department has a process of making calls to seek customer feedback and grievances proactively. This has been done considering that the customer profile served by the MFI leaves possibilities that many of them may not complain even if they are not satisfied with services. Ujjivan has partnered with professional Business Process Outsourcing (BPO) service providers to outsource the call centre programme in each region. The call centre service providers have been carefully chosen in line with its social mission; for instance, Vindhya E-Info Media Pvt Ltd. based at Bangalore employs differently abled persons and Indian Association for the Blind, Madurai, employs visually impaired people. Currently there are 45 tele-callers at five call-centres across India. Ujjivan has also started a policy of making welcome calls to all customers post loan disbursement with the objective of seeking their feedback on their satisfaction on loan application process, verifying the accuracy of a few important data provided by the customer and cross-verifying loan purpose as well as to check their understanding on fees and charges, repayment amount and repayment dates.

Overall the sector has displayed good progress on putting in place grievance redressal systems and it is hoped that in line with expectations of MFIN, all MFIs will move up from minimum framework to best practices. Evidence on active use of channels comes from the data on CPP certifications done in India. On an average, 2.64% of the combined client base of certified MFIs had called on the customer care number either to seek information or to register complaints.

2.4.2.4 Collection practices: Codified and backed by training but is something missing?

Newspaper reports of harassed and abused clients and in some cases reports of client suicide on account of excessive pressure brought on clients by the field staff precipitated the action of the Andhra Pradesh government in 2010. The measures prescribed by the Andhra Pradesh ordinance went to the other extreme of hurting MFI operations and RBI regulations and UCoC have restored the balance. Sections 2.3.1.1 and 2.3.1.2 detailed the requirements for MFIs. As these are mandatory guidelines, which are checked through CoC assessments, industry has seen a dramatic change in policies post 2010.

Almost all MFIs have developed their CoC for staff and also follow RBI's FPC in conjunction with the industry CoC. In most MFIs, staff, especially the field staff, receive training on the institution's adopted CoC and are also required to sign an undertaking in which they agree to abide by the rules and regulations of the institution.

Arohan's staff code prohibits 'coercive collection practices' which includes rude or aggressive behaviour and approaching clients for repayment during odd hours, bereavement or sickness. The ethics code includes courteous conduct, prohibits staff members from acting in an intimidating manner and using abusive language with any customer, colleague or stakeholder. It further prohibits staff from engaging in mental, physical, sexual or any other form of abuse. Arohan uses role plays to educate field staff distinguish between acceptable and unacceptable conduct towards clients. Staff is appraised according to the key performance indicators (KPI) communicated at the beginning of the year and accorded an alpha-numeric grade. The numeric part of the grade corresponds to the business achievements whereas the alphabet part determines the assessment of the soft skills. GFSPL has designed a special e-module to train staff on CoC. All branch staff has to take an e-quiz on CoC after the training. ESAF's CoClike others contains instructions for staff detailing the expected and prohibited behaviour and possible acts of misconduct. Induction training for the staff includes a session on CoC and CPP. Similar process of codification, trainings and action on erring staff is seen across most MFIs. Interviews with industry experts and author's own field experience reveal that the earlier practice of sitting at client's home beyond office hours to exert pressure in cases of default have lessened to a considerable degree. Industry associations have also been active in dealing with reported cases of client distress. In recent past, MFIN investigated incidents in Amroha (UP), Azamgarh (UP), Narsinghpur (MP) and Burhanpur (MP) and in not so distant past (September 2014), it got the events in Erode and Nanded investigated by two external agencies.

But despite all these steps, many experts believe that there might be a missing link between policies and practice. Overall the sector is reporting ~99% recovery and this is more noteworthy considering much of the sector has moved away from weekly repayments to fortnightly or monthly repayments.

Average loan size has also gone up in recent years (₹16,327 in 2014–15). It seems difficult to register near perfect recovery rates with higher loan instalments on account of increased repayment frequency—more so while catering to poor clients who often have income fluctuations. In the past, despite smaller loan sizes and weekly repayments, there were cases of excessive pressure on clients to achieve zero delinquency. The near absence of policies in the sector to reschedule loans in cases of wilful default further adds to the mystery, though the MFIs counter it with saying that the rescheduling policies are an anachronism in a near perfect recovery scenario. Moreover, having such policies and informing clients about it can lead to defaults. Though as per codified policies, MFIs do not follow zero tolerance policy on defaults, portfolio quality is one of the parameters for staff incentive in most of the MFIs. The recent events in Madhya Pradesh and Uttar Pradesh point that the reality is not as hunky dory as the data and policies suggest. It is a sensitive issue and needs to be examined empirically; MFIs need to be watchful and invest more resources in monitoring of field practices to ensure that repayments are genuine and not causing any client distress.

2.4.3 Including staff as part of social performance and balancing financial and social performance (USSPM dimensions 5 and 6)

Client protection has been the key focus area in the rebuilding phase and rightly so; social performance framework however places equal importance on employees as satisfied and motivated work force is critical to delivering client-centric services. Responsibility to staff is not the subject matter of prudential regulation and labour laws only prescribe basic conditions like minimum wages, provident fund and mandatory leaves. Industry CoC also leaves it at that point. Going beyond minimum stipulations requires intent and the realisation that human capital is as important as financial capital, if not more. Not surprisingly in an industry majorly shaped by regulations in post 2010 phase, this aspect has not received much attention. The consequences of Andhra Pradesh crisis have been analysed more from the perspective of clients losing access to financial services. The story of thousands of field staff losing their jobs due to contraction of the microfinance industry remains untold. Being not a focus area is also reflected in lack of data and studies pertaining to it. Post 2010, only one study[24] has been done in this area and as the sector has moved towards mainstream financial ratings, the data available on staff related aspect is limited and relates to staff productivity, percentage of women staff and whether or not minimum prescribed working conditions are being met. This section therefore uses some limited data and proxy indicators to analyse responsibility to staff.

Compensation is an important issue concerning responsibility to the staff especially field staff who constitute around 60–70% of MFI workforce. Data analysis from rating reports shows that while all MFIs meet the minimum wages and perks requirement, the wage structure for field staff veers towards being at 150% of per capita gross national income (GNI) for India[25] with some variations and has shown marginal increase over the years. The HR study report referred to earlier confirms this by stating: 'In majority of the cases, the tendency was to comply with the provisions of law by paying the minimum wage' and goes on to say that other comparable industries provide better monetary compensation and reduced working hours to candidates of similar background.

It needs to be examined whether the depressed wages and labour intensive nature of field jobs in the sector contributes to high rates of staff turnover averaging at 25%.[26] High staff turnover not only points towards strengthening responsibility to staff but also has an adverse effect on financial performance (Figure 2.10). Recruitment, training and attuning new staff to institutional ethos takes time and resources and increases cost.

To be fair to MFIs, it needs to be mentioned that in post 2010 scenario, MFIs have invested substantial resources in training systems for staff and meeting regulatory compliances within the tight margin cap on pricing. Even larger MFIs have to meet their operational cost, make provisions for risky assets and be profitable within the allowable margin of 10% over cost of borrowings, leaving little room for increasing salaries. From the angle of social performance, external limitations of regulatory guidelines can be justified if the constraint has been applicable across the workforce rather than being limited to the field staff. Examination of this aspect requires time series data on movement of salaries of field staff and senior management, which is unfortunately not available with either MIX or MFIN database.

Staff satisfaction surveys and gender balance can be other metrics of measuring responsibility to staff. It is heartening that nearly 50% of MFIs (out of 28 which submitted data to the questionnaire for this report) reported conducting staff satisfaction study or survey during last one year. All surveys were done in-house and despite the limitation of positive bias, all surveys showed high level of staff satisfaction (Box 2.6). Another matter of pride for the sector in this area comes from recognition of Ujjivan as 24th best place to work in India and 16th best place to work in Asia in the category of best large workplaces.[27]

Gender balance remains skewed in the industry with the HR study of 2013 reporting average percentage of women staff in 25 MFIs at 19%. Data from M-CRIL social rating reports of 12 MFIs done in last two years confirms this with an average of 18% women staff with even smaller share in the

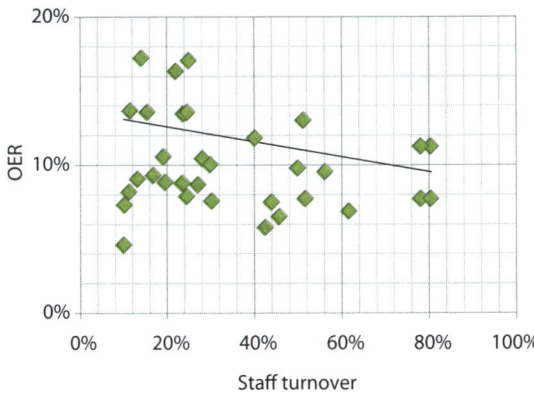

Figure 2.10 Effect of staff turnover on operating expense ratio (OER) of MFIs

Source: M-CRIL Microfinance Review 2014.

Box 2.6 Highlights from Satin's staff satisfaction survey in 2014–15 (n=763)

- 98% felt being integral part of the organisation.
- 63% were satisfied with leave days.
- 69% were satisfied with salary.
- 73% reported having adequate training for the job.
- 85% considered level of communication between staff and management as good.

Source: Employee Job Satisfaction and Engagement Report, 2014–15, Satin Creditcare Betwork Ltd.

middle and senior management. *M-CRIL Microfinance Review 2014* drawing on MIX data of 28 MFIs puts the share of women staff at 13.2%. The MFIs reason that the loan officers' job requires long hours of work and extensive field travel, an arduous task that is difficult for women to perform, particularly in rural areas. However, unlike in the case of salaries where regulation is often cited as the impediment, this argument on gender skewness does not stand the test of logic. If the argument is valid, it should result in lesser percentage of women staff at field level and higher percentage at managerial level, but it is not so. The HR study 2013 showed similar levels of women staff at both field level and head office. Considering that the sector is focused on women clients, it is imperative that more efforts are made at increasing the share of women staff.

Overall, while the sector has moved positively in adequately meeting minimum stipulations of working conditions, formulating human resource policies, fair and unbiased recruitment and staff training, it needs to do more to address gender balance, arresting staff attrition and having a relook at the salary structure for the field staff.

2.4.3.1 Balancing financial with social: Double bottom line

This USSPM dimension has three core elements. First, institutions committed to double bottom line performance should grow responsibly, thereby not hurting clients' interests. Second, investors, lenders, board and management should be committed to double bottom line performance, and finally compensation structure for senior management should be appropriate for a double bottom line performance.

Growth rates need to be monitored to ensure that clients are not over-indebted by expansion in saturated markets and have to be matched by proportionate investments in controls and systems. Indian microfinance market seems to be back on the growth path with MFIN members (which account for nearly 90% market share) growing their loan book by 64% during 2014–15 as compared to 43% and 4% in 2013–14 and 2012–13, respectively. Among the top 10 NBFC-MFIs, the annual growth rates ranged from 18% to 106%. While growth is back, the assurance that clients interest are not jeopardised comes from adherence to CoC guidelines, mandatory check of indebtedness through credit bureau and establishment of multiple channel grievance system across the industry. Clients have

also benefitted from increased operational efficiency in the form of reduced interest rates. As per *M-CRIL Microfinance Review 2014*, average yield fell to 24% in 2013–14 as compared to 28.3% in 2009–10. This fall in yield is more significant considering that lending rates of banks have not reduced as compared to 2009–10. Seen with RBI's cap on interest rate, it implies that the fall is a result of improved efficiencies. However, there are very few examples of institutions capping growth rates or profitability and the paradigm of fund availability based growth continues to be the dominant driving theme. CASHPOR has adopted a policy of capping operational self-sustainability at 110% and any increase in operational surplus is passed on to clients by way of reduced interest rates. Equitas has a board-approved policy of capping return on assets (RoA) at 5% and in case of profitability exceeding it, the same is passed on to clients. Even though the policy of capping growth rates or profitability is not widespread in the industry, stakeholders derive comfort from MFI's compliance to client protection guidelines especially prevention of over-indebtedness, multiple loans and cap on interest rates. The question whether despite these regulatory prescriptions, hidden risks in terms of geographical skew in growth, drivers of increased efficiency and robustness of measures taken to prevent over-indebtedness are emerging again is examined in Chapter 3 dealing with potential risks.

Compensation structure of senior executives has been a contentious issue and there is no unanimity on which metrics should be adopted to judge its appropriateness. On one hand, some quote Infosys founder Narayana Murthy's interview of 2012[28] wherein he suggested a ratio of 20 to 25 between the salary of the lowest-level professional and the highest compensation paid in the corporation, the other side talks about the need to give flexibility in deciding senior management compensation to retain high performing managers. Sector experts also think that comparing microfinance sector, wherein the gap between the skill set of the lowest and highest rung is too wide, to other industries is a wrong benchmark. The survey questionnaire for this report sought information on this aspect but of the 28 MFIs who responded, only 18 MFIs answered this question. Of these 18, only two belong to the list of top 10 MFIs by asset size. The data shows that the ratio of loan officer to CEO salary ranges from 1:10 to 1:60 with lower ranges seen amongst smaller-sized NBFC-MFIs and NGO-MFIs. Only one large MFI—Equitas has a stated policy of keeping the CEO compensation not above 40 times of base staff salary. While the concern on salary structure for field-level staff has been mentioned in the section on responsibility to staff, it is difficult to comment on the fairness of the prevalent ratio in the industry in the absence of data for all MFIs and any defined benchmark for measuring the adequacy of this ratio. It is better left to the board and shareholders to decide it based on the institution's mission and profitability.

2.5 NEED TO GO BEYOND 'DO NO HARM' TO 'DOING GOOD'

There is an overwhelming consensus amongst all stakeholders including MFIs that different initiatives post 2010 have had a significant impact on the sector especially relating to client protection and veering the sector towards balanced social and financial performance. Much progress has been achieved by way of improved governance and transparency, lowering costs, establishing multiple channel based grievance redressal system and appropriate collection practices. Indian MFIs also do well on poverty outreach and focusing on non-financial services. This performance is more appreciable as it has come in the wake of high degree of regulation bordering on micro-management and at a time when people had started writing its epitaph.

Since the industry caters to vulnerable sections of the society and has a double bottom line commitment, there are areas of improvement which will enable the sector to move to 'do good' paradigm. Now that the sector is well and truly back on its feet and profitable, it is expected that it moves beyond mandatory to desirable changes. The recent relaxations given by the RBI on use of loans as well as loan sizes open up the right opportunity to work on product diversity. In addition, MFIs also need to focus on working conditions of staff, integration of social goals/metrics aligned to institutional mission and balancing social and financial performance. These are 'intent' issues that cannot be induced by external guidelines but have to evolve from institutional commitment to best practices in social performance.

ANNEXURES

ANNEXURE 2.1
Major initiatives taken by SIDBI during 2014–15

- SIDBI introduced a product which offers longer tenor loans and instruments for well-performing MFIs.
- SIDBI focused on capacity building of MFI personnel and nominated about 90 mid- and senior-level microfinance professionals for various inland and foreign trainings.
- The cumulative assistance [including loans, equity and quasi equity but excluding India Microfinance Equity Fund (IMEF) and (PSIG)] sanctioned under SIDBI's microfinance initiatives up to 31 March 2015 aggregated ₹10,719.01 crore, while cumulative disbursements aggregated ₹9,373.59 crore. The number of MFIs assisted by SIDBI and having loan outstanding with the bank as on 31 March 2015 stood at 93. The assistance through SIDBI has benefitted around 332 lakh (approx.) disadvantaged people, most of them being women. The comparative operational highlights of SIDBI's microfinance support are given in the following table.

Assistance under Micro Credit Loans and Equity/Quasi Equity Assistance (₹ Crores)

S. No.	Particulars	FY 2013–14		FY 2014–15		Cumulative
		Disbursement	Outstanding	Disbursement	Outstanding	Disbursement
1.	Term loans to MFIs	581.00	1,276.31	950.02	1,482.09	8,593.60
2.	Missing middle assistance to PFIs/NBFCs	33.00	75.29	210.00	267.37	346.14
3.	Long-dated loans to MFIs	0.00	0.00	92.00	142.00	142.00
4.	MEL—direct lending	0.00	1.42	0.00	0.77	12.25

(Continued)

(Continued)

| S. No. | Particulars | FY 2013–14 | | FY 2014–15 | | Cumulative |
		Disbursement	Outstanding	Disbursement	Outstanding	Disbursement
5.	Transformation loan (TL)/corpus support for transformation	0.00	1.85	0.00	1.85	19.05
6.	Subordinate debt.	0.00	100.00	0.00	100	175.00
7.	Equity support	0.00	84.89	0.00	84.89	85.55
8.	Optionally convertible cumulative preference shares	0.00	275.04	0.00	247.46	0.00
9.	Compulsory convertible preference shares	0.00	109.20	0.00	109.20	0.00
	Total	614.00	1,924.00	1,252.02	2,435.63	9,373.59

- Continued support under IMEF set up in 2011–12 by the Government of India with the primary objective of providing equity and quasi-equity to smaller MFIs. As at the end of March 2015, SIDBI commited an amount of ₹162.25 crore to 56 MFIs under the scheme.
- Under the debt fund scheme of PSIG programme supported by the Department for International Developent (DFID), Government of UK, out of total sanction of ₹71.29 crore, ₹64.73 crore was disbursed up to 31 March 2015.
- Based on Capacity Building Needs Assessment (CBNA) exercise, SIDBI extended support to MFIs under PSIG for loan portfolio audit, social performance management, client protection assessment, expansion of other financial services, technology upgradation, human resource development, strengthening risk management and governance, etc. Grant assistance of ₹10.78 crore was sanctioned to 28 MFIs.

Initiatives on responsible finance

- SIDBI has created a lenders' forum comprising key lenders of MFI with a view to promote cooperation among MFI lenders for leveraging support to MFIs across the sector. Pursuant to initiatives of SIDBI, regional chapters of 'lenders' forum' have been set up for better coordination among lenders and closer interaction with the MFIs. So far, SIDBI has conducted nine meetings of lenders' forum.
- Continued its support for CoC assessments by reimbursing 75% of the cost of Code of Conduct Assessments (COCA) subject to a maximum reimbursement of ₹1,50,000. A total of 82 assessments have since been undertaken and reports of 69 MFIs have been placed in the public domain. During 2014–15, SIDBI took up a fresh round of COCA exercise for 16 MFIs including repeat assessments of eight MFIs.
- SIDBI has supported the India Microfinance Platform (IMFP) developed by MIX to provide and disseminate various financial and operational information on Indian MFIs. It is a global, Web-based, microfinance information platform, a MIX market tailored for India, i.e., IMFP—meant to provide and disseminate valuable information on the Indian MFIs. The IMFP project has resulted in enhanced data coverage for India's microfinance sector through growth in the number of reporting MFIs as well as development of granular, district-level datasets.
- SIDBI engaged Access Assist for undertaking identified policy advocacy initiatives in PSIG states. A National Think Tank comprising of eminent experts in the microfinance/development sector has been set up to provide overall direction and guidance to the policy advocacy initiatives. During the year, three meetings of the Think Tank were held. Further, state financial inclusion forums (SFIF) comprising all important stakeholders have been set up in each of the four PSIG states with the objective of bringing synergy and coordination among their work and to identify areas where PSIG can make a catalytic intervention.
- A pilot project on providing financial literacy and women empowerment training has been started in Uttar Pradesh and Bihar in partnership with seven MFIs. The pilot envisages creating a cadre of 80 master trainers and training of about 60,000 women clients of these seven MFIs.
- SIDBI organised five gender sensitisation workshops for senior executives and leaders of partner MFI's.

ANNEXURE 2.2
Global responsible finance initiatives for retail institutions

Stating commitment	Tools for self-assessment	Tools for implementation	Demonstrating commitment	Evaluations, audits and ratings	Certifications
SMART Campaign Endorsement	SMART Getting Started Questionnaire	SMART Tools	Reporting to MF Transparency	Microfinance Institutional Ratings	Smart Campaign Certification
Global Appeal for Responsible Microfinance	Microfinance Transparency: Calculating Transparent Pricing Tool v2.2	USSPM—Implementation Series	Reporting to MIX	Social Ratings	Progress Out of Poverty Certification
MF Transparency	MIX/SAVIX Reports		Truelift Milestones	Truelift	Microfinance Transparency Seal of Excellence
Social Performance Task Force	USSPM			SPI-4	MIX S.T.A.R Recognition
Truelift Community of Practice	Truelift Community of Practice			Code of Conduct Assessments	
	SPI-4				
	Responsible Business Index				

Legends		
Client Protection Tools	Social Performance Tools	Social Performance Tools Applicable Only to Indian MFIs

Social Goals

Source: Microfinance Barometer 2013. Only retail finance initiatives have been focused upon as the tools for direct and indirect investors are not applicable in the Indian context.

ANNEXURE 2.3
FY 2013–18: Social goals—Grameen Financial Services Pvt Ltd.

Particulars	FY14	FY15	FY16	FY17	FY18
Sanitation Coverage	60%	70%	80%	90%	100%
Healthcare Insurance Coverage	30%	40%	50%	60%	70%
Pension Scheme Coverage	20%	30%	40%	50%	60%
Safe Drinking Water Coverage	70%	80%	90%	100%	100%
Socioeconomic Development Workshops	2 per branch	2 per branch	2 per branch	2 per branch	2 per branch
Husband's Workshops	1 per branch	1 per branch	1 per branch	1 per branch	1 per branch
Financial Literacy Training Coverage	30%	60%	80%	100%	100%

Source: Grameen Financial Services Pvt. Ltd.

SKS Microfinance Limited has been providing microfinance services in 15 Indian states since 1997. It is imperative for SKS to ascertain whether their services are providing 'high value' to the low-income households (social empowerment, expansion and strengthening of household businesses and finances). For this purpose, the 'SKS Quick Impact' report assessed the social and economic impact of loans on 514 female borrowers in Maharashtra and Madhya Pradesh.

Impact on household income generation activities

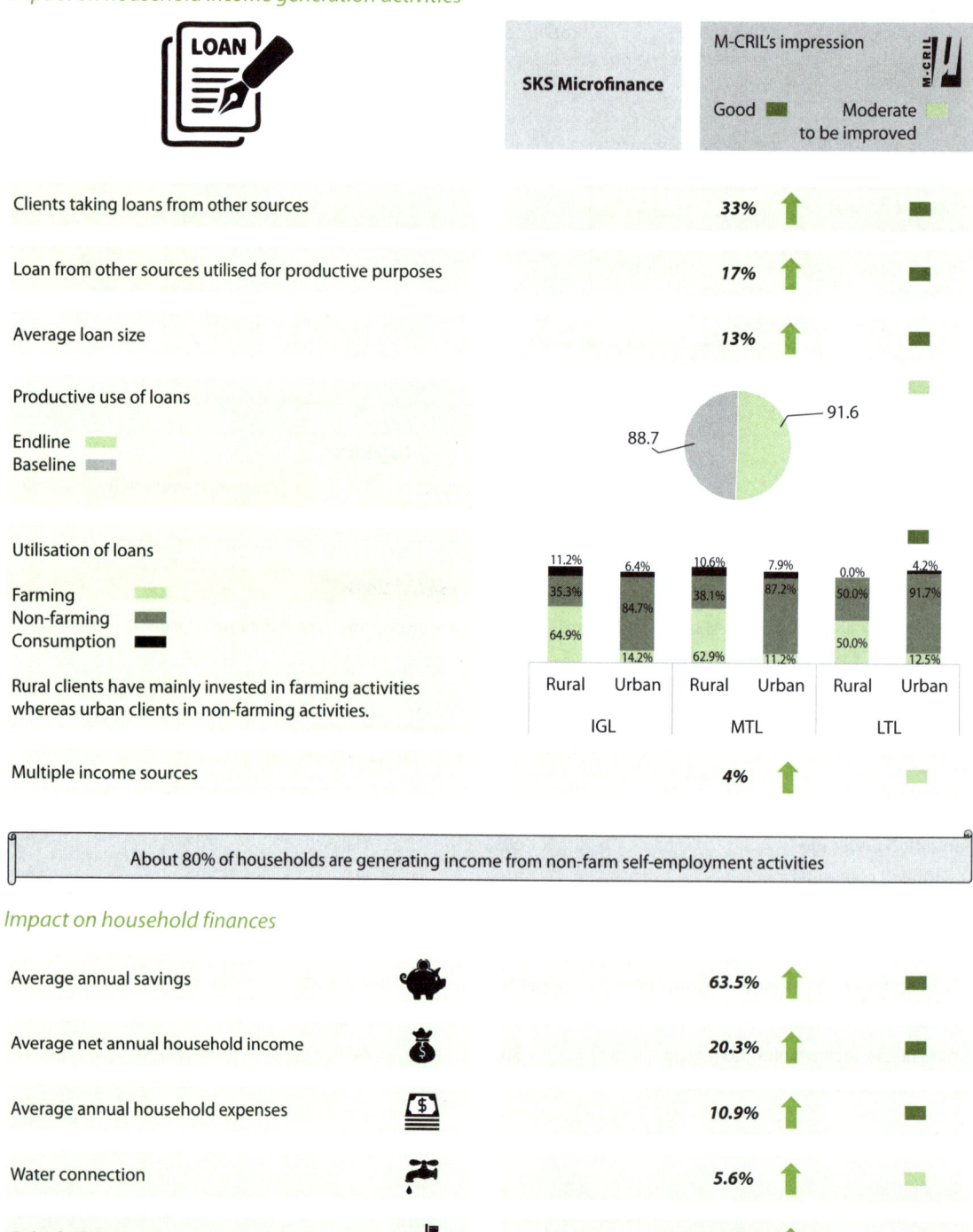

About 80% of households are generating income from non-farm self-employment activities

Impact on household finances

Average annual savings — 63.5%

Average net annual household income — 20.3%

Average annual household expenses — 10.9%

Water connection — 5.6%

Toilet facility — 5.6%

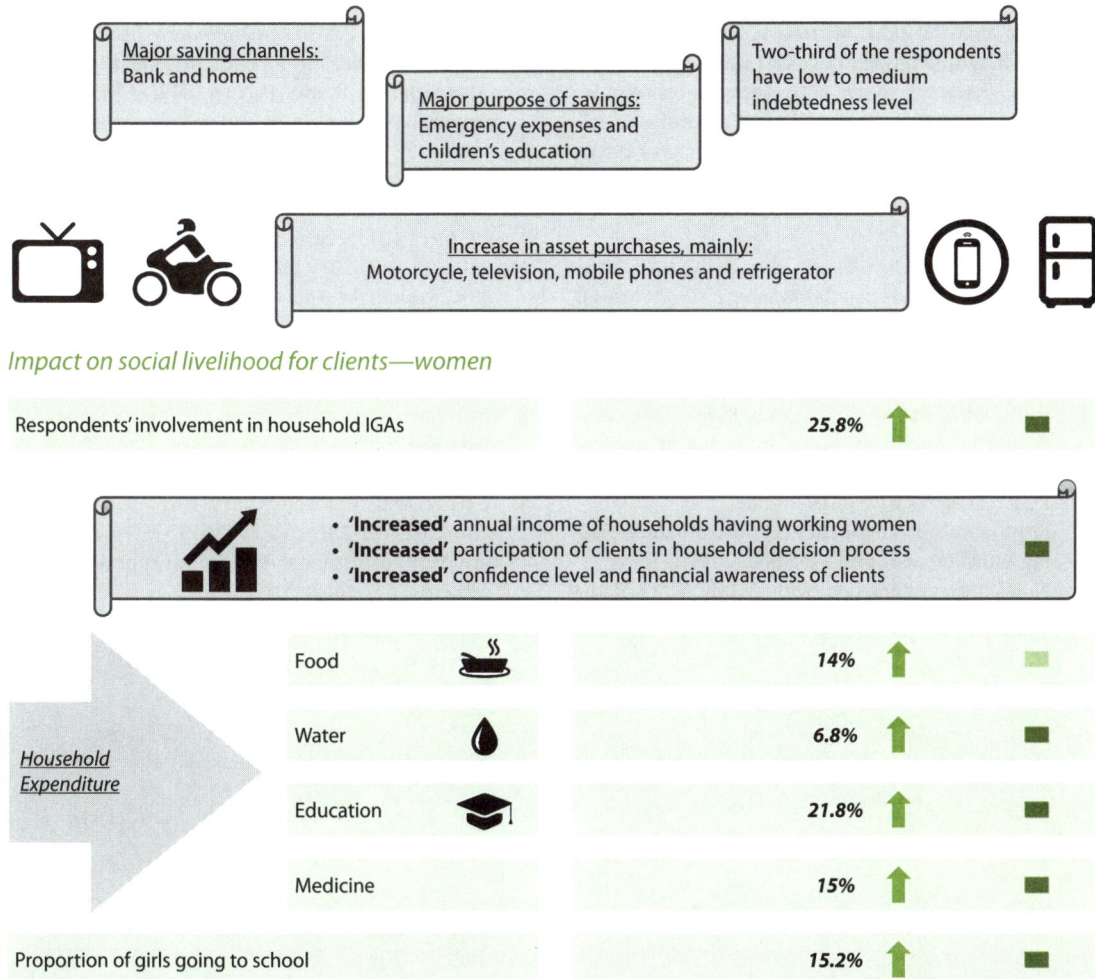

Impact on social livelihood for clients—women

Respondents' involvement in household IGAs	25.8% ↑

- **'Increased'** annual income of households having working women
- **'Increased'** participation of clients in household decision process
- **'Increased'** confidence level and financial awareness of clients

Household Expenditure

Food	14% ↑
Water	6.8% ↑
Education	21.8% ↑
Medicine	15% ↑
Proportion of girls going to school	15.2% ↑

NOTES AND REFERENCES

1. All India Debt and Investment Survey, 1991.
2. M-CRIL. 2009. *M-CRIL Microfinance Analytics 2009*, New Delhi.
3. Sriram, M.S. 2010. 'Commercialisation of Microfinance in India: A Discussion of the Emperor's Apparel', *Economic and Political Weekly*, XLV (24), 12 June 2010.
4. Consultative Group to Assist the Poor (CGAP). 2009. 'Shedding Light on Microfinance Equity Valuation: Past and Present'. http://www.cgap.org/publications/shedding-light-microfinance-equity-valuation-past-and-present (accessed 5 October 2015).
5. DNBR.CC.PD.No. 027/03.10.01/2014-15, dated 8 April 2015.
6. DNBS (PD) CC No. 388/03.10.042/2014-15, dated 1 July 2014 (Master Circular on FPC).
7. Asset size more than ₹500 crore.
8. Srinivasan, Girija. 2013. *Microfinance India: The Social Performance Report 2012*. New Delhi: SAGE Publications.
9. MicroSave. 2015. 'Code of Conduct Assessment for Microfinance Sector'. http://www.microsave.net/resource/code_of_conduct_assessment_for_the_microfinance_sector (accessed 1 October 2015).
10. At present, the four microfinance rating agencies are the licensed certifiers globally. M-CRIL based in India is one of them and has till date certified 10 MFIs in India.
11. One thousand six hundred MFIs, 186 networks, 184 investors and donors, 354 support organisations, 40 certified organisations and 2,207 individuals.
12. Ujjivan, GFSPL, Cashpor, Swadhar, Equitas, SKS, Arohan, Sonata, Janalakshmi and Utkarsh.
13. SPTF. The Universal Standards for Social Performance Implementation guide. http://www.sptf.info/images/usspm%20impl%20guide_english_20141217.pdf (accessed on 21 October 2015).
14. CGAP Brief. May 2014. Embedding Social Performance Management in Financial Services Delivery. http://www.cgap.org/publications/embedding-social-performance-management-financial-service-delivery (accessed on 6 October 2015).

15. Responsible Microfinance Practices by Microfinance Institutions in India, MicroSave. 2015. 'Governance Practices among Microfinance Institutions in India'. http://www.microsave.net/resource/governance_practices_among_microfinance_institutions_in_india_2#.VhNwK_mqqko (accessed 6 October 2015).

16. Shukla, Rajesh et al. 2011. *Assessing the Effectiveness of Small Borrowing in India*, NCAER.

17. See note 9.

18. CSFI. 2014. *Microfinance Banana Skins 2014: The CSFI Survey of Microfinance Risk.* https://centerforfinancialinclusionblog.files.wordpress.com/2014/07/2014_microfinance_banana_skins.pdf (accessed 5 October 2015).

19. RBI guidelines require that only 85% of net assets should be 'qualifying assets' by virtue of meeting stipulated operational guidelines.

20. Different banks have different rates.

21. http://www.mftransparency.org/microfinance-pricing/india/ (accessed on 4 October 2015).

22. Notes from interaction with MFIN CEO Ratna Vishwanathan.

23. SKS Terminology for Loan officer.

24. Access Assist. 2013. *Microfinance Institutions in India: The State of Practice in Human Resource Management.* Study Partner HR AXIS. http://www.microfinanceindia.org/uploads/news_attachments/20140120114855_hr-study-for-web.pdf (accessed 6 October 2015).

25. http://data.worldbank.org/indicator/NY.GNP.PCAP.PP.CD (accessed on 6 October 2015).

26. M-CRIL. 2015. *M-CRIL Microfinance Review 2014: Risk, Regulation & Reward.* http://www.m-cril.com/BackEnd/ModulesFiles/Publication/M-CRIL%20Microfinance%20Review%202014.pdf (accessed 6 October 2015).

27. http://www.greatplacetowork.in/best-companies/best-workplaces-in-asia/best-large-workplaces-in-asia (accessed on 5 October 2015).

28. http://articles.economictimes.indiatimes.com/2012-12-28/news/36036337_1_compassionate-capitalism-global-mindset-corporate-leaders (accessed 6 October 2015).

Emerging risks in MFI model: Let the leaves not wilt

3

Chapter

3.1 MICROFINANCE RISKS AND RESPONSIBLE FINANCE

Despite being one of the most tightly regulated, rather 'micro-managed' sector, and having achieved quite a bit in the journey towards responsible finance, this is no time for slackness in the MFI sector. The sector has been de-risked to a large extent by the extensive regulatory guidelines, especially pertaining to limits on lending, checks on over-indebtedness, collection practices and transparency. The general perception is that without these, the situation could have spiralled out of control. The very fact that the RBI is regulating the dominant part of the sector and ensuring adherence to its guidelines has restored confidence in the sector—the flocking back of investors and banks proves this. However, the sector needs to be watchful and intensify its efforts to be client centric on two counts.

First, it must consider that the business model of unsecured lending to the poor and vulnerable can possibly never be ring-fenced from risks—both external and internal. However, sound client-centric practices and keeping the welfare of clients at the core of operations can definitely ensure client loyalty and lower the risks to manageable levels. To do this, not only will the sector needs to consolidate the present compliance-based approach, but also move to creating added value to clients, in line with its double bottom-line mission. In this journey into the future, past experiences, especially during 2–3 years preceding the Andhra Pradesh crisis should be kept in mind. The exuberance of growth and greater credibility should not lead to diluted focus on client-centric practices, as well as investments in human resources and control systems.

Second, history shows that the financial sector is to a large extent dependent on perception, and the perception of MFIs—despite recognition from the RBI, continues to be not very favourable—time and again one hears such comments either from individuals or policy institutions. In February 2014, the Standing Committee on Finance, while considering the Microfinance Institutions (Development & Regulation) Bill 2012 said, in its report, 'The Committee notes with alarm that the rate of interest on individual loans by NBFC-MFI may exceed 26 per cent as per RBI's guidelines'.[1] The expert group constituted by the Ministry of Rural Development to consider feasibility of a financial institution for women SHGs reported[2] that as MFIs offer much better return to lenders (banks), it leads to bias in extending loans to SHGs. A former Mumbai Police Commissioner, who now works with the poor in Mumbai, said in his article, 'Incredibly industrious micro-entrepreneurs could only borrow paltry sums for earning their daily bread at usurious rates from unsavoury elements or even micro-finance institutions'.[3] While much of the criticism is ill-informed and primarily focused on pricing, these statements do influence perception, and the recourse available to MFIs is not only to educate but also to ensure that their work remains client centric. Even though an unfair situation, the onus of disproving such negatively motivated claims with facts and empirical studies lie with the MFIs.

To add to these, the advent of SFBs and PMJDY linked with overdraft will add to the competition in near future, so the MFIs need to consolidate their advantage in the last mile connectivity to effectively meet these challenges. This is the right time to do so, as the sector has demonstrated its viability within the tight regulatory space, restored its credibility and is being recognised as a vital cog in the financial inclusion landscape. Amidst all these 'confidence building measures', there are a few areas which merit closer attention of the sector to ensure that risks are managed and the sector continues to grow sustainably. The close link between responsible finance and sector or institutional risks is often ignored. Institutional viability and sustainability is inextricably linked to a client-centric approach as the interruption of services affects the clients equally, if not more, in fact, more. In Andhra Pradesh, when MFIs had to stop their operations in 2010, the study by Institute for Financial Management and Research (IFMR) and MicroSave showed that 59% of clients had to take recourse to informal credit and 85% clients reported reduction in consumption expenses.[4] Thus, being a client-centric industry, MFI sector has to ensure that it proactively mitigates the emerging risks or possible risks.

3.2 GROWTH AND ITS POSSIBLE RISKS

The return to the high growth path during 2014–15 (NBFC-MFIs reporting an annual increase of 61%) with growth in higher microfinance concentration states like Odisha and Bihar touching 75%, make us return to the lingering question—is the sector growing sustainably? There are different views on this—some quite contradictory to each other. The India ratings in its report on microfinance[5] earlier this year opined that the RBI regulations have de-risked the sector to a large extent, and the sector is expected to record sustained and stable growth rates for next 4–5 years. On the other hand, a recent sector report by Religare Capital Markets[6] sounded alarm bells, suggesting that another crisis is brewing in the sector. The alarmist stand taken by it was based on the logic that high growth and high return expectations have been the common precursors of past six crises in the international microfinance markets, and three crisis events in Indian microfinance market. While these two agencies are more focused on mainstream financial sector, M-CRIL, an agency specialising in microfinance in its 2014 review also sounded caution:

> To some extent this scenario defies the fundamental principles of economics: there is supposed to

be a trade-off between return and risk. If return is high then risk must also be high, if risk is low it must be because investors are being cautious, not taking much risk and accepting a low return. In the context of excellent portfolio quality (low risk) combined with high growth, this review has already raised the possibility of strains on MIS and internal control systems that resemble conditions in the sector in 2010, just before the Andhra Pradesh crisis. While the present rosy conditions could endure for some more time, a cautious approach to the future outlook would seem appropriate.

Amidst these divergent opinions, it is worthwhile to examine the commonly associated risks with high growth, namely, regional concentration, robustness of credit appraisal and drivers of growth in outreach and depth.

3.2.1 Is the portfolio growth concentrated or diversified across regions/states?[7]

This dimension of growth is closely associated with risk, as concentration in a few markets could lead to saturation of those markets. In 2010, the microfinance market in India had a distinct southern region concentration as well as state-specific concentration, with the southern region accounting for 54.8% of MFIs loan portfolio (Figure 3.1). As compared to that, the sector in 2015 seems much more balanced. Though the highest share in portfolio is still accounted for by southern region, its share has fallen to 30%—this excludes non-performing loans being carried on books by MFIs with Andhra Pradesh portfolios. In this new, more balanced and comforting picture of regional distribution in 2015, the region having the lowest share, i.e., Western region now accounts for 20% of loan portfolio (Figure 3.2).

Though the regional spread is balancing out, if the data is analysed in terms of state-specific concentration, the change is not significant. In 2010, top five states in terms of loan portfolio accounted for 72% of total sector outstanding and while the names of states have changed places a bit in 2015, top five states still account for 58% share in total loan portfolio (Table 3.1).

Nearly 60% share in total portfolio being accounted for by the five states does point to state-specific concentration, and the concentration becomes more pronounced if population share of these states is brought into analysis. Top three states in 2015 accounted for 40% of microfinance portfolio, while their share in total population of the country is

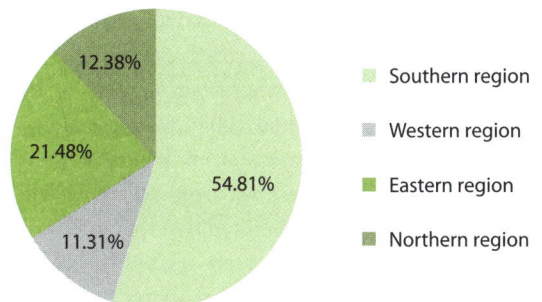

Figure 3.1 Region-wise share in MFI portfolio, 2010
Source: State of Sector Report, 2010.

Figure 3.2 Region-wise share in MFI portfolio, 2015
Source: MFIN Micrometer, Issue 13.

Table 3.1 **Loan portfolio share of top five states in 2010 and 2015**

| | **2010** | | | | **2015** | | |
State	**Portfolio (₹ Cr)**	**% share in total**	**% share in population**	**State**	**Portfolio (₹ Cr)**	**% share in total**	**% share in population**
Andhra Pradesh	5,210.71	29.53	6.99	West Bengal	6,019	14.99	7.54
Tamil Nadu	2,387.09	13.52	5.96	Tamil Nadu	5,700	14.20	5.96
West Bengal	2,106.28	11.93	7.54	Karnataka	4,370	10.88	5.05
Karnataka	1,897.69	10.75	5.05	Maharashtra	3,872	9.65	9.29
Odisha	1,200.41	6.80	3.47	Uttar Pradesh	3,391	8.45	16.51

Source: State of Sector Report 2010, MFIN Micrometer Issue No. 13 and Census of India 2011.
Note: This excludes non-performing assets (NPA) portfolio in Andhra Pradesh.

18.55%. Details of state-wise portfolio in 2010 and 2015 are provided in Annexure 3.1. Analysis of the top 80 districts in the country in terms of microfinance portfolio of MFIs also shows that the five states accounting for the highest portfolio account for 58 districts in the list of top 80 districts in terms of highest loan portfolio (Table 3.2). This clearly shows that MFI activity continues to be concentrated in certain states as well as certain districts within these states. It also sits oddly with the fact that 110 districts in the country have no MFI operations.

The growth rate of MFI portfolio is another indicator to show whether the share of these states is on account of higher existing base or due to portfolio growth during last year. States already having higher microfinance portfolio are bound to have higher share but if the rate of growth in these states is also higher than the national average,[8] it adds to concentration risk. Figure 3.3 shows that

Table 3.2 **State-wise number of districts in top 80 districts with microfinance loans**

State	**No. of districts in top 80**
West Bengal	15
Tamil Nadu	19
Karnataka	08
Maharashtra	09
Uttar Pradesh	07

Source: CRIF High Mark Credit Bureau.

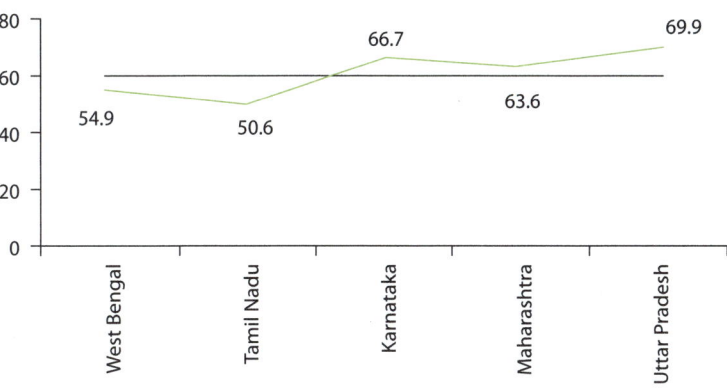

Figure 3.3 Annual growth rate in top five states compared with annual growth for the sector

Source: MFIN Micrometer.

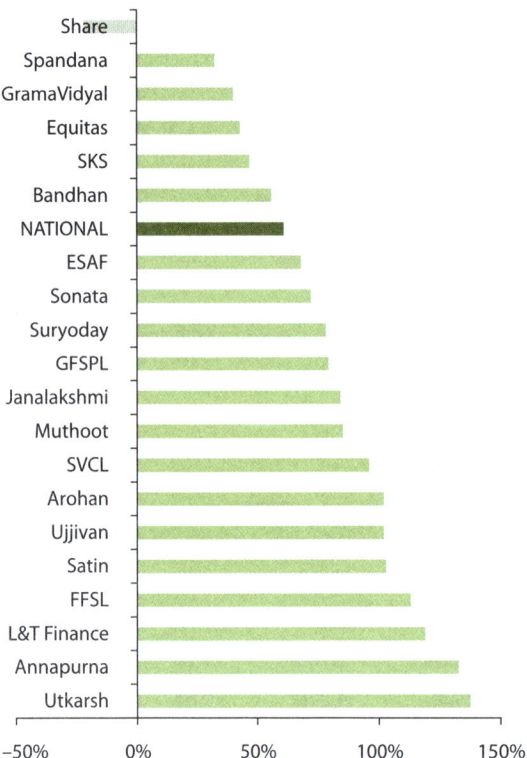

Figure 3.4 Annual growth rate of top 20 NBFC-MFIs during 2014–15

Source: MFIN Micrometer.

other than West Bengal and Tamil Nadu (which are marginally lower than the sector's overall annual portfolio growth), the rate of portfolio growth in remaining three states is higher than the overall growth rate. Maharashtra and Uttar Pradesh, are the two new states which form part of top five states in 2015 and both have a higher than national growth rate in portfolio.

The annual growth rate achieved during 2014–15 by top 20 NBFC-MFIs by portfolio size also shows that 14 of them had growth rates in excess of the national average of 61% (Figure 3.4). Further, it is disconcerting that seven MFIs in top 20 had growth rates in excess of 100%. As these big MFIs account for majority market share amongst NBFC-MFIs, if the bottom 30 are excluded from analysis, the annual growth touches 100%. This is giving rise to concerns related to risks associated with high growth—in 2009–10 the year preceding the Andhra Pradesh crisis the sector had grown by 56%.

The analysis clearly shows that while region-specific concentration has been addressed, it has been replaced by state-specific concentration as

also concentration in certain districts within those states. Further, the annual growth rate in 2014–15 for top 20 NBFC-MFIs representing 90% of the NBFC-MFI sector touched 100%, which is almost double of the growth rate seen in 2009–10. While these parameters suggest we need to move with caution, it needs to be reiterated that this in no way implies that growth is inversely related to quality. It only suggests, based on past experience, that often such growth is achieved by short-circuiting processes, and aggressively pushing credit. In a country with a vast majority of financially excluded people, speed is key to ensuring access for all, but speed without proper controls can lead to possibility of over-indebting clients through excessive credit. Hence, it is necessary to examine whether the growth is coming from increased depth or increased outreach.

3.2.2 Increase in number of clients lags behind significantly: Focus on depth over outreach

Considering the high levels of exclusion from a responsible finance lens, it would be optimal if the high portfolio growth is matched with growth in client numbers. This would imply that MFIs are spreading their outreach to cover the excluded. The comparative annual growth rate of portfolio and annual growth in client numbers in top 10 states with microfinance portfolio is shown in Figure 3.5. The comparison shows that accretion in client numbers

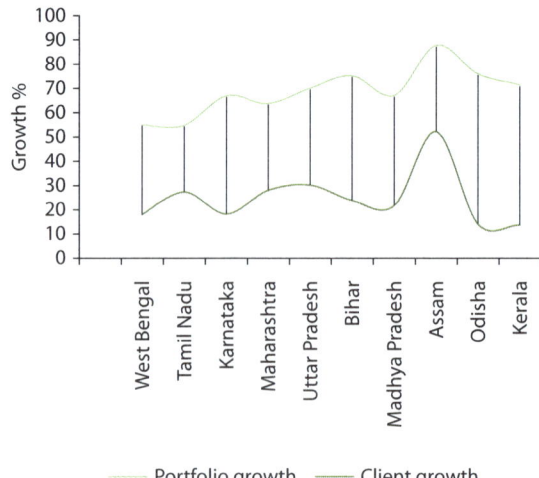

Figure 3.5 Annual growth rate of loan portfolio and clients in top 10 states

Source: MFIN Micrometer.

lags far behind portfolio growth and more importantly the gap between these two indicators is more or less consistent across states. While similar situation prevails in other states too, for sake of clarity, data pertaining to 10 states is presented. It may be noted that it is also representative of the sector, as these 10 states account for 85% of All India portfolio of NBFC-MFIs.

With NBFC-MFIs relying on the strategy of increasing depth rather than outreach, the other area which merits analysis is whether the increased depth is achieved by increase in loan size, or by more institutions lending to the same client. In the same 10 states, it is seen that while the increase in average loan size disbursed during the year 2014–15 ranges from no increase to 16.97%, implying that the loan sizes being disbursed by MFIs have not gone up in proportion to portfolio growth. The gap between growth in loan portfolio and average size of loans disbursed is accounted for by more lending to the same client by other MFIs, and is reflected in significant increase in loan outstanding per client (Figure 3.6).

From an economic view point as also the client's view point, it is more efficient if a client's needs are met from a single source rather than from two or

three different institutions. Each of the institutions lending to the same client incur operational cost. The client also faces additional hassles and loss of time in meeting the requirements of different institutions. A single loan which meets client's needs is more manageable and serviceable for the client, rather than managing different loans with different repayment amount and frequency. CGAP's note[9] on the subject of growth and vulnerabilities also says that while competition enables greater efficiency by lowering operating expenses, it undermines credit discipline by providing borrowers with alternatives and opportunities for multiple borrowing, that enable them to juggle payments and skip between MFIs, to avoid the restraints of rigid payment schedules, defaulting with one while retaining their relationship with another.

The drivers of current portfolio growth in the MFI sector seem to come from certain states/regions, as also through lending by many institutions to the same clients. Regional concentration is definitely a risk, and considering the past experience of Andhra Pradesh, it will be prudent if MFIs diversify to other areas rather than focusing on certain states/districts. Such an approach will not only diversify their risk, but also serve the cause of financial inclusion more efficiently. The increased depth of outreach is not so much a risk, provided the credit bureau check is foolproof and all institutions abide by the regulations on indebtedness. While adherence to mandatory credit bureau reporting and checks is ensured by CoC assessments and adherence to RBI guidelines, the dependence on credit bureau needs to be examined to ensure that depth does not lead to indebtedness.

3.3 IS IT WISE TO DEPEND SOLELY ON CREDIT BUREAU?

Though the analysis shows that the loan sizes have not increased significantly, the increase is not so insignificant on two counts. First, the average loan outstanding amount has increased by 28% in the last two years, going up from ₹12,757 to ₹16,327. This assumes importance if we consider the fact that in previous five years (2008–13), the average loan outstanding amount for the sector stagnated at around ₹11,000. Second, the average loan size does not capture the variations in loan sizes, and the sector has in last one or two years seen a rapid shift to

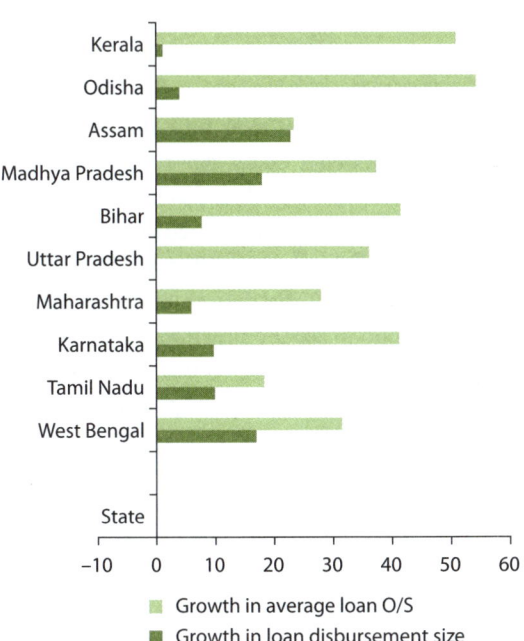

Figure 3.6 Comparison of percentage growth in average loan outstanding per client and average loan disbursement size

Source: MFIN Micrometer.

much higher-sized loans by a few players. Industry experts believe that by end of the next year, the average loan size will go up to around ₹25,000. The data for top 20 NBFC-MFIs also shows a considerable variation in average loan size ranging from ₹11,029 to ₹22,868.

In such a scenario, it is imperative that the loan approval process incorporates cash flow analysis of the client. The effectiveness of earlier paradigm of smaller loan sizes coupled with group guarantee as the primary default mitigation strategy has reduced to a considerable extent. However, even though the loan size is increasing, the dominant practice in Indian MFIs under group lending continues to be the reliance on joint liability, albeit with an additional cushion of credit bureau checks. Many organisations do have cash flow analysis as part of loan appraisal, as well as a prescription of debt threshold, but the field practices do not reflect the required rigour, and often the calculations are simply made to justify the loan size. The issue has been highlighted in recent sectoral reports, with the *Social Performance Report 2013*, observing 'Grameen model with group guarantee mechanism is followed by many of the MFIs and detailed household debt and household analysis is traditionally not part of the analysis. MFI staff rely on the self-reported data of clients on income, debt repayments and other expenditure'.[10] Though organisations that have ventured into individual lending have started doing cash flow analysis, in case of group loans, most MFI lenders remain dependent on self-reported data and credit bureau checks. Many studies have commented on weakening of group guarantee beyond a certain threshold, as the members are reluctant to make good higher amount of defaults. CGAP in its blog on the Kolar crisis says, 'MFIs typically attempted to enforce joint liability in the mass default towns. Enforcing individual liability rather than joint liability may result in better repayment performance when a critical threshold of a center has already defaulted'.[11] Nevertheless, given the way the sector is witnessing increase in loan sizes, it is prudent to back the group guarantee with rigorous cash flow analysis.

The establishment of microfinance focused credit bureaus in India and the regulatory requirement of checking client bureau data do mitigate the risk to a certain extent, but do not eliminate it. The limitations of credit bureaus arise from several counts. First, in the absence of a unique ID, there exists a possibility that the same client using different know your customer (KYC) documents can take multiple loans under different identities. Discussions with credit bureaus reveal that there are several other factors that can lead to multiple loans beyond the prescribed limit. Institutions can exploit the gap between the two credit bureau records and use the bureau report which enables them to disburse loans—there can be cases where one credit bureau shows more than two loans against a client, while the other shows less than two loans. Further, some institutions do 'inquiry softening' by manipulating the input so that the inquiry gives erroneous result.

SIDBI, under the DFID supported PSIG programme commissioned High Mark Credit Information Services to do a deep dive study into microfinance activity in all of the four states covered by PSIG.[12] The study period was January–March 2014 and though it is a bit dated, but it still shows that in all the four states there were few clients with more than two loans (Figure 3.7 shows the situation in Madhya Pradesh).

The percentage of clients having more than two loans was quite small across the four states (ranging from 1.03 in Madhya Pradesh to 0.2 in Bihar and Odisha), as shown in Figure 3.6. It spreads across all districts.

To examine whether over time the position has improved with better credit reporting and compliance, the data on microfinance clients with more than two loans as on 31 March 2015 was requested from CRIF High Mark Credit Bureau. The data was obtained for top 80 districts in terms of microfinance portfolio to see the situation in microfinance concentration areas. These 80 districts account for around 60% of the microfinance portfolio. The data shows that while there is no link between higher portfolio in the district and percentage of clients having more than two loans, all districts have such clients, and the incidence level ranges from 3.61% to 0.01%. The data for top 20 districts and frequency distribution for all eight districts is shown in Tables 3.3 and 3.4, while the detailed district-wise position is given in Annexure 3.2.

Though the data from credit bureau does show some incidence of more than two loans across

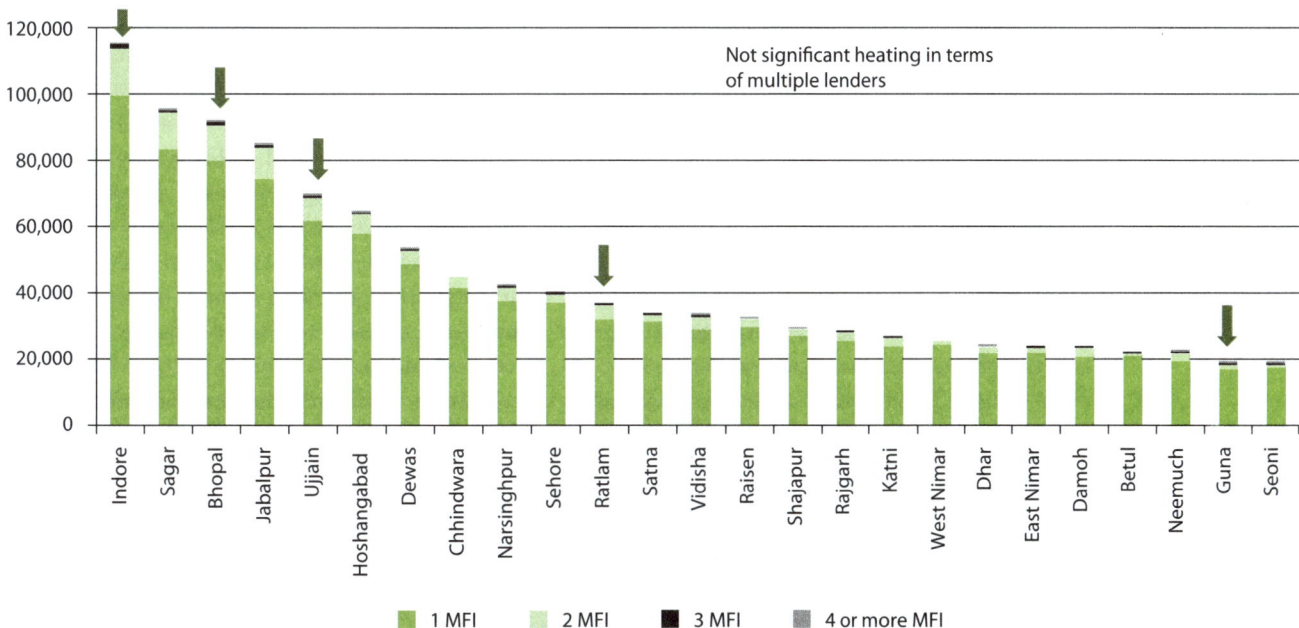

Figure 3.7 Extent of multiple loans with microfinance clients in 25 districts of Madhya Pradesh

Source: Microfinance Activity in Madhya Pradesh: A Study for SIDBI PSIG Program, High Mark Credit Information Services.

Table 3.3 Top 10 districts with clients having >2 loans as on 31 March 2015

District	Percentage
Kolhapur	3.61
Pune	2.95
Vadodara	2.92
Dharwad	2.85
Coimbatore	2.72
Solapur	2.61
Belgaum	2.41
Nagpur	2.33
Jaipur	2.22
Tiruchirappalli	2.14

Source: CRIF High Mark Credit Bureau.

Table 3.4 Frequency distribution of 80 districts

% of clients with >2 loans	Number of districts
>2.5	06
2 to 2.5	05
1.5 to 2	15
1 to 1.5	18
<1	36

Source: CRIF High Mark Credit Bureau.

all the 80 districts, it is comforting that the incidence is within manageable limits. But this data has to be read with a caveat that it misses clients who manage to obtain loans (more details on this in the next section). Discussions with industry stakeholders suggest that this problem can be addressed to a large extent by moving to a national identification or any unique identification. CGAP & IFC in their publication on credit reporting in

case of microfinance clients stress the point of unique identity saying that

> [T]he challenge of uniquely identifying base-of-the-pyramid customers for credit reporting purposes is significant in many countries. Yet, without a reliable means of uniquely identifying borrowers, credit reporting mechanisms are more costly to implement, and the quality of data is reduced—in some cases to the point of rendering the data of little or no value.[13]

This view is confirmed by the experience in Indian microfinance sector where despite the sophisticated matching algorithms of credit bureaus, many gaps exist for both the institution and the client to circumvent the maximum borrowing guideline.

Aadhaar has emerged as the answer to this issue in India and despite occasional policy hiccups relating to its scope and applicability, it has been able to enrol 74% of the population by 5 September 2015.[14] The Unique Identification Authority of India (UIDAI) has also clarified that the purview of unique identification numbers (Aadhaar) will be limited to establishing identity based on a person's demographic and biometric information. More promising is the fact that the coverage rates in top five microfinance states ranges from 64.4% to 88.7% (West Bengal, Tamil Nadu, Karnataka, Maharashtra and Uttar Pradesh). MFIN has rightly decided that its member NBFC-MFIs should endeavour to increasingly rely on the UID and also stipulated that from 1 January 2016, new loans have to match the state UID coverage rate. While complete population coverage and movement of MFIs to UID-based KYC can be expected over next one to two years, a recent newspaper report suggests that the path may not be smooth, as a recent interim ruling by the Supreme Court restricted the use of Aadhaar data to ration shops and cooking gas, and referred the petitions on the validity of Aadhaar to a Constitution bench on 11 August 2015.[15] However, both MFIN and Sa-Dhan are confident that use of Aadhaar for lending decisions does not go against the court ruling as that is directed towards government entitlements.

It seems plausible that in near future, the problem of multiple KYCs and inquiry softening can be adequately dealt with by moving to Aadhaar based identification. However, even that will not eliminate the risk, as a parallel microfinance programme—SBLP has similar clients, and its data is not part of the credit bureau record. MFIs got the blame for Andhra Pradesh crisis based on charges of pushing excessive debt but an analysis by M-CRIL in its Microfinance Review 2011 showed that SHG loans far outweighed the MFI loans. The analysis used two assumptions—one that typically financially excluded people will be either SHG or MFI clients and two, it used multi-dimensional poverty index (MPI) based poverty rates to calculate the microfinance market for financially excluded families in each state. It showed that in Andhra Pradesh, while the number of MFI loans was just over 100% of the number of eligible financially excluded families, SHG loans were 310% of that number (Figure 3.8).

Though the analysis did use certain assumptions on perfect overlap of SBLP and MFI clients, the field realities do show a great amount of overlap. CRIF High Mark Credit Bureau, in its study of microfinance for SIDBI in four states (referred above) also found nearly 50% common clients between SBLP and MFIs. Considering significant client overlap, and the fact that the average loan outstanding per SHG under SBLP has gone up to ₹115,295 implying per member outstanding loan of ₹8,800,[16] the significance of the SHG-MFI overlap assumes criticality.

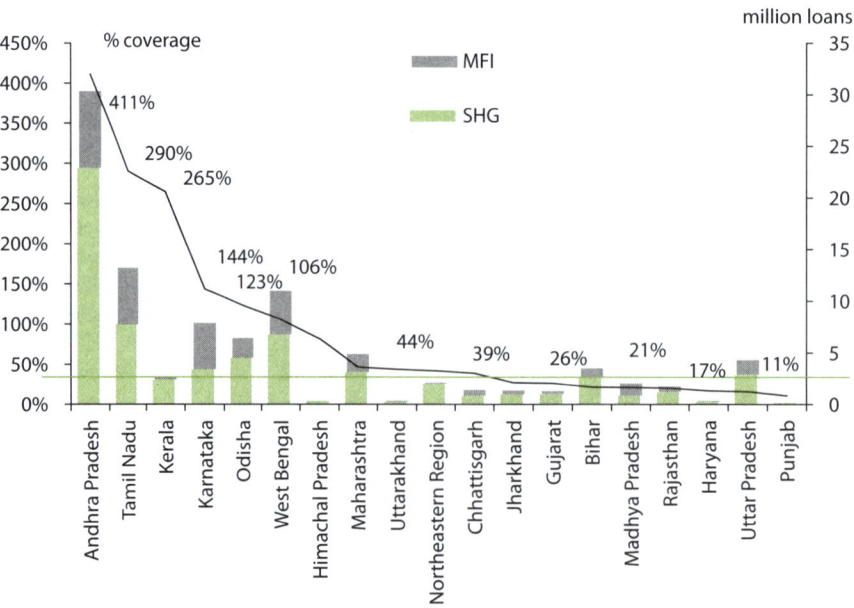

Figure 3.8 Coverage of eligible population by microfinance loans (MFIs + SHGs)

Source: M-CRIL. 2011. *M-CRIL Microfinance Review 2011: Anatomy of a Crisis.*

The other missing piece relates to small borrowal accounts of scheduled commercial banks, which includes rural banks and lending by cooperative banks. The data on accounts with loan facility less than ₹25,000 shows 32 million accounts as on 31 March 2014, which is almost same as number of MFI clients in 2015. This data is not part of microfinance credit bureaus. Similarly, cooperative banks, especially the Primary Agricultural Credit Societies (PACS) also give small-size loans in rural areas which at present are not part of either CIBIL (credit bureau for banks) or microfinance credit bureaus.

Thus, SBLP, small loan accounts of scheduled commercial banks and lending by PACS taken together represent a significant gap in reported credit bureau data for microfinance clients. The problem is likely to be accentuated with the roll out of full features of PMJDY, which includes provision for an overdraft of ₹5,000 for all account holders.

Thus, all the three vital issues in credit reporting relating to microfinance clients identified by CGAP & IFC in the paper referred above namely '(i) the extent to which available credit reporting systems cover all significant lenders targeting low-income borrowers; (ii) the feasibility of uniquely identifying base-of-the-pyramid borrowers; and (iii) the quality of the data on such borrowers that can be assembled' are exhibited in India. These aspects significantly affect the reliability of credit bureau data for microfinance clients. Even if in near to medium term, graduation to Aadhaar as KYC and 360 degree credit reporting across all channels is put in place, it will take care of one aspect of credit assessment—correct estimation of client's liability and cash flow analysis would still be required to measure income. Further, the increasing loan size of microfinance loans which is inversely related to the strength of group guarantee, as well as gaps in credit bureau data add to the immediate need to shift to robust cash flow analysis—credit bureau checks can increase the effectiveness of analysis but cannot substitute the appraisal skills.

3.4 EXTERNAL RISKS CONTINUE TO CROP UP NOW AND THEN

The march of the microfinance sector in pre-2010 years was halted frequently by several external events, including some major ones like the Krishna crisis in 2007, Kolar crisis of 2009 and finally the Andhra Pradesh crisis in 2010. As detailed in Chapter 2, the sector has moved significantly to address the major causative factors leading to previous crises through regulation as well as industry initiatives. But even with the elaborate architecture of guidelines and assessments to check compliance, one continues to hear occasional recurrences of incidents due to external factors, and this has all become a bit too frequent in the past one year or so. It is an accepted fact that external risks in the form of interference in normal lending operations by either the executive or socio-political organisations is not within the control of affected organisations, but the responsibility of institutions in particular and the sector in general lies in ensuring that their practices and behaviour do not lead to external interventions. In this context, it is useful to analyse the factors leading to past events to see if there is a common pattern between them and the recent events, and identify issues requiring corrective action.

The Krishna crisis (2006) started with the district administration seizing the records of MFI branches and closing their operations, and also giving the borrowers an impression that they need not repay MFI loans, and the government and banks will meet their credit needs. Prabhu Ghate[17] in his analysis of the crisis gives a detailed account of enabling as well as underlying causes leading to action by the state government. The enabling causes were near saturation of coastal Andhra Pradesh with microfinance loans, surfeit of bank funding of MFIs especially after introduction of ICICI's partnership model and state government's concern on interest rates being charged by MFIs, as the government had pitchforked cheap credit to poor borrowers through the SHG programme as part of its election plank. Despite the coverage of 95% of poor households under the Velugu programme of the government, the area was lucrative for MFIs on account of its high population density. Among the underlying causes, the prominent ones related to the excessive focus on growth by MFIs, leading to dilution of controls and client selection processes, non-transparency in interest rates and fees, over lending, leading to debt overhang and excesses in collection practices in order to maintain zero delinquency rates. As a response to the Krishna crisis, Sa-Dhan brought out a voluntary CoC in March 2006, which was replaced by statement of 'core values and a voluntary code of mutual conduct' in January 2007. RBI on its part issued guidelines for NBFCs to abide by an FPC.

EDA Rural Systems and CGAP have examined Kolar crisis of 2009 in detail.[18] Multiple loans with microfinance clients'[19] new institutions entering the market despite market saturation, and engagement of agents for faster enrolment of clients have been flagged as the causes which created a volatile situation. While these conditions had led to overheating of the market, suicide by one borrower allegedly on account of debt stress proved to be the last straw. Initially, religious leaders picked up the cause and encouraged members of their community to stop paying MFI loans and later local leaders latched on to it and flared it further affecting nearby places like Sidlaghatta and Mysore. The report surmises that aggressive growth plans followed by excessive credit supply, coupled with insistence on zero delinquency for the field officers, led to this incident. In a situation where institutions insisted on zero delinquency, even clients having repayment problems due to genuine business failures were denied any relief by way of stoppage of loan recovery or rescheduling of loans for a longer period.[20]

As events like Krishna and Kolar were happening, the sector went about in business as usual mode, ignoring voices of sanity and caution. These incidents were rationalised as one off incidents, in pursuit of the massive inclusion required in India. Unfortunately, the heavy handed ordinance of Andhra Pradesh government in October 2010 proved to be the straw that proved to be the turning point for the sector to look seriously at client protection practices. Though some reports and commentators have linked it to the SKS's IPO or government's genuine concern for microfinance borrowers, sector experts have pointed to a variety of reasons like overlap with the SHG programme, multiple borrowings and rising default rates under the SHG programme as the major factors. The intense media scrutiny of SKS IPO, possible envy/concern owing to the profitability of MFIs and adverse press reports linking suicides to MFI's coercive recovery practices added fuel to the tinderbox conditions.[21] The ordinance of the state government changed things so drastically that it forced the RBI to shake off its passive stance leading to the formation of Malegam Committee and subsequent issue of regulatory guidelines to ensure fair pricing, avoidance of multiple lending and appropriate collection practices. Industry associations MFIN and Sa-Dhan not only framed a more comprehensive CoC but also importantly made its compliance mandatory as opposed to the earlier stance of keeping it voluntary.

One common thread runs through all the three major flash points discussed above—excessive lending in saturated areas leading to build up of debt, beyond servicing capacity of the clients, isolated incidents of staff forcing clients to repay, linking of random incidents of suicide to microfinance or local leaders approached by clients, leading to the flare up. In most cases, the issue remained confined to the local area, like Krishna and Kolar and on rare occasions like 2010 went beyond and engulfed the entire microfinance sector. All these events in pre-2010 period happened in the southern region as that region accounted for nearly 60% market share till 2010.

What is worrying is that similar local incidents have started happening again with great regularity in the past one year or so, and this time the geographical location is vastly different. Late last year, there were two reported incidents in Erode (Tamil Nadu) and Nanded (Maharashtra) of client unrest due to problems in repayment. Since the middle of 2015, there have been several such incidents like Amroha and Azamgarh (both Uttar Pradesh), Narsinghpur and Burhanpur (both Madhya Pradesh), and as this report goes to press in September, another incident is being reported from Sagar in Madhya Pradesh. Discussions with MFIs involved in these areas disturbingly show that there is a striking similarity between these events and the events of pre-2010 years. The events have been pieced together based on discussions with MFIs and bankers. Though MFIN has been proactive in dealing with these flashpoints and ensuring that they remain contained, it did not share its field investigation reports. MFIN got last year's incidents in Erode and Nanded investigated by two external agencies, but the reports are not public.

What happened in Amroha (Box 3.1) is similar to other places with the additional angle of client suicide in few places like Narsighpur and Azamgarh. In Narsinghpur, suicide of a client was linked by the local press to debt-related stress on account of multiple loans. House visit by a field officer of one MFI and use of harsh and abusive words to shame the client to repay has also come to light. Though the credit bureau check of the deceased client showed only one loan, she had four loans obtained through different KYCs as well as through 'pipelining'—a term used for cases where

Amroha has recently been added to the microfinance market, and in few years there are already quite a few MFIs operating there. The competition for market share is intense, with not much differentiation among MFIs in terms of products. In a matter of 2–3 years, it has moved from less penetration to multiple borrowings. In May 2015, clients approached the local politician who also happens to be a minister in the state government with stories of problems in making loan payments and subsequent pressure by field staff to repay. The politician in his zeal without ascertaining the other side of the story announced publicly that nobody has to repay MFI loans. Community angle was also prominent in local events.

MFIs affected by the 'No Pay' announcement approached MFIN. Parleys were held with the politician and district officials to explain the situation and legitimacy of MFIs operations. As a compromise (can be termed face saver), MFIs agreed to give 4% interest rebate on loans and it was worked out that interest relief will amount to ₹3 crore. The politician communicated to locals that he has won an important concession for them but it did not go well with the locals and there were localised protests. The situation is reported to be under control but it is not sure whether MFIs will continue to be as eager as before in disbursing loans in Amroha.

Source: Author's discussions with MFIs and other stakeholders.

there is difference between borrower on MFI record and the actual user of the loan. With the swift and active involvement of MFIN, the issue did not go out of hand and remained confined.

In Burhanpur, a particular community leader was approached by clients complaining of rude behaviour by MFI and the leader asked clients not to repay MFI loans. In the heated atmosphere, clients also beat up staff of two MFIs and a police case was registered. Post-crisis inquiry revealed that even though MFIs have disbursed loans after eligibility check with credit bureau, there were clients having loans from more than two MFIs, and in some cases from four or five MFIs.

The MFIN coordinator, on behalf of all member institutions, met local administration officials, local leaders and clients. It was decided that MFIs will ensure courteous behaviour by their field staff and the loan tenure of clients having problems in repayment will be extended. Clients agreed to pay after Ramzan festival; however, field reports suggest that only few members have started repaying but the majority is still not repaying. As the majority of clients have not started repaying, MFIs have also not extended the loan tenure.

The purpose of highlighting these events is not to give a detailed blow-by-blow account of what happened, but to draw attention to two key learnings. First, it shows that regulation and guidelines can only goad the institutions towards responsible practices, but if the institutional intent is guided by considerations of fast growth, it is possible to find loopholes. As discussed in the earlier section, it also shows that substituting due diligence process, while sanctioning loans, with credit bureau checks, can have negative consequences. Recent history shows that a period of fast-paced growth often results in dilution of processes—there is nothing wrong in growth per se if it is backed by commensurate focus on processes. These events clearly point towards the link of growth and saturated markets with over lending. All these events happened in states of Tamil Nadu, Maharashtra, Uttar Pradesh and Madhya Pradesh; the first three states figure in the list of top five states with microfinance portfolio and Madhya Pradesh is seventh in the list.

Second, it is worrisome that practices like multiple lending, inappropriate collection practices and culture of enforcing zero delinquency continue to exist despite existence of elaborate guidelines to prevent them. In Chapter 2, the subject of near perfect recovery rates was mentioned, and these events reinforce the point.

The sector needs to take into cognizance that when loan sizes have almost doubled and repayment instalments have gone up on an average by three times due to shift in repayment frequency from weekly to fortnightly/monthly, while the clientele has remained same, some level of delinquency cannot be wished away. It is better to acknowledge it and devise policies to accommodate genuine cases of default, rather than sticking to perfect recovery paradigm, which in turn leads to pressure on the field staff to somehow or the other prevent potential defaults, and make good on recovery. One never knows which of these isolated events will spread across the state or states and lead to another major crisis. Experts believe that the industry is not in a position to withstand another Andhra Pradesh like event. Another large scale event like that has the potential to completely derail the painstaking work of decades.

One part of the sector comprising NGO-MFIs faces another type of risk—regulatory risk. These institutions continue to suffer from the long-standing confusion between form of incorporation and nature of business, and last year's rejection by the Parliamentary Standing Committee of Microfinance Institutions (Development & Regulation) Bill, 2012 has meant that these institutions continue to remain at the mercy of state authorities and poor regulatory oversight. Paradoxically, though these institutions are not covered by the RBI guidelines for NBFC-MFIs, lenders insist on compliance with these guidelines. Funding has gone down for NGO-MFIs and reports suggest that their share in microfinance market portfolio is as low as 10%, and a large share of it is accounted by two institutions—CASHPOR and Sri Kshetra Dharmasthala Rural Development Project (SKDRDP). While their share in the portfolio is small, according to Sa-Dhan's[22] member list, there are nearly 150 such NGO-MFIs. The policy stance seems to suggest that the legal form of NGO-MFIs is not considered suitable for financial intermediation. In fact, this was acknowledged by the Task Force[23] on microfinance regulation way back in 1997 by saying 'NGOs are structurally not the right type of institutions for undertaking financial intermediation activities as the bye-laws of these institutions are generally restrictive in allowing any commercial operations'. Their inability to attract equity capital also limits their growth.

From the lens of responsible finance, the shrinking operations of NGO-MFIs imply that clients once included are getting financially excluded. This needs to be addressed through providing these institutions a graduated path to transform to more suitable legal form, and by bringing them under a central regulatory purview, rather than leaving them to be governed by state-specific laws. However, their numbers and small-sized operations are a challenge for any potential regulator, and this seems to have influenced the reluctance of NABARD and SIDBI to take up that role, in their submissions to the

standing committee examining the microfinance bill. But the challenge should not lead to inaction and the gradual withering away of these grassroots institutions providing diversity to the ecosystem of responsible finance. Policymakers need to find ways to mainstream them.

While the regulatory challenge is more for a smaller subset of the sector, for the dominant set of NBFC-MFIs, high growth rates and its effect in the form of pockets of saturated markets and over lending are the major risks.

3.5 FACTORS FUELLING GROWTH AND ITS IMPACT ON HUMAN RESOURCES

3.5.1 Business as usual for investors and lenders: Impact on responsible finance

Business growth of microfinance institutions is dependent on funding both capital and debt, as the regulations do not permit mobilisation of deposits. Insistence on debt and equity ratio by the debt lenders requires that the institutions maintain comfortable level of equity ranging from the stipulated minimum of 15–20%. Equity investors were drawn to the sector in the years preceding 2010 based on the promise of sustained high profitability and growth in portfolio and clients. In the early years of post-2010 crisis, both equity and debt lenders stayed cautious, being initially not sure about the policy stance and later about the ability of the sector to be profitable. RBI's extensive guidelines for NBFC-MFIs dispelled the policy ambivalence on the role of MFIs and continuance of the policy to treat loans to NBFC-MFIs under priority sector further comforted the lenders.

While these two steps cleared the air, investors and lenders were initially not sure whether the MFIs will be able to maintain profitability levels in the wake of interest rate caps. However, the sector demonstrated its ability to remain profitable within the prescribed ceiling; this has been majorly achieved by lowering operating expenses (Figure 3.9). The reduction in operating expenses has been a big game changer as it enabled MFIs regain previous levels of profitability within the regulatory ceiling; this is more noteworthy as the OER of Indian MFIs is already well below that of MFIs in Bangladesh (11.3%), Africa (20%) and Latin America (14.5%). In terms of model and socio-economic similarity, Bangladesh

Figure 3.9 Return on assets and operating expense ratio over the years

Source: M-CRIL Microfinance Review 2014.

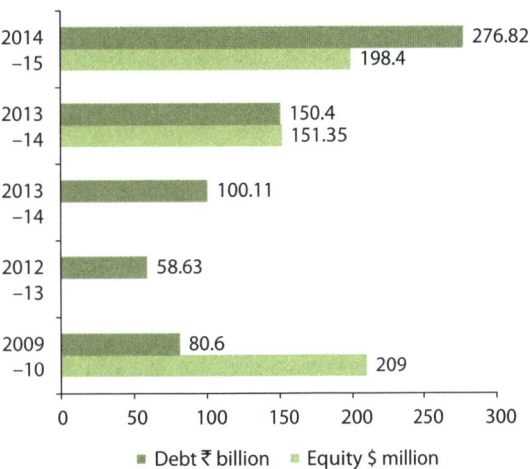

Figure 3.10 Amount of equity and debt flow in the last five years

Sources: State of the Sector Report, 2010; www.VCCircle.com; MFIN Micrometer.
Note: Equity figures for 2012–13 and 2013–14 are not available.

is closer to Indian situation. The figures for return on assets exclude the non-performing portfolio in Andhra Pradesh. Early analysis of the data for the year 2014–15 shows further reduction in operating expenses and increase in profitability. Riding primarily on reduced operating costs, the sector has almost regained profitability levels of 2010.

With policy certainty in place and sector's return to profitability, both equity investors and debt lenders are well and truly back in the market. Investors never had it so good, as the current deals are being done at 1.7 times to 2.2 times book value,[24] which is much lower than the high levels of 7–10 times book value reached during the build up to 2010 crisis.[25] But the reduction in acquisition price is not reflected in reduced return expectations. Discussions with industry players revealed that equity investors (both private equity and microfinance investment vehicles) still expect an annual return of 16–18%, which is only marginally lower than the earlier expectations of ~20%. With this win-win proposition, the equity investments in last one year have touched 2010 levels (Figure 3.10).

Banks as providers of debt shrunk their lending drastically in 2011–12 but over last three years bank lending to NBFC-MFIs has gone up substantially; in the last financial year 2014–15, bank lending recorded an annual growth of 86% reaching ₹27,682 crores. The increased scale of bank lending shows confidence of banks in the sector, and should have logically led to reduction in interest rates, but the

risk assessment has not translated in any rate cuts, and the average lending rate continues to be in the range of 14–15%. At present, NBFC-MFIs, especially the top 25, are flushed with funds, and interaction with MFIs reveals that banks are pushing for additional sanctions, even if the MFI has excess liquidity. Industry observers believe that two factors will further aggravate the situation. First, with the largest MFI (Bandhan) becoming a bank and the prospect of an eight, other large MFIs transforming as SFB in near future, banks will have a much smaller market to lend. This can lead to more aggressive debt funding to remaining players. Second, RBI has now mandated compliance with priority sector lending targets on a quarterly basis, in place of earlier norm of annual compliance.[26] This will lead to year-round pressure on banks to achieve targets.

The current pattern of equity and debt investments in the sector has significant implications on responsible finance practice. Equity investors continue to have high return expectations, which can be only met through high growth and by keeping costs low. The short time horizon (3–5 years) of investors, coupled with high return expectations, is leading microfinance institutions to take the high growth path. High growth necessitates that innovations in product design and investments in control systems take a backseat, and credit is pushed aggressively. It is quite plausible that the recent events of client unrest have a direct link to return of the sector to high growth path. Foreign investors dominate the equity investment scene, and barring SIDBI, there is no other source of domestic patient capital for MFIs in India. While all major foreign investors are signatories of PIIF, the investment deals seem to find more comfort in normal business numbers of growth and profitability. Innovative aspects like tolerance for lower growth and profitability, in case of institutions showing greater commitment to social performance, are hardly seen.

Bankers on their part are also hooked to the paradigm of growth and profitability, and lending decisions attach more importance to financial aspects like capital adequacy and solvency ratios. The lending decisions are based on internal appraisal and external ratings, wherever available. Banks do not have the practice of attaching importance to social performance, and while CoC assessments are included as part of documents wherever available, neither are these compulsory nor their scores/grades have any bearing on the interest rate.

Further, on account of RBI's policy of New Capital Adequacy Framework (NCAF), external assessments/ratings of MFIs in India has moved from microfinance specialist agencies to mainstream rating agencies accredited by SEBI and RBI. Globally, the microfinance rating framework has evolved to incorporate elements of social performance like client protection, and balancing social and financial performance (Figure 3.11). However, India, ironically, seems to have moved back to emphasis on financial performance. In the Microfinance Institutional Rating (MIR) framework,[27] the section on responsible practices includes client protection principles and balancing of social and financial performance. Similarly, Governance and Management section

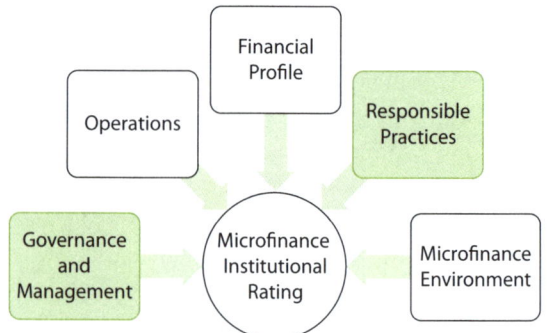

Figure 3.11 Microfinance institutional rating framework

Source: Rating guide, The Rating Initiative.

includes elements of social governance and alignment of system and processes with mission. The mainstream rating agencies have played their part in boosting investor and lenders' confidence and that is reflected in their strong endorsement of the sector—during FY 2015, out of 26 ratings done by mainstream rating agencies, 25 ratings entailed an upgrade of the rating grade, implying improved performance.[28]

The decision matrix of investors and lenders seems to mirror the past, and they have to take the responsibility of high growth and its likely negative impacts on clients as well as institutions. Surprisingly, while the lending volumes show strong faith in the sector, in response to a questionnaire on emerging risks in the sector, all four major equity investors listed quite similar risks—with high growth and staff turnover emerging as the two main risks (Table 3.5).

Though the investors seem to be well aware of the risks, especially high growth, it is yet to translate

Table 3.5 Risks in microfinance in India listed by investors

Investor (1)	Investor (2)	Investor (3)	Investor (4)
• Resumption of high growth	• High growth	• Over dependence on credit bureau	• Growth and saturation
• Issues of mission drift	• Lack of domestic capital	• Dominance of international investors—political risk	• Absence of unified legal framework
• Staff attrition levels		• Field staff turnover	• Operational risk—staff turnover
• Dependence on priority sector funding from banks		• Weaknesses in risk framework	

Source: Response to emails sent by the author.

into mitigating action. Unlike in the past though, where investors could cite their minority holding as an excuse, the higher equity requirement at present has entailed shift in majority ownership of NBFC-MFIs from original promoters to investors and have to take responsibility. The dexterity of MFIs in maintaining earlier profitability levels by reducing operating expenses—which has brought back investors and lenders—is examined next.

3.5.2 Mechanics of reduced operating expenses: Implications for responsible finance

The regulatory regime, post 2010, has capped interest rates charged to clients. This started with an absolute cap of 26%, but over the years has moved to the principle of average borrowing rate plus 10–12% margin to cover costs. The MFIs have to cover operational costs, make provisions for risky assets and earn surplus within the ceiling. Provisions based on asset quality are mandated by regulation, and there was little scope for reduction in provisions, as the sector has been maintaining near perfect recovery rate. Reduction in profitability depended on investors and lenders expectations of returns, and this left only operational costs, wherein the institutions had some degree of control. Typically operational costs can be reduced by financial institutions by way of reducing salaries and increasing productivity—productivity can be increased either by adding more clients with the same set of staff strength (outreach expansion) or by increasing the loan sizes to existing clients (deepening). The choice for MFIs narrowed down to increase in productivity as salary levels in case of field officers are already close to minimum prescribed levels (Chapter 2, section 2.4.3). The importance of this parameter for cost implications is spelt out in *M-CRIL Microfinance Review 2014,*

> As financial service agencies operating in a low technology arena, microfinance institutions are heavily dependent on staff for ensuring efficient and effective operations. Staff productivity measured by the number of clients served per staff member is, therefore an important factor determining the efficiency of MFIs, and feeds directly into the determination of the average cost per borrower.

The productivity levels of Indian MFIs measured as number of clients handled per staff/field officers has historically been higher than other countries, resulting in lowest operating expenses (section 3.5.1). Yet, despite an already high productivity,

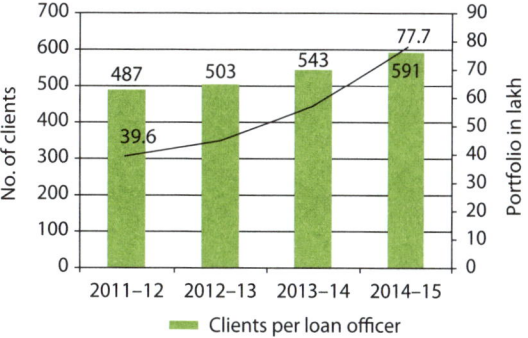

Figure 3.12 Movement in clients per loan officer and portfolio per loan officer—NBFC-MFIs
Source: MFIN Micrometer.

pressure to maintain profitability within the prescribed ceiling has led Indian MFIs to further step up the productivity. Figure 3.12 shows that over the last four years, the number of clients handled per loan officer has gone up from 487 to 591, and loan portfolio handled by each loan officer has gone up from ₹39.6 lakh to ₹77.7 lakh. In percentage terms, the growth in clients handled per loan officer (21.35%) lags substantially behind growth in portfolio per loan officer (96%). This shows that though the productivity increase is on both counts, the contribution of increased loan sizes is significantly higher. Detailed institution-wise figures are provided in Annexure 3.3.

The deepening of outreach is necessitated as it is difficult for any loan officer to handle clients beyond a number. Frequent interactions by way of weekly group meetings, collection of repayments and maintaining cohesion in the group requires time and has been historically cited as the main reason for higher transaction costs in loan delivery. Post 2010, realising this limitation, the sector has increasingly moved away from weekly repayments to fortnightly or monthly repayments. With this change in repayment frequency, the same loan officer can handle more clients, as the frequency of group meetings decreases from weekly to fortnightly or monthly.

If the data for top 80 districts in the country in terms of microfinance portfolio is examined, the number of districts having more than 50% weekly repayment loans is mere 22, while in remaining 58 districts the share of weekly loans has fallen to less than 50% (Figure 3.13). Field observations suggest that the shift has become more pronounced

Figure 3.13 Frequency distribution of top 80 districts across percentage of weekly repayment portfolio share
Source: CRIF High Mark Credit Bureau.

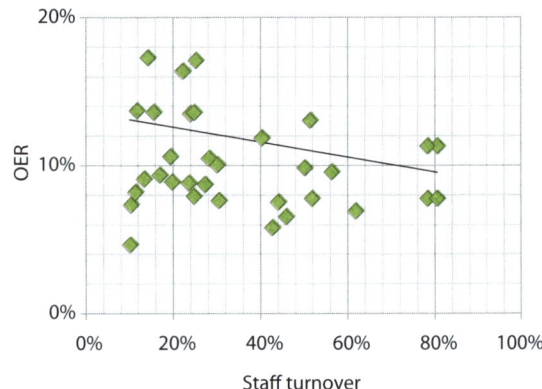

Figure 3.14 Effect of staff turnover on operating expense ratio
Source: M-CRIL Microfinance Review 2014.

recently, and in one or two years, nearly all loans will be of fortnightly or monthly repayment cycle. Udaya Kumar, MD & CEO of GFSPL observed 'it is difficult for us to expand in certain areas, especially north and west, as other players offer loans with fortnightly or monthly option, while GFSPL is focused on weekly repayments'.[29]

This shift in repayment frequency, coupled with the increasing depth of outreach (higher size of loans), is the major driving force in productivity increase, and has implications for responsible finance. Weekly loans à la Grameen style originated with the idea that microfinance loans require constant touch and the importance of keeping loan instalments manageable for the group, as well as for effectiveness of joint liability. It seemed logical, as typical microfinance clients do not have a steady source of income and find it difficult to make lumpy repayments. But this logic does not hold for what is being witnessed now, as the instalment amounts have gone up substantially due to the combined effect of increased loan size and increased duration of repayment frequency. Linking this to recent events of client distress does not have any empirical base but it surely needs examination. It is quite feasible that the mix of clients facing repayment stress due to lumpy repayments and field officers enforcing timely recovery leads to flare ups. Industry stakeholders need to get this aspect examined by an external agency through a pan India study. It is learnt that MFIN has commissioned a study to study the impact of high growth on clients in four districts (Kolhapur, Vadodara, 24 Parganas and Madurai). Hopefully, the study will examine this angle.

Related to this is the issue of high staff attrition and staff competencies. The staff attrition rate in Indian MFIs has continued to remain high. M-CRIL[30] in its review gives the average staff turnover rate of 25% in the sector with as many as 11 MFIs in a sample of 33 reporting turnover in excess of 40%. This also has an adverse impact on the operating costs of the institutions, as recruitment and training of new staff take up substantial resources (Figure 3.14). MFIs need to examine it deeply, as retaining staff can be a more responsible strategy to cut costs than increasing the loan repayment frequency and field staff productivity. Over the years, the challenge has become more acute as the skill set of field staff has not kept pace with increased work load, as well as the product diversity. The role of a loan officer has changed from forming groups and attending weekly group meetings, to incorporate additional tasks of purveying higher-sized loans, using technology like POS and retailing of other products like pensions. Industry observers feel that this will require massive investments in capacity building. The current state of practice seems not to accord this issue the priority it deserves. Left unattended, it can lead to increased levels of attrition at the field level.

3.6 LET THE LEAVES NOT WILT

The previous chapter detailed numerous initiatives taken in last five years to ensure that the sector returns to its client-centric roots. To the credit of MFIs in India, the sector has been able to meet the extensive regulatory and industry guidelines in a short period of time, even while demonstrating profitability. This is the right time for the sector to go beyond seeing client centricity from a compliance perspective, and integrate it as the core working philosophy. As it moves in that direction in the coming months and years, it also needs to simultaneously address the inherent and emerging risks. The sector scan shows that quite a few conditions similar to pre-2010 situation have re-emerged, while certain legacy issues continue to persist. High growth and market saturation in certain areas require cautious approach in lending, as also moving to cash flow based assessments, in place of depending solely on credit bureau checks. Industry associations (MFIN and Sa-Dhan) need to take a more proactive role in monitoring such markets and restraining imprudent action by their members. External risks are exacerbated by excessive lending in saturated markets, as this leads to debt stress, and cases of friction between MFI field staff and clients. For a sector which continues to remain under scrutiny, it will be a collective failure if any such sporadic event snowballs into a major crisis. A client-centric approach also requires the industry to examine whether increasing repayment frequency is what the clients want, or it is merely a method to increase productivity. Investments in staff capacity building, especially field staff, has become more critical with a number of additional tasks being handled by the field staff.

The paradigm of achieving growth, by lending in easy markets and reducing costs by increasing case load of field staff, has proven to be costly in the past. Investors and bankers have a critical role in facilitating this change. At present, their focus on responsible finance seems missing or restricted to meeting basic standards of regulation. They need to build in procedures to factor in social performance in their lending decisions, rather than relying solely on financial strength.

The current phase is crucial for the MFIs, as the financial landscape is changing fast, and in the near future, MFIs will have to compete with SFBs, banks downscaling to reach excluded segments through banking correspondents as well as with schemes like PMJDY. These are new initiatives and will take time to gain traction. To meet the challenge, MFIs need to build on their advantage in last mile delivery. Deepening client relationship, continuing to work on customer friendly products and processes, and addressing risks proactively can achieve this. Weakening of client relationship, aggressive growth and absence of significant product innovation will severely dent the advantage and make MFIs similar to mainstream financial institutions. This is something, which the sector wedded to responsible finance, and catering to excluded segments of the society can ill afford.

ANNEXURES

ANNEXURE 3.1
State-wise position of MFI loan portfolio and client outreach

State	Total portfolio (₹ Crore)		No. of MFIs (2015)	No. of clients		
	2010	2015		2010	2013–14	2014–15
North						
Haryana	48.77	455	12	65,454	203,440	313,269
Himachal Pradesh	5.96	NA	4	8,027	NA	NA
Punjab	5.98	NA	5	7,670	NA	NA
Chandigarh	0.23	NA	2	232	NA	NA
Rajasthan	346.56	862	14	429,840	645,151	687,177
Delhi	346.42	424	10	113,181	214,980	257,006
Bihar	493.55	2,723	19	747,352	1,725,668	2,134,493
Uttar Pradesh	890.14	3,391	17	1,205,005	1,839,875	2,392,318
Uttaranchal	47.8	439	NA	83,093	NA	NA
Sub-total	2,185.41	8,294	83	2,659,854	4,629,114	5,784,263

(Continued)

(Continued)

State	Total portfolio (₹ Crore)		No. of MFIs (2015)	No. of clients		
	2010	2015		2010	2013–14	2014–15
East						
Assam	218.19	2,087	7	369,016	877,920	1,334,806
Jharkhand	175.03	566	14	345,678	436,136	512,579
Odisha	1,200.41	1,930	14	1,598,352	1,468,654	1,673,288
West Bengal	2,106.28	6,019	13	3,513,955	3,886,914	4,579,767
Sub-total	3699.91	10,602	48	5,827,001	6,669,624	8,100,440
West						
Chhattisgarh	211.82	544	14	464,273	364,386	471,781
Goa	7.83	NA	4	6,986	NA	NA
Gujarat	216.22	1,242	19	246,601	719,410	1,083,431
Maharashtra	967.14	3,872	27	3,867,064	2,362,155	3,020,680
Madhya Pradesh	593.81	2,491	27	1,005,870	1,706,541	2,073,357
Sub-total	1,996.82	8,149	91	5,590,794	5,152,492	6,649,249
South						
Andhra Pradesh	5,210.71	86	6	6,244,648	365,657	122,574
Karnataka	1,897.69	4,370	21	3,743,190	2,492,444	2,942,949
Kerala	159.83	1,765	8	280,281	902,514	1,023,933
Tamil Nadu	2,387.09	5,700	19	4,550,289	3,825,377	4,868,056
Pondicherry	15.53	113	9	22,517	74,781	91,934
Sub-total	9,670.85	12,034	63	14,840,925	7,660,773	9,049,446
Total	**17,553.01**	**40,138**	**285**	**28,918,574**	**24,112,003**	**29,583,398**

Source: FY 2010: Srinivasan, N. *Microfinance India – State of the Sector Report 2010*; FY 13–14 and FY 14–15: MFIN MicroMeter, Issue 13 as of 31 March 2015.
Notes: Data for FY 13–14 and FY 14–15 are shown only for states where six or more MFIs are operating.
Gross loan portfolio (GLP) and clients data for FY 13–14 and FY 14–15 excludes non-performing (PAR > 180 days) portfolio + SKS portfolio in Andhra Pradesh.

ANNEXURE 3.2
Extent of multiple loans in top 80 districts with microfinance loans (sorted as per extent of multiple loans)

S. No.	State	District name	Portfolio outstanding (₹ billion)	No. of active micro lenders	Borrowers with >2 loans (%)	District rank*
1.	Maharashtra	Kolhapur	3.52	28	3.61	268
2.	Maharashtra	Pune	5.23	25	2.95	175
3.	Gujarat	Vadodara	2.43	24	2.92	111
4.	Karnataka	Dharwad	2.26	21	2.85	11
5.	Tamil Nadu	Coimbatore	5.47	27	2.72	1
6.	Maharashtra	Solapur	3.16	29	2.61	302
7.	Karnataka	Belgaum	4.51	24	2.41	70
8.	Maharashtra	Nagpur	5.13	28	2.33	106
9.	Rajasthan	Jaipur	2.61	30	2.22	236

(Continued)

(Continued)

S. No.	State	District name	Portfolio outstanding (₹ billion)	No. of active micro lenders	Borrowers with >2 loans (%)	District rank*
10.	Tamil Nadu	Tiruchirapalli	3.33	32	2.14	25
11.	Maharashtra	Mumbai	2.17	31	2.08	12
12.	Gujarat	Ahmedabad	2.26	28	1.95	235
13.	Tamil Nadu	Thiruvallur	2.60	29	1.83	84
14.	Madhya Pradesh	Indore	3.79	36	1.82	103
15.	Maharashtra	Ahmednagar	3.37	22	1.81	389
16.	Tamil Nadu	Madurai	3.73	24	1.79	20
17.	Maharashtra	Amravati	3.29	29	1.77	185
18.	Tamil Nadu	Kancheepuram	3.33	29	1.77	18
19.	Madhya Pradesh	Sagar	2.79	28	1.72	281
20.	Tamil Nadu	Erode	3.08	34	1.70	29
21.	Karnataka	Davanagere	2.34	21	1.66	68
22.	Tamil Nadu	Salem	3.34	33	1.60	80
23.	Tamil Nadu	Dindigul	2.20	27	1.58	47
24.	Tamil Nadu	Namakkal	2.44	26	1.53	35
25.	Bihar	Patna	3.96	21	1.53	212
26.	Uttar Pradesh	Varanasi	2.80	22	1.51	263
27.	Maharashtra	Thane	2.28	30	1.49	480
28.	Karnataka	Mysore	4.74	16	1.46	27
29.	Bihar	Saran	2.70	18	1.39	493
30.	Odisha	Khordha	2.50	19	1.37	13
31.	Tamil Nadu	Tiruppur	2.69	27	1.32	96
32.	Tamil Nadu	Thanjavur	4.99	26	1.31	36
33.	Gujarat	Kheda	2.49	25	1.29	273
34.	Uttar Pradesh	Allahabad	2.63	24	1.27	423
35.	Uttarakhand	Haridwar	2.16	18	1.27	194
36.	Karnataka	Mandya	2.29	14	1.25	58
37.	Karnataka	Tumkur	2.81	25	1.23	52
38.	Karnataka	Bangalore	10.29	26	1.13	66
39.	Uttar Pradesh	Saharanpur	3.57	16	1.12	278
40.	Tamil Nadu	Chennai	2.90	31	1.07	14
41.	Kerala	Palakkad	2.45	13	1.07	32
42.	Uttar Pradesh	Gorakhpur	2.31	15	1.05	358
43.	West Bengal	Kolkata	3.72	18	1.03	59
44.	Gujarat	Surat	2.34	22	1.01	427
45.	Tamil Nadu	Virudhunagar	2.15	26	0.98	46
46.	Karnataka	Hassan	2.51	19	0.93	22
47.	Gujarat	Panch Mahal	2.70	25	0.90	479

(Continued)

(Continued)

S. No.	State	District name	Portfolio outstanding (₹ billion)	No. of active micro lenders	Borrowers with >2 loans (%)	District rank*
48.	Uttar Pradesh	Ghaziabad	3.64	19	0.86	241
49.	Maharashtra	Yavatmal	2.15	22	0.75	316
50.	Tamil Nadu	Vellore	2.75	27	0.69	69
51.	Delhi	New Delhi	2.83	12	0.67	94
52.	Tamil Nadu	Tirunelvali	2.85	21	0.65	49
53.	Kerala	Thrissur	2.47	10	0.63	1
54.	Assam	Kamrup Metropolitan	2.42	15	0.58	83
55.	Tamil Nadu	Cuddalore	3.03	23	0.58	76
56.	Odisha	Cuttack	2.58	20	0.56	104
57.	Bihar	Muzaffarpur	2.53	19	0.53	487
58.	Odisha	Ganjam	2.87	17	0.51	137
59.	West Bengal	Haora	5.31	17	0.50	283
60.	West Bengal	Maldah	2.90	14	0.49	464
61.	West Bengal	Hugli	5.09	17	0.46	252
62.	Tamil Nadu	Thiruvarur	2.55	23	0.45	37
63.	Tamil Nadu	Viluppuram	2.31	27	0.42	148
64.	West Bengal	Barddhaman	5.30	20	0.39	279
65.	West Bengal	Darjiling	2.19	10	0.38	81
66.	Tamil Nadu	Nagapattinam	2.24	23	0.36	61
67.	West Bengal	North 24 Parganas	8.11	26	0.35	287
68.	West Bengal	Nadia	5.15	18	0.34	276
69.	Uttar Pradesh	Bulandshahr	2.45	13	0.33	405
70.	West Bengal	South 24 Parganas	6.94	23	0.30	408
71.	West Bengal	Murshidabad	5.09	15	0.30	357
72.	West Bengal	Birbhum	2.34	13	0.29	311
73.	Kerala	Alapuzha	2.27	7	0.27	1
74.	West Bengal	Uttar Dinajpur	3.61	13	0.24	338
75.	West Bengal	Jalpaiguri	5.04	10	0.23	200
76.	Bihar	Begusarai	2.23	15	0.23	509
77.	Assam	Kamrup	2.36	15	0.19	147
78.	West Bengal	Purba Medinipur	2.75	20	0.18	432
79.	West Bengal	Koch Bihar	5.79	8	0.11	145
80.	Assam	Nagaon	2.18	9	0.01	504

Sources: CRIF High Mark Credit Bureau.
*CRISIL Inclusix Ranks 2013; CRISIL Inclusix, Volume III, June 2015.

ANNEXURE 3.3
Growth in gross loan portfolio (GLP) and clients handled per loan officer (NBFC-MFIs)

S. No.	MFI	FY 2011–12		FY 2014–15	
		GLp per loan officer (₹ lakh)	Clients per Loan Officer	GLP per loan officer (₹ lakh)	Clients per loan officer
1.	Bandhan	52.0	504	94.3	646
2.	SKS^	16.2	312	89.9	787
3.	Janalakshmai	41.0	353	61.9	384
4.	Ujjivan	37.6	438	84.7	568
5.	Equitas	60.8	1,002	96.4	1,031
6.	Satin	36.1	345	155.5	866
7.	Muthoot	36.0	408	79.2	517
8.	GFSPL	65.5	433	73.5	434
9.	Spandana*	49.6	631	59.1	557
10.	ESAF	32.9	403	82.7	461
11.	Gramavidiyal	30.3	476	93.1	794
12.	L & T Finance⁺	64.6	1,431	68.8	644
13.	Utkarsh	34.9	492	74.9	626
14.	Share	74.2	760	31.5	348
15.	Sonata	32.5	426	68.9	471
16.	Suryoday	66.9	733	84.2	706
17.	FFSL*	75.1	1,018	112.6	722
18.	SVCL	26.2	375	68.4	540
19.	Annapurna	16.1	230	76.3	643
20.	Arohan	9.8	195	67.1	564
21.	Madura#	114.7	1,716	56.9	489
22.	Asirvad	29.8	651	108.7	881
23.	BSS			108.8	603
24.	Asmitha	74.2	672	31.1	324
25.	Fusion	58.2	578	82.8	620
26.	RGVN			78.2	773
27.	Belstar	35.1	379	77.8	679
28.	Disha	52.1	563	81.3	723
29.	BSFL	10.4	204	25.4	363
30.	Smile	38.2	609	37.0	622
31.	Saija	5.2	124	63.6	568
32.	VFS	25.2	397	38.9	486
33.	Margdarshak	22.3	303	67.2	533
34.	Chaitanya	34.3	373	39.6	278
35.	Jagaran	4.3	432	41.1	507
36.	Sahayog	22.5	178	27.4	246

(Continued)

(Continued)

S. No.	MFI	FY 2011–12		FY 2014–15	
		GLp per loan officer (₹ lakh)	Clients per Loan Officer	GLP per loan officer (₹ lakh)	Clients per loan officer
37.	Pahal			55.9	565
38.	Namra	16.1	259	43.1	537
39.	M Power	21.9	199	59.1	449
40.	ASA	13.9	245	24.8	395
41.	Samasta	31.1	401	47.4	380
42.	Varam	33.9	774	187.2	1,013
43.	Navachetna	14.1	228	65.7	523
44.	Adhikar	29.8	629	74.1	578
45.	Sambandh			119.5	855
46.	Svasti	19.0	243	56.7	437
47.	Svatantra			37.1	383
48.	Shikhar			59.6	614
49.	Nirantara			70.4	414
50.	Agora	10.4	86	28.8	282

Source: MFIN MicroMeter, Issue 13, data as of 31 March 2015.
Notes: ^Data shown for SKS excludes GLP, branches, employee and loan officers in Andhra Pradesh.
*Excluding non-performing portfolio (PAR > 180 days) in Andhra Pradesh.
+L&T data only for microfinance portfolio.
#Number of clients for Madura is not available as loans are provided to SHGs. Estimated number of clients is calculated by multiplying the SHG number by 13.

NOTES AND REFERENCES

1. http://www.prsindia.org/uploads/media/Micro%20Finance%20Institutions/SCR-%20Micro%20finance%20bill.pdf (accessed on 7 October 2015).
2. Ministry of Rural Development, Government of India. November 2014. *Report of the Expert Group on Setting Up a Developmental Financial Institution for Women SHGs.* http://www.aajeevika.gov.in/sites/default/files/nrlp_repository/Report%20of%20the%20Expert%20group%20-%20Final-PMO.pdf (accessed on 7 October 2015).
3. http://www.ndtv.com/opinion/mumbais-former-police-chief-has-a-new-stirring-job-1206844
4. IFMR & MicroSave. June 2012. *Andhra Pradesh MFI Crisis and Its Impact on Clients.* http://www.microsave.net/files/pdf/AP_MFI_Crisis_Report_MicroSave_CMF_Ghiyazuddin_Gupta.pdf (accessed on 7 October 2015).
5. India Ratings & Research. January 2015. Microfinance: Strong Comeback. https://www.indiaratings.co.in/showDetails.jsp%3Bjsessionid=2E397D694CCC2388FE4C9E126FDD89A6?fileName=/upload/sectors/pressReleases/normal/2015/1/30/indra-30Micro.htm (accessed on 7 October 2015).
6. Religare Capital Markets. August 2015. *India Microfinance: Crisis Brewing.* http://research.religarecm.com/INDIA/India%20Microfinance%20-%20Sector%20Report%2019Aug15.pdf (accessed on 7 October 2015).
7. Based on NBFC-MFIs data reported by MFIN—constituting ~90% of market share.
8. The loan portfolio of NBFC-MFIs grew by 61% during 2014–15.
9. Chen, Greg, Stephen Rasmussen and Xavier Reille. 2010. 'Growth and Vulnerabilities in Microfinance'. *Focus Note*, No. 61. Washington DC: CGAP.
10. Srinivasan, Girija. 2014. *Microfinance India: The Social Performance Report 2013.* New Delhi: SAGE Publications.
11. http://www.cgap.org/blog/what-caused-mass-defaults-karnataka-india (accessed on 7 October 2015).
12. Microfinance Activity in Uttar Pradesh, Odisha, Bihar and Madhya Pradesh: A Study for SIDBI PSIG Program, High Mark Credit Information Services.
13. CGAP & IFC. 'Credit Reporting at the Base of the Pyramid: Key Issues and Success Factors'. *Access to Finance Forum*, No. 1, September 2011.

14. https://data.uidai.gov.in/uiddatacatalog/get DatsetInfo.do?dataset=UIDAI-ENR-DBTL-DIST (accessed on 8 September 2015).

15. http://www.livemint.com/Industry/Xkj3V-lBtApvAfJhMCD7OsO/MFI-plans-for-Aadhaar-as-primary-identity-may-face-legal-hur.html (accessed on 10 September 2015).

16. Provisional data for 31.3.2015 from NABARD. Assumes average SHG membership of 13 members.

17. Ghate, Prabhu. 2007. *Microfinance in India: A State of the Sector Report, 2006.* New Delhi: Microfinance India.

18. EDA Rural Systems Private Limited and CGAP. *Competition & the Role of External agents: The 2009 Delinquency Crisis in Southern Karnataka.* http://www.m-cril.com/BackEnd/ModulesFiles/Publication/Karnataka-delinquency-crisis-2010.pdf (accessed on 7 October 2015).

19. The study says microfinance clients in Kolar had an average of three loans.

20. The study report shows that clients in Sidlaghatta stopped repaying on account of losses in silk reeling business.

21. World Microfinance Forum (WMFG). 2010. *Working Group on Inclusive Finance in China Research Compendium I, The Indian Microfinance Crisis 2010—Lessons for China*; Srinivasan, N. 2011. *Microfinance India: State of the Sector Report 2011.* New Delhi: SAGE Publications.

22. http://www.sa-dhan.net/Adls/Microfinance/member%20list.pdf

23. Task Force for Supportive Policy and Regulatory Framework for microfinance, NABARD, 1999.

24. Religare Capital Markets. August 2015. *India Microfinance: Crisis Brewing.*

25. Consultative Group to Assist the Poor (CGAP). 2009. 'Shedding Light on Microfinance Equity Valuation: Past and Present'. http://www.cgap.org/publications/shedding-light-microfinance-equity-valuation-past-and-present (accessed on 7 October 2015).

26. RBI circular no. FIDD.CO.Plan.BC.54/04.09.01/2014-15, dated 23 April 2015.

27. http://www.microfinancegateway.org/library/rating-guide (accessed on 8 October 2015).

28. Religare Capital Markets. August 2015. *India Microfinance: Crisis Brewing*, page 99.

29. Phone interview with the author.

30. M-CRIL. 2015. *M-CRIL Microfinance Review 2014: Risk, Regulation & Reward.*

SHG-bank linkage programme: Time for consolidation and innovation

4.1 STRENGTHENING EXISTING INFORMAL GROUPS OF POOR: CLIENT-CENTRIC IDEA SHAPING DESIGN OF SHG-BANK LINKAGE PROGRAMME (SBLP)

Microfinance in India can be broadly distinguished as following two main approaches. The first approach discussed in previous chapters based on Grameen model uses individual clients organised as joint liability groups and adopts credit as the primary intervention. The other approach catalysed by NABARD as the Apex agency for rural development originated with the realisation that poor tended to come together in a variety of informal ways for pooling their savings and dispensing small and unsecured loans at varying costs to group members on the basis of need. This concept of self-help was discovered by social development NGOs[1] in 1980s, who catalysed this informal structure to form groups for pooling savings into microloans for internal lending. NABARD funded an action-research project in collaboration with Mysore Resettlement and Development Agency (MYRADA) in 1986–87 on Savings and Credit Management of self-help groups (SHGs) to assess its efficacy. The democratic nature of these groups, flexible operation and prudent use of savings and loans was impressive. The only constraining factor being the small nature of financial resources available with such groups, NABARD explored the concept of linking these groups with banks to overcome the financial constraint. Conception of this synergistic relationship between SHGs and banks paved the way forward and is aptly summed up by the Ex-Chairman of NABARD, Y.S.P. Thorat[2] 'The essential genius of NABARD in the SHG-Bank programme was to

recognise this empirical observation that had been catalysed by NGOs and to create a formal interface of these informal arrangements of the poor with the banking system. This is the beginning of the story of SHG-Bank linkage programme.' NABARD launched the pilot project of linking 500 SHGs with banks in 1992. The programme has come a long way since 1992 passing through stages of pilot (1992–95), mainstreaming (1995–98) and expansion phase (1998 onwards) and emerged as the world's biggest microfinance programme in terms of outreach, covering 7.7 million groups as on March 2015.

The design of the programme has a strong client-centric approach. The operational model conceptualises nurturing existing groups of homogeneous poor, strengthening of their egalitarian functioning and encouraging them to follow the concept of thrift-based internal lending as the first step. Once the nurtured groups demonstrate characteristics of member-based informal group with regular thrift, the group can be credit linked with banks. SBLP model requires three roles: (i) borrower (SHG), (ii) a self-help promoting agency (SHPA) which forms and nurtures the group and facilitates the linkage of group with bank for savings and credit, and (c) financing institution, i.e., banks. The role of SHPA in mobilising and strengthening groups is critical as SHPA is the link between groups and banks and is supposed to identify potential group, assess its homogeneity, nurture the group and inculcate regular savings habit among group members. Being a savings led model, the programme emphasises thrift as the essential activity and leaves the borrowing decision to the groups. If the group decides to borrow from the bank, banks are supposed to assess the formation process, homogeneity of members to avoid dominance by few, group's internal processes and quality of record keeping with special emphasis on transparency. To maintain the focus on savings, guidelines suggest providing bank credit without collateral in a specified ratio to group savings ranging from 1:1 to 1:4.

Considering the focus of the programme on empowering people's groups, the programme envisages loans to the group leaving the flexibility of deciding individual loans to members, loan purpose, tenure and rates of interest to the group. The margin earned on the difference between rate of interest on bank loan and loan from the group to members accrues to the group corpus. The entire design has no subsidy element and policy support is limited to capacity building of SHPAs, banks and creating a facilitating policy atmosphere. The SBLP can thus be truly considered as a 'people's programme' with group members driving the course of their financial lives aided by the SHPA's and funding support from banks.

4.1.1 Dilution of core design principles over time

From the modest start of pilot project in 1992 covering 500 groups, the SBLP has travelled much ground reaching an outreach of 7.7 million groups by March 2015. While the numbers are impressive and SBLP has emerged as the world's largest microfinance programme, the programme has witnessed enormous changes, which have substantially diluted the core principles. It is necessary to outline the two broad changes before analysing the operational and financial numbers.

4.1.1.1 Transformation of SBLP from mobilisation of social capital to quantitative targets

Growth rates under SBLP in initial years were modest as bankers were being convinced of the business proposition and capacity of NGOs was being built. Observance of operational norms in letter and spirit such as minimum period of group functioning before credit linkage contributed to slow and steady growth. Substantiation comes from the fact that total number of SHGs credit linked with banks (cumulative) were only ~1 million by 2004 (12 years after the launch of the programme in 1992).

Establishment of a critical mass of SHGs, active savings and credit linkage support from banks and near perfect recovery caught the fancy of public

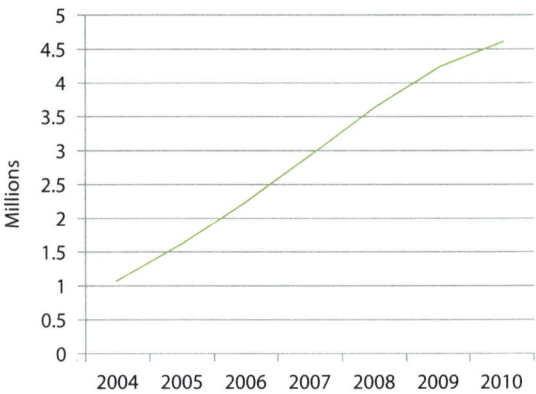

Figure 4.1 Growth in SBLP—cumulative number of SHGs credit linked
Source: NABARD.

policy as a quick and easy means of furthering inclusion and poverty alleviation efforts. Starting from 2002, targets for linkage of SHGs started to figure in the budget speeches of Union Finance Minister. Having achieved its earlier target of one million SHGs, NABARD revised the target to four million SHGs by 2011–12. Targets were described as 'aspirational', but ground realities differed significantly with a frenetic rush to link more and more SHGs on the part of banks, NGOs and government agencies. Achieving numbers became the sole focus, with success solely being described in terms of SHGs linked to banks. Critical factors like poverty outreach, time taken to identify and nurture groups and client satisfaction started to get ignored. A comprehensive study on SHGs in India by EDA Rural Systems and Andhra Pradesh Mahila Abhivruddhi Society (APMAS) in 2006[3] found that 40% of groups had very weak records and another 39% had moderate quality of records. The study covered 215 SHGs spread across four states of Andhra Pradesh, Karnataka, Odisha and Rajasthan.

What followed is captured in Figure 4.1. The programme kept adding numbers year on year at a phenomenal pace and it seems the effects are being seen now with a lag.

4.1.1.2 People's programme to state programme

The advent of Swarnjayanti Swarojgar Yojana (SGSY) in 1999 changed things drastically. The popularity of group-based lending under SBLP influenced the policy governing implementation of Integrated Rural Development Programme (IRDP). Despite massive injection of funds under IRDP, the programme suffered from extensive malpractices and leakage of funds. The repayment rates under IRDP were abysmally low ranging from 25% to 33%, forcing a rethink on its operation. In 1999, the government merged IRDP and its allied schemes into a new programme named SGSY. The core approach adopted in SGSY to obviate the past lacunae was adoption of SHG mode of lending and the concept of back end subsidy. The scheme was implemented by District Rural Development Agency (DRDAs)/ Zilla Parishads through Panchayat Samithis with active involvement of Panchayats based on the funds provided for the SGSY. Despite the expected improved programme results with these correctives, the decline continued. ADB noted that 'though the SGSY also lends mainly through SHGs, the quality of SHGs under it are not very strong and often groups are formed with the lure of a larger loan along with a subsidy'.[4] Expansion of SGSY and involvement of government agencies in SHG promotion became a thorny issue leading MYRADA to rename its groups as Self Affinity Groups (SAGs) to have distinction from the target driven government formed groups. This started the co-option of SHGs by the state. While state was right in using the SHG mode for effective delivery, the focus on target-based approach, introduction of subsidy element and short-circuiting group formation and nurturing process seriously affected quality of SHGs, negatively influenced the empowerment approach and also dampened the enthusiasm of banks. The committee[5] formed to look into functioning of SGSY observed several deficiencies like (i) no effective monitoring after sanctioning loans, (ii) many SHGs were formed with the intension of availing the revolving fund and subsidy, and influential persons in the village were found to own a group. Based on the recommendations of the committee, the Government of India restructured SGSY as National Rural Livelihoods Mission (NRLM).

NRLM is being implemented by the government in a mission mode and is based on three pillars—enhancing and expanding existing livelihoods options of the poor; building skills for the job market; and nurturing self-employed and entrepreneurs. The key differentiating features of NRLM with SGSY are (i) building village-level and higher-level federations to provide space, voice and resources for the poor and for reducing their dependence on external agencies, (ii) promoting specialised institutions like livelihoods collectives, producers' cooperatives/ companies for livelihoods promotion and (iii) working towards achieving universal financial inclusion, beyond basic banking services to all the poor households (conceived ecosystem under NRLM shown on next page). NRLM had set a target of reaching at least one member from each identified rural poor household, preferably a woman through the SHG. Apart from this welcome change in approach, it however continues with target mode, interest rate subsidy and other type of financial support to the SHGs (revolving fund of ₹10,000 to ₹15,000) and upper-level structures (community investment fund to SHG federations at cluster level). The provision of financial support through revolving fund is based on the logic that it will provide catalytic capital for leveraging repeat bank finance. NRLM envisages that with this support, each SHG would be able to leverage cumulative bank credit of ₹1,000,000.

Besides continuing with reliance on capital support and interest subsidy, which goes against the grain of SHG concept, what is more worrying is the fact that it shortens the period between group formation to bank credit (Figure 4.2).

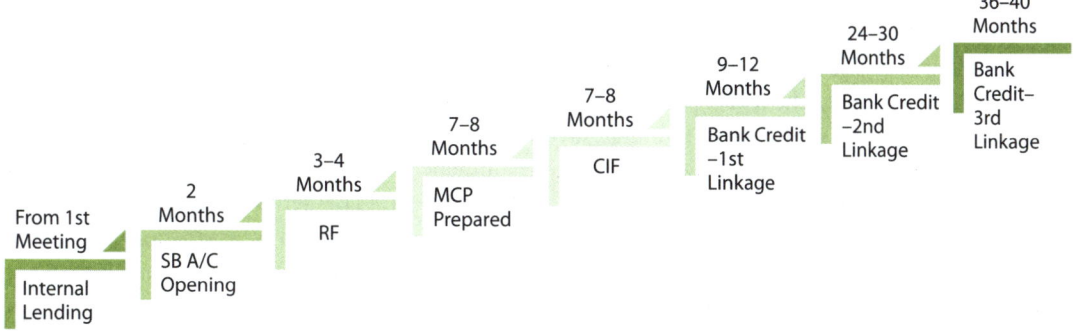

Figure 4.2 Group formation and bank linkage process and timeline under NRLM

Source: http://www.aajeevika.gov.in/content/components/financial-inclusion

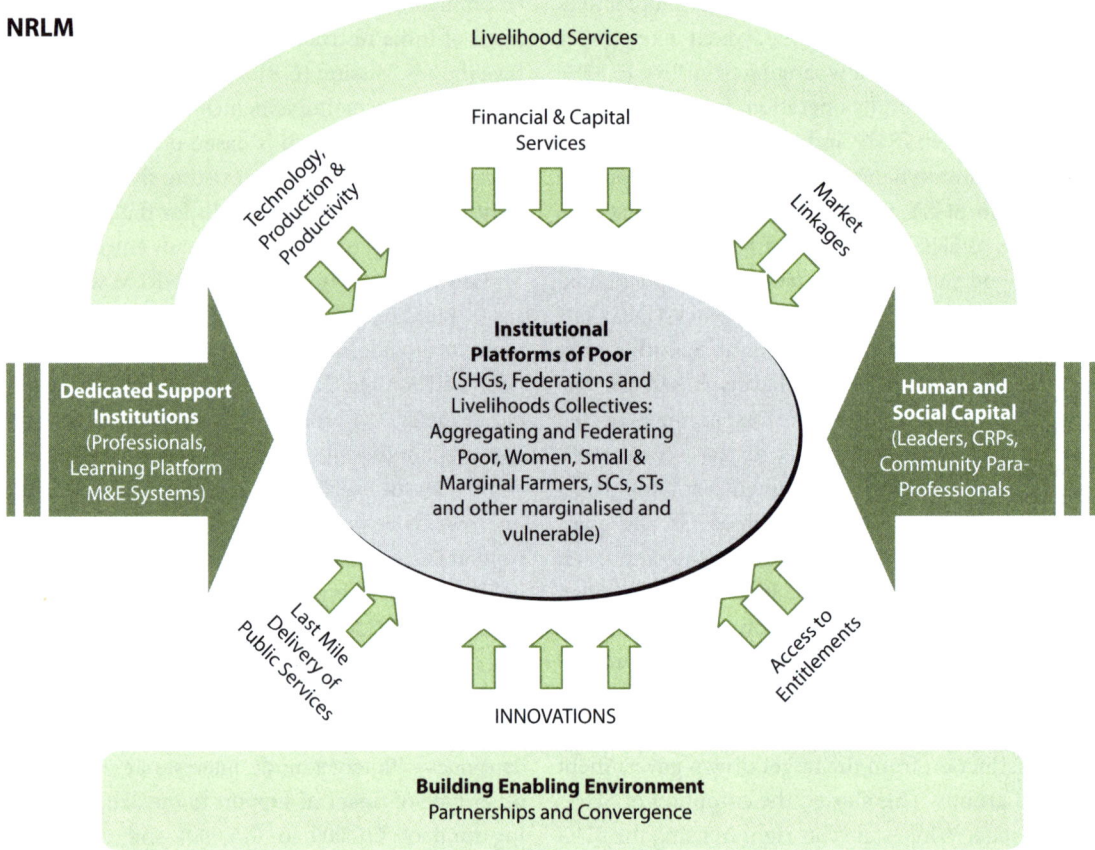

NRLM ecosystem

The mid-term review of NRLM[6] done this year reports that by December 2014, a total of about 1.44 lakh new SHGs were promoted and 1.31 lakh pre-project SHGs were revived. As per report, on an average, about 738 SHGs were promoted per project block, while the expected number of SHGs in a block after two years of intensive implementation is 720. While the programme has been successful in creating SHGs and higher-level structures, not much has happened in other segments of the ecosystem conceived for NRLM. The mid-term review report has negligible mention of livelihood services, market linkages or innovations but is primarily focused on financial side. The report primarily talks about the number of SHGs mobilised, trainings, savings, loans, revolving fund and capital support provided to SHGs and federations. Field interactions reveal that the primary focus of the programme is on formation, opening of savings account followed by provision of revolving fund and capital support as per timelines (Figure 4.2). Hopefully, NRLM will take up other needed services like livelihood support and

market linkages with same 'mission mode' approach in near future. As discussed later, at present its interplay with NABARD SHG programme is creating confusion in the field with stakeholders placing nametags on SHGs as 'NABARD SHG' or 'NRLM SHG'. Even though both programmes have inherent differences, it is hoped that both programmes can work together benefitting SHG members. Key differences in features of SBLP and NRLM are provided in Annexure 4.1.

4.2 PROGRESS UNDER SBLP

Comprised of different types of interventions as discussed earlier, SBLP has emerged as a significant component of financial inclusion for the poor and the excluded. The period of rapid growth (Figure 4.1) has been followed by stagnation with number of SHGs credit linked with banks showing a decline over the all-time high of 4.8 million SHGs in 2010. However, during 2014–15, the period of negative growth has been arrested and the number grew

Table 4.1 **SHG-bank linkage programme: Key highlights over the years**

Particulars	2009	2010	2011	2012	2013	2014	2015[†]
No. of SHGs with outstanding bank loans*	4,224,338	4,851,356	4,786,763	4,354,442	4,451,434	4,197,338	4,486,018
Of which in southern region*	2,283,992	2,582,112	2,706,408	2,355,732	2,415,191	2,221,038	2,406,461
Share of southern region (%)	54	53	57	54	54	53	54
NPA % under SHG loans*		2.9	4.7	6.1	7.1	6.8	7.40
Share of SGSY/NRLM groups (%)	23	26	27	28	27	23	NA
Share of women's groups (%)	79	80	83	84	84	81	NA
Loans disbursed to SHGs during the year (₹ billion)[#]	122.54	144.53	145.48	165.35	205.85	240.17	303.34
Average loan disbursed during the year per group (₹)[#]	76,131	91,081	121,625	144,048	168,754	175,768	184,551
Total bank loan outstanding to SHGs (₹ billion)*	226.79	280.38	312.21	363.41	393.75	429.27	517.22
Average loan outstanding per SHG* (₹)	53,687	57,794	65,224	83,457	88,455	102,273	115,295
Incremental groups with outstanding loans (million)	0.6	0.63	(–)0.06	(–)0.43	0.1	(−0.25)	0.29
Incremental loans outstanding (₹ billion)	56.77	45.9	33.53	57.22	30.35	35.52	87.95
No. of SHGs with savings accounts with banks* (million)	6.12	6.95	7.46	7.96	7.32	7.42	7.71
Total savings of SHGs with banks* (₹ billion)	55.46	61.99	70.16	65.51	82.17	98.97	113.07
Average savings of SHGs with banks*(₹)	9,060	8,915	9,402	8,230	11,229	13,321	14,661

Source: SHG Data from NABARD (2009–14), 2015 provisional data provided by mCID, NABARD.
Notes: *As on 31 March.
[#]during the year ended 31 March.
[†]Provisional.

by 6.8% over last year to reach 4.48 million SHGs. However, the figures are still lower than 2010. The stagnation extends to savings linked SHGs also–with the current outreach at 7.71 million lower than the all-time high reached in 2012 (Table 4.1).

The stagnation in outreach numbers happening after a five-year exponential growth seen with increasing NPA suggests that the chase of numbers diluted quality of SHGs and many SHGs being formed for availing financial support under earlier SGSY scheme. Field interactions and discussions with bankers reinforce this with some bankers doubting the numbers being reported. Hopefully, the rolling out of SHG digitisation project (discussed in section 4.3) will be able to bring out the full picture. The Chairman, NABARD,[7] also pointed out that more sanitised data being reported by banks now is also responsible for the decline in numbers and added that the digitisation project is being piloted with a view to get an accurate picture. On the positive side, the financial progress in terms of year end loan

outstanding amount and amount disbursed during the year has been unidirectional and positive. Despite dip/stagnation in outreach numbers, group savings with banks, annual flow of funds to the sector and the bank loan outstanding has been increasing steadily. This shows deepening of credit outreach.

As data on various responsible finance indicators like poverty outreach, nature of loan facility, member-wise loans or use of loans is not available; the available macro data has been analysed on aspects having a direct bearing on clients. The data analysis focuses on regional balance, link between savings and loans, adequacy of financing and NPAs.

4.2.1 Highly concentrated outreach

The SBLP started with a predominant share of southern region in outreach and credit flow (Table 4.2). Realising that the progress in SBLP showed a distinct regional skew with southern states accounting for more than 70% of SBLP numbers in 2000–01, a strategic approach was adopted by NABARD for

Table 4.2 **Regional share in number of SHGs credit linked (2009–15)**

Region/Year	2009	2010	2011	2012	2013	2014	2015
Northern	3.9	3.1	3.1	4.9	4.8	4.4	3.94
North-eastern	2.8	2.8	3.1	3.7	3.2	3	2.75
Eastern	22.1	21.2	23.1	22.6	22.9	23.3	23.84
Central	7.9	10.3	7.5	8.1	8.1	10	9.77
Western	9.3	9.4	6.6	6.6	6.6	6.4	6.05
Southern	54	53.2	56.5	54.1	54.3	52.9	53.64

Source: SHG Data from NABARD (2009–14), 2015 provisional data provided by mCID, NABARD.

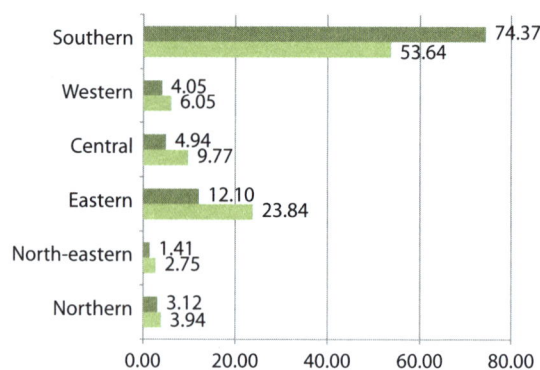

■ Share in Portfolio O/S ■ Share in no. of SHGs credit linked

Figure 4.3 Regional-wise share in loans outstanding and number of groups credit linked 2015
Source: NABARD.

expansion of SBLP in 13 priority states. It included capacity building efforts of NGOs and government agencies, widening the scope of SHPAs and increasing the participation of cooperative banks. The concerted strategy has yielded some positive results as the share of southern states came down to 54% by March 2006 but has remained at that level since then.

The situation shows more imbalance when the share in loan portfolio outstanding with SHGs is viewed. The southern region accounts for ~75% share in loans outstanding, much higher than its 53% share in number of groups. This contrasts with all other regions, in which the portfolio share is lower than their share in number of groups (Figure 4.3). This is a very telling pointer of the highly uneven spread of SBLP.

The analysis of MFIs on similar dimension (Chapter 3) showed that regional spread has been addressed by MFIs, though the state concentration still exists. The unbalanced growth of SBLP exhibits both concentrations with top 10 states accounting for 89.60% share on loans outstanding. It is significant that there is significant overlap between top five states of MFI outreach and SBLP outreach with West Bengal, Tamil Nadu and Karnataka figuring in both lists and if the non-performing portfolio of Andhra Pradesh is considered, the names are exactly similar (Table 4.3). This has great importance relating to prevention of over-indebtedness of clients. With SBLP outreach not being part of credit bureau, it makes it difficult for MFIs to ascertain the true debt profile of

Table 4.3 **Top 10 states with SBLP outstanding loans as on 31 March 2015**

States	Savings linked SHGs (lakhs)	Savings (₹ billion)	SHGs with loan O/S (lakhs)	Loan O/S (₹ billion)	% of SHGs credit linked
Andhra Pradesh	8.84	26.29	8.11	159.01	91.74
Telangana	5.11	9.96	4.73	74.80	47.48
Tamil Nadu	9.88	10.35	4.27	63.81	43.22
Karnataka	7.34	13.16	5.46	62.89	74.39
West Bengal	7.62	14.04	5.85	28.67	76.77
Kerala	5.85	6.45	1.43	23.41	24.50
Odisha	4.52	4.97	2.36	19.36	52.21
Maharashtra	7.31	9.18	2.09	15.76	28.59
Uttar Pradesh	3.92	3.56	2.22	15.72	56.63
Total top 10	60.39	97.97	36.52	463.43	60.48
Other 24 states	16.74	15.10	8.34	53.78	49.80
Total	**77.13**	**113.07**	**44.86**	**517.21**	58.16

Source: SHG Data from NABARD (2009–14), 2015 provisional data provided by mCID, NABARD.

clients. What compounds the problem is that these states also have the highest per SHG loan outstanding amount implying greater per client debt.

Such lopsided regional growth is not in line with the developmental mission of SBLP and more so as the southern states have a higher human development index (HDI) ranking. This implies that SBLP outreach is less in states with lower development levels. The steps taken by NABARD in diversifying outreach and the learning from the evaluation of SGSY which commented on lopsided growth of the programme have not had much effect.

Even as the programme suffers from predominant regional bias with overall outreach numbers stagnating, there is confusion in the field among borrowers with interplay of NRLM and NABARD promoted SHGs. Members of NABARD promoted SHGs feel discriminated on account of revolving fund and interest subsidy being provided to groups formed under NRLM. The speed in group formation and linkage process under NRLM is another pain point. At the policy level, NRLM talks about building synergies with its mission statement stating: 'There are existing institutions of the poor women formed by Government efforts and efforts of NGOs. NRLM would strengthen all existing institutions of the poor in a partnership mode',[8] but in most areas, NRLM structure is forming new groups rather than strengthening existing groups. The field reality is supported by the data provided by the mid-term review of NRLM, which states: 'The age analysis of the sample SHGs reveals that 8% are about 1 year old, 31% are in the age group 12 to 18 months, 26% in the group 18 to 24 months and 34% over two years old'.[9] The predominance of SHGs less than two years old shows that the programme is working with newer SHGs. This is causing disruption and feeling of discrimination among older SHGs not covered under NRLM and needs to be sorted out at the earliest.

4.2.2 Are clients' loan requirements being met adequately?

Under SBLP, loans are disbursed in the name of groups and member-wise data is not captured. Further, published information does not provide data on difference between loan amount applied by the group and sanctioned by the bank, which could provide concrete evidence on adequacy of financing. The available data can however be analysed to see bank-wise loan outstanding per SHG across states and region. Though the group has the flexibility to decide individual member loan in the absence of member-level data, the analysis assumes equal division of the loan amount. The analysis (Table 4.4) shows that other than southern region and northern region, the average per member loan outstanding is quite low at around ₹5,000.

Compared with MFIs, this level of depth is quite inadequate. Average loan amount in case of NBFC-MFIs stands at ₹16,327 as on 31 March 2015. The extension of analysis across agencies shows that cooperative banks are the most conservative in financing SHGs, followed by regional rural banks (RRBs). The conservatism in loan amount among cooperative banks extends to their low share in All India outreach under SBLP at 6.41%. Considering the extensive rural outreach of cooperative banks, it is disconcerting that their share is negligible and has remained so over the years. Such pervasive underfinancing can lead to SHG members seeking loans from other sources as well as unviability of their micro businesses, which in turn leads to NPAs.

Table 4.4 Depth of outreach across regions and agencies, 2015

	Region average loan O/S per SHG	Per member loan O/S[@]	Average loan O/S per SHG—commercial banks	Average loan O/S per SHG—RRBs	Average loan O/S per SHG—cooperative banks
South	159,835	12,295	167,961	158,920	97,562
North	91,357	7,027	109,274	65,288	48,115
Western	77,131	5,933	90,691	66,455	35,247
North-east	59,263	4,559	63,908	56,025	39,836
East	58,531	4,502	65,014	72,196	31,631
Central	58,333	4,487	95,153	37,827	25,908

Source: NABARD.
[@] Assuming 13 members per SHG.

Table 4.5 Savings and loans of SHGs (2008–15)

	2008	2009	2011	2012	2013	2014	2015
No. of SHGs with savings accounts with banks	6,120,000	6,950,000	7,460,000	7,960,000	7,320,000	7,420,000	7,712,653
No. of SHGs with outstanding bank loans	4,224,338	4,851,356	4,786,763	4,354,442	4,451,434	4,197,338	4,486,018
Percentage of SHGs not credit linked	31.0	30.2	35.8	45.3	39.19	43.4	41.8
Amount of SHG savings with banks (₹ billion)	55.46	61.99	70.16	65.51	82.17	98.97	113.07
Amount of loan O/S against SHGs (₹ billion)	226.79	280.38	312.21	363.41	393.75	429.27	517.22
Ratio of credit to savings (%)	409	452	445	555	479	434	457

Source: SHG Data from NABARD (2009–14), 2015 provisional data provided by mCID, NABARD.

As the programme is based on the design of linking savings with loans, it is necessary to examine the link of savings with credit. The pattern of SHGs not credit linked over the years shows that the percentage of such SHGs is gradually going up. In 2009, only 30% of SHGs were not credit linked but over the years it has steadily moved upwards to reach 42% in the year 2015 (Table 4.5). The existence of higher number of SHGs yet to be provided loans seen alongside with not so significant increase in outreach over past three years suggests that even mature SHGs are finding it difficult to assess loans. The aspect of linking savings with loans also seems to be losing operational effectiveness. Though the loan outstanding amount for all credit linked SHGs has remained around 4 to 5 times of savings, if ~40% of SHGs not having loans are taken out, the savings to credit ratio goes much beyond the prescribed norm. This needs to be addressed as while 40% SHGs have no loans, others have loans much in excess of four times of group savings.

The breach of link between ratio of savings and credit in case of credit-linked SHGs implies that the programme has not been able to build savings in proportion to the credit requirement.

Agency-wise performance reflects that cooperative banks have 18% share in SHG deposits but their share in loans outstanding is mere 6%. Cooperatives also have the lowest per SHG loan amount; the amount of credit extended by cooperatives is less than half the all India average (Figure 4.4). Thus, the SHGs of cooperatives are more likely to be underfinanced. This is further proved by the fact that loan to savings multiple is less than 2 in the case of cooperative banks while it is 4.6 for the country as a whole.

■ Cooperative banks   ■ RRBs   □ Commercial banks

Figure 4.4 Share of agencies in SHG savings and loan outstanding (March 2015) inner pie (savings), outer (loans)

Source: 2015 SHG Provisional Data by mCID, NABARD.

4.2.3 Portfolio quality: Cause for concern

The success of both strands of microfinance—MFIs and SBLP—was to a large extent based on having almost 100% recovery rates. While MFIs have continued to maintain that, SBLP has seen slippages. It started with a slight increase in NPA reported in 2002 but it is worrisome that over time it has kept inching upwards to reach 7.4% by March 2015. Rising NPAs under SBLP seen with the aspect of possible underfinancing of SHGs in most regions are the two main causes of concern. The problem for clients is getting compounded as rising NPAs make banks more conservative in sanctioning loans.

The corresponding effect of it is also seen in rise of unlinked SHGs—it has gone up to 42% by March 2015 against 30% in 2008.

The NPA position is similar across agencies but has regional/state dimensions. The figures for various agencies shows an almost equal percentage of NPAs—commercial banks have 7.73% NPA as on 31 March 2015, while cooperatives had the highest NPA at 8.55% with RRBs falling in between at 8.36%. Similar levels of NPAs across agencies show that the strategy of cooperative banks being conservative in loan amounts to minimise risks is not working; it is leading to underfinancing but is not able to contain loan defaults. However, some states have an alarmingly high level of NPAs (Table 4.6), but the effect is reduced on account of lower SBLP portfolio in these states. The combined share of these states in all India loan portfolio is 11.17%. What is more comforting is the fact that none of the states in southern and western region have NPAs in excess of 10%. Detailed state-wise NPA information is given in Annexure 4.2.

Field interactions with bankers and SHPAs bring out two common strands. Bankers feel that considering their workload, it is difficult for them to do continuous follow-up with groups and suggest that this should be the responsibility of SHPAs. Branch managers responsible for lending to groups also feel that the quality of SHGs being promoted by different agencies especially government departments leaves much to be desired. Induction of diverse SHPAs ranging from NGOs, individual volunteers to government agencies without much coordination on having a basic understanding on quality aspects is leading to formation of groups with an eye

on loans and subsidy. The quality of SHPAs has not got the attention it deserves. NABARD provides financial support to SHPAs for group formation and linkage with banks, and by March 2014 had supported 3,545 SHPAs with a grant support of ₹228.97 crore.[10] Over the years, number of SHPAs has multiplied manifold and resulted in involvement of NGOs without any social mobilisation skills. On one hand, banks under other work commitments relegate SHG appraisal work to desk review or occasional field visit to the group and rely more on SHPA; on the other hand, the quality of SHPAs had deteriorated. Experts believe that involvement of such large number of SHPAs in itself is a pointer to quality dilution as in many parts of India there is an acute shortage of mature NGOs with experience in social mobilisation.

Various studies have brought out this aspect. During the year, 2014–15, NABARD commissioned APMAS to study the quality of SHGs in Bihar and Odisha.[11] The study report mentions that while state through Bihar Rural Livelihoods Promotion Society (BRLPS) is the predominant promoter of SHGs in Bihar, in Odisha the role of NGO-SHPAs and Mission Shakti programme of the government is equally important. While Box 4.1 gives the key findings, the report adds to the evidence of negative impact of state involvement. It reports that government agencies generally follow a target-oriented approach to the promotion of SHGs resulting in poor quality. The haste with which groups are being formed leads

Table 4.6 States with more than 10% NPA under SBLP—31 March 2015

States	NPA %
Jharkhand	22.69
Uttar Pradesh	19.04
Haryana	16.46
Himachal Pradesh	15.64
Odisha	15.28
Madhya Pradesh	14.12
Chhattisgarh	11.75
Punjab	10.32

Source: 2015 SHG Provisional Data by mCID, NABARD.

Box 4.1 Key findings from APMAS study of SHGs in Odisha and Bihar

- Fifty-six per cent of SHGs in Bihar and 33% in Odisha are SGSY groups.
- Average per member per month savings is ₹55.
- Rating on NABARD tool shows 24% SHGs in Odisha and 20% in Bihar as 'C'—lowest rating grade.
- Thirty per cent of SHGs have loans from banks.
- Fifty-four per cent of SHGs defaulted on bank loans—average default amount being ₹27,951.

Source: APMAS. *Quality and Sustainability of Self Help Groups in Bihar and Odisha.* https://www.nabard.org/Publication/QualitySustainabilityofSHGsinBiharandOdisaH.pdf (accessed on 8 October 2015).

to low awareness among members on the objectives of the group, responsibilities of members and leaders and low financial literacy. The report finds that SHG meetings are mostly confined to financial transactions, and non-financial and social agenda figure in only a few SHG meetings.

While the quality of groups has deteriorated, the report also mentions certain weak points on the financial side. At group level, about one-third of the SHGs had no internal lending operations from savings as banks did not allow for savings withdrawal during loan tenure and in some cases groups keep depositing incremental savings with the bank in the hope of getting larger loan. While only 30% of SHGs had loan outstanding from banks, there was an average of ₹19,940 in the savings account of each SHG. On multiple loans, the report mentions that SHGs accessed funds and grants from multiple sources, i.e., DRDA, SHG federations, banks as well as MFIs. The confidence of bankers in financing SHGs in these states is on the wane with only 30% of SHGs having loans from banks. The poor quality of groups and the reported high default rate of 33% in Bihar and 44% in Odisha are the contributing factors. The report findings show that there is lot of dilution of the original design ideas factored in the SBLP—group quality is weak, groups being formed with primary objective of obtaining loans and grants, poor record keeping, high defaults and low focus on non-financial aspects. Though the report is focussed on two states, discussions with bankers and other stakeholders reveal that these typify position in other states as well. These weaknesses have severely constrained the responsible finance agenda of SBLP and adoption of quantitative targets and active involvement of the state has almost taken over the 'people's movement'.

4.2.4 Grievance redressal and pricing

Grievance redressal is an important piece of client protection. The SBLP continue to depend on the formal grievance channel applicable to banks or the group dynamics to resolve it. There is no defined and dedicated grievance redressal channel for SHG clients and the nature of the programme makes it more critical. SHGs, besides their group dynamics, depend on SHPAs and banks and government agencies for capacity building, as well as financial support. In such a multi-agency scenario, the only formal channel open to them for lodging complaints is with the bank as a first step, followed by escalation to banking ombudsman. The common grievances of SHGs on issue of subsidy and reported cases of financial cuts in releasing it, as well as the persistent issue of underfinancing relate to the bank, while lack of adequate support and guidance relate to SHPAs. Within the group also there are cases of internal conflict, capture of resources by dominant members and unfair division of surplus, which have a major role in dissolution of the groups. It is not practical to expect group members to complain to banks and ombudsman due to their literacy levels, psychological barriers with the formal system as well as in the absence of any dedicated initiative to make them aware of this mechanism. In MFIs, there is a practice of printing phone number of branch managers and grievance redressal cell but there is no such practice in case of SHGs. As grievances can pertain to various agencies, the problem of whom to complain in a particular situation compounds the issue. For example, if the member has grievance against the SHPA, even making a complaint to banking ombudsman would not be productive. A dedicated grievance redressal mechanism covering all agencies needs to be evolved by NABARD and NRLM. The issue was flagged in the *Social Performance Report 2013* and it had mentioned that SHG members are not aware of the grievance redressal procedures based on a study by GIZ.[12] However, this crucial aspect has been left unattended.

The dimension of responsible pricing was considered to be the strong point of SBLP. Lending by banks directly to SHGs implied much lower cost as compared to MFIs and typically the lending rates by banks on SHG lending have remained lower than normal lending by banks. The lower interest rate feature still holds true, as the lending rates under SBLP are nearly half compared to interest rates charged by MFIs. However, the aspect of other costs besides interest rate in the form of transaction cost and opportunity cost tend to be ignored. In the past, studies have commented on these aspects saying that because of time spent in securing a loan, cost of paperwork and sometimes not getting the desired amount, there is not much variance in total cost to the client under both SBLP and MFIs. National Council of Applied Economic Research (NCAER)[13] in its study took sample of borrowers of banks, SBLP and MFIs and computed actual cost to the client. The report found that considering costs other than the interest rate, clients had to pay maximum for bank loans, followed by SBLP and MFI. For a ₹1,000 loan, client had to bear an additional cost of ₹30 in case of direct loan from banks, ₹24 if the loan was availed as SHG member and ₹13 in case of loan from MFIs. This additional cost component included wage loss due to time spent in getting the loan, travel cost, document charges and bribes.

Last year, a similar study[14] was done by IIM Lucknow for NABARD covering MFI and SBLP clients in Uttar Pradesh. The study split the transaction cost into direct and indirect cost with indirect cost component representing opportunity cost and direct cost covering costs directly related to getting a loan like travel cost and documentation cost. The study notes that even though under the SBLP the group absorbs a lot of transaction cost on behalf of the individual members yet the transaction cost of borrowing under SBLP at 7.18% is higher than MFIs at 6.20%. It further observes (referring to the issue of under financing discussed earlier) that the average amount of borrowing under SBLP is 40% less in SBLP and considering the fixed nature of transaction costs, it results in even further increased cost seen as percentage of the borrowed amount. The report finds that to secure a loan under SBLP, six visits to the bank are required as against one in case of MFIs. The findings are almost similar to earlier studies. The examination of total costs including interest rate is what should drive SBLP policy; absence of this erodes the huge advantage of the programme in terms of interest rate. Process streamlining, sensitisation of bankers and building group capacity is needed so that clients incur minimum other costs in availing loan.

4.3 DIGITISATION OF SHG RECORDS: SMALL BEGINNING WITH ENORMOUS POTENTIAL FOR RESPONSIBLE FINANCE

As SBLP grapples with issues relating to slow growth, dip in ratio of savings to credit-linked groups, and rising defaults, a small but significant step has been taken last year by NABARD in digitisation of SHG records. This has the potential to substantially transform the microfinance landscape by not only addressing issues of SBLP but also by supporting the responsible finance agenda of other institutions like MFIs catering to a similar segment.

Non-reporting of SBLP data to credit bureau has been flagged as an area of concern with possibilities of leading to over-indebtedness of clients. Credit decisions under SBLP are based without any checks on individual group member's credit history and MFIs, which lend to similar clients face the issue of not being able to correctly assess the existing indebtedness of their clients. The situation as of now shows that the outreach of both channels is concentrated in similar states, aggravating the situation. The Puri committee[15] set by the RBI to look into credit information data reporting in its report in 2014 suggested that it is critical that lenders (banks) should consider prior borrowings from SBLP and MFIs and hence it is needed that banks may capture and provide credit related information of individual borrowers within the SHG to the credit bureaus. The importance attached to it is evident from the fact that despite banks contention that SHG loans are given and tracked at group level, the committee recommended that banks may be required within a reasonable period of, say, 18 months, to arrange for capturing the required data from SHGs for reporting to Credit Information Companies (CICs).

The issue was also examined by the Expert Group[16] set up by the Ministry of Rural Development, Government of India, to set up a financial institution for financing of women SHGs. While acknowledging the importance of Puri Committee recommendations, it was observed that this can be used by the banks to rationalise exclusion and as such suggested a cautious approach. The Expert Group observed:

> The EG acknowledges that it is necessary to have the details of the members of the SHGs to enable their identification and ensure that they are not members of several JLGs/SHGs to avoid multiple lending and over-borrowing. However the individual credit record is private information of the member and the SHG, and using this for providing further finance to the group could undermine the concept of the SHG which is based on mutuality and consensus. It is appreciated that going forward, when members mature from SHG loans to individual loans their track record in the CICs will help them better their credit scores. However, in the early stages, the concern for the EG is that such data should not be used by the banks for exclusion rather than inclusion at the very low levels of finance being discussed and hence may be used with caution.

Apart from non-reporting of individual member-level or even group-level data to the credit bureau,

SBLP is also beset with the problems of varied book keeping and accounting. The problem is twofold—in many cases, the financial transactions are not up to date and the records kept vary across groups. This not only impedes transparency but also acts as a constraining factor for banks. Banks unable to get a clear picture of financial records in standardised format tend to either not consider giving loans or limit the loan size. MIS is another issue being faced by all stakeholders. As the outreach has gone up substantially to 7.7 million SHGs, the collation of data at national level from different banks and agencies has become an onerous task. The sheer volume of data being compiled manually at national level is not only prone to errors but also acts as a limiting factor in reported data points.

To address the above issues, NABARD started a digitisation pilot project in two districts of Ramgarh (Jharkhand) and Dhule (Maharashtra) during 2014–15. The project is at present using the Tablet-based software developed by Leaps & Bounds. Leaps and Bounds software allows for multifuntionality (Box 4.2) and importantly considering the locational issue of SHGs can be used in both online and offline mode. However, going ahead, the project envisages integrating it with android-based phone application. The digitisation of SHG records is a well thought out process and starts with mapping of the existing SHGs in the district (bank wise, branch wise) covering all SHGs including SGSY/NRLM promoted SHGs. Under the pilot project in two districts, SHPAs were trained on collecting SHG wise/member-wise data. The SHG data captured covers both individual

---

Box 4.2 Features of leaps and bounds SHG accounting software

- All Indian languages on tablet.
- Requires basic functional literacy.
- Generation of all financial statements like Balance Sheet and P&L.
- Both offline and online mode.
- Web-based system—all stakeholders can access same information.
- Provision to connect with core banking system (CBS).
- SAAS (Software As A Service) model—no huge investment in purchase of the software.
- Cloud computing compatible model.

Source: Leaps and Bounds booklet, NABARD.

Box 4.3 Data points captured in SHG digitisation

MEMBER LEVEL

Name, address, gender, marital status, Aadhaar number, Voter ID card, mobile number, BPL/APL status, membership of any Joint Liability Group (JLG), house type, availability of toilets, electricity connection and other financial details like saving bank account number, savings, borrowing and repayment, life/medical insurance, micro-pension policy (if any).

SHG LEVEL

Name, address, date of formation, name of SHPA/NGO, programme under which supported, savings habits, lending policy, bank linkage, details of periodic savings collected and internal lending, utilisation of bank credit availed for members.

Source: Concept Note on Digitisation, NABARD.

---

member and group data. The list of data points being captured is extensive (Box 4.3) and based on that financial statements can be generated automatically besides giving an insight into intra-group dynamics. The client identity is captured based on multiple eligible IDs but the prime focus is on Aadhaar. Group-level identity is generated by the system based on village number format used by Census. To establish the authenticity of records captured in the software, the pilot project got the group and members to physically sign the records. It is noteworthy that using the extensive data points being captured, the system has been so designed that it can produce SHG grading based on NABARD SHG grading tool.

The audited data is then uploaded through a customised software in the central server. NABARD has launched a web portal www.eshakti.nabard.org for hosting the SHG data under the digitisation project. The project envisages that bank branches will be given login-based access to SHGs financed by them or in their area. The pilot project in Ramgarh started in March 2014 and will be completed by September 2015, and Dhule district is likely to be completed a bit later. The process flow of the digitisation process is shown in Figure 4.5.

Buoyed by the success and positive response from other stakeholders like banks, NABARD proposes to start extension of the pilot project for digitisation

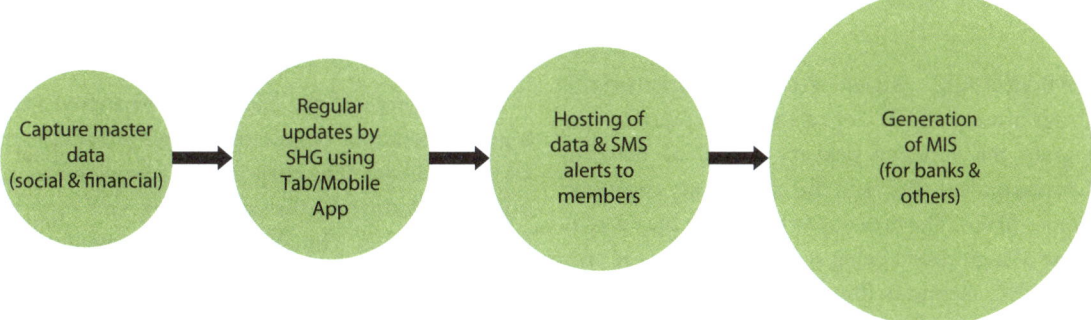

Figure 4.5 Digitisation of SHG data—process flow
Source: mCID, NABARD.

of all SHGs in 10 districts across 10 states of the country. The pilot is to be executed over a two-year period and is expected to cover 75,000 SHGs touching the lives of over 11 lakh rural households.

4.3.1 Benefits of digitisation

The success of the project has opened up many possibilities. Capturing bank account details and Aadhaar based identity of group members, it opens up the enabling ecosystem for integrating SHG members with the national financial inclusion agenda. It will allow ease of transfer of social benefits and direct benefit transfer (DBT) through Aadhaar linked accounts and convergence with other government benefits as well as facilitate suitable interventions and convergence of other programme for social and financial empowerment.

At a more concrete level and in near future, it will lead to standardisation of book keeping across SHGs, insights into intra-group functioning, ready financial and operational information for banks to assess the performance of SHGs and collation of national-level database on almost real-time basis. Banks can also reduce their time on appraisal as the grading can be generated from the software leaving banks to focus on sample field-based checks. The most significant impact on responsible financing of the excluded lies in possibility of migrating the data to credit bureaus—tracking of individual member financial transactions coupled with Aadhaar based KYC will facilitate this process. Often field functionaries as well as bankers question the veracity of national-level data reported every year; digitisation addresses this question. The pilot project in two districts has shown that nearly 25% of SHGs listed in the first phase could not be traced,[17] thus data sanitisation is an in-built part of the process.

4.3.2 Issues going ahead

The positive experience of digitisation pilot has to be taken forward and some issues need to be considered. The pilot programme cost in terms of training of SHPAs, infrastructure costs, cost of Tablets, software cost and personnel cost has been borne by NABARD. Discussions with the project advisor on per district cost suggest an approximate figure of ₹2 crore. This does not include recurring costs. As such, one-time digitisation cost across the country will be high but considering its immense usefulness, it is hoped that funding will not be a problem. Pilots in two districts show that it takes around six months to digitise one district's data. Even though going ahead with more experience, the process time may get slightly reduced, discussions reveal that it might still take 4–5 years. Operationally, this pilot relied on SHPAs for the digitisation work and intensive training and handholding by NABARD. It is doubtful whether NABARD will have the bandwidth to undertake such intensive handholding pan India and the possibility of outsourcing this to external agencies needs to be considered. While the system claims to have the functionality of integrating with core banking system of banks, it has not been tested. For the project to achieve its full potential, this must be tried out from the pilot stage.

4.4 CLIENT-CENTRIC INNOVATIONS UNDER SBLP

During last year, NABARD kept up a high pace on revitalising the SBLP. Besides the digitisation pilot, which has enormous potential to transform the financial inclusion landscape, NABARD initiated few pilot projects to benefit the SHG members.

4.4.1 SHG members as banking correspondent agents: NABARD-GIZ pilot project[18]

NABARD-GIZ Rural Financial Institutions Programme (RFIP) conceived this pilot to integrate the doorstep delivery model of Banking Correspondent (BC) and the community organisations—SHGs. The idea was to overcome the current issue of high churn being seen in BC agents as also help SHG members improve their earnings. SHG members were chosen on account of their integration with the community and experience in dealing with money and banks. It was also felt that given that SHG members were women, this approach would help the bank reach out to more women clients. Above all, the agent-driven doorstep delivery model would enable the bank to track the flow of credit and have a longer time float on account of doorstep convenience. In order to assess the potential of using SHG members as agents, extent of uptake by SHGs and the challenges encountered, two pilots were conducted with Gramin Bank of Aryavat (GBA) in Unnao district in Uttar Pradesh in May 2013 and Narmada Jhabua Gramin Bank (NJGB) in Madhya Pradesh in 2014. Though the model (Figure 4.6) was broadly the same, some tweaking was done to suit the contextual variations.

Also, different partners and technology solutions were used in each pilot to test the efficacy of the model.

In both projects, the banks have partnered with a local federation, corporate BC and a technology service provider. The corporate BC provided technology including hardware, software and support for maintenance. The SHG members having prior experience in facilitating transactions and record keeping were appointed as agents known as 'Bank Sakhis'. While SHG federations were responsible for capacity development, training and providing monitoring support to the Sakhis and also in helping them to raise financial awareness in the communities, the Sakhis were to offer a range of bank products and other non-financial services to SHG members. In return, they were paid differential commission for the various services provided.

Under conventional BC model, the customer service point (CSP) can only serve individual accounts and SHGs with group accounts still need to go to branch as signature of multiple office bearers are needed. To overcome this limitation, the banks under the pilot customised their Micro-ATM devices to support biometric authentication of multiple signatories of one account and thereby allow deposits

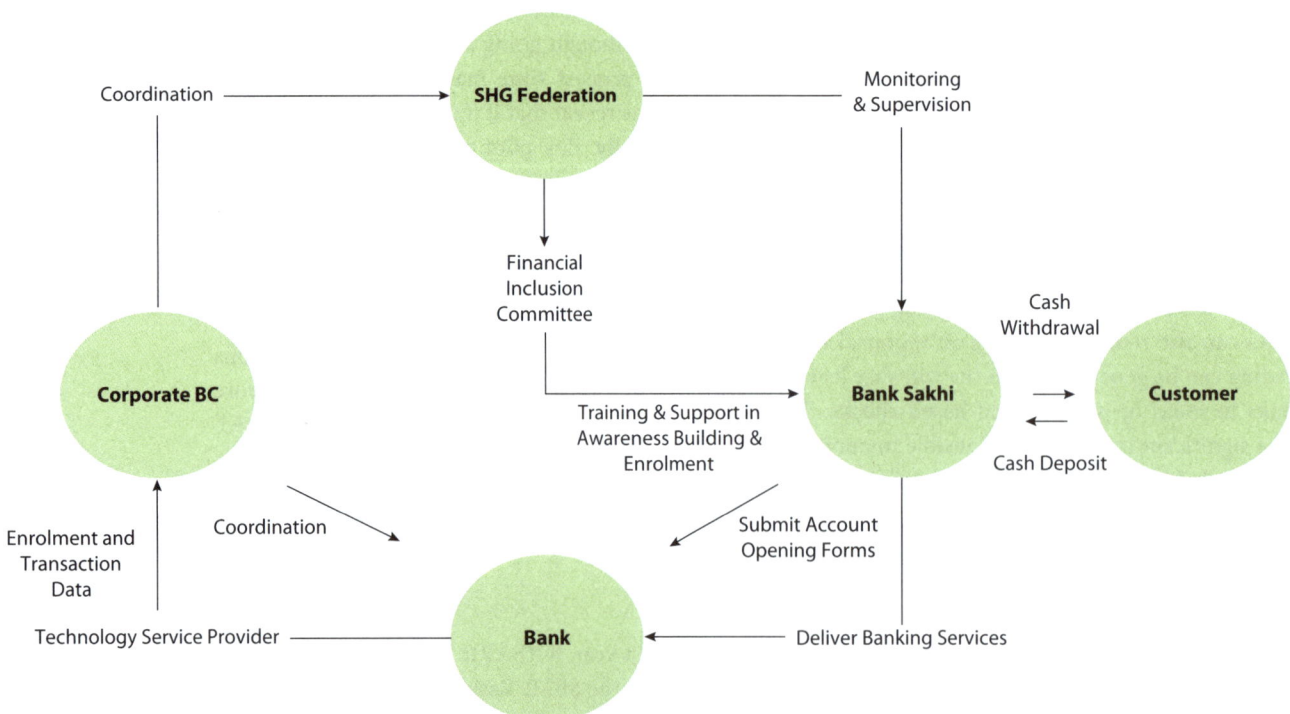

Figure 4.6 Process flow in SHG members as banking correspondent pilot

Source: NABARD-GIZ. June 2015. *SHG Members as Bank Agents: Case Studies from Unnao, Uttar Pradesh.* New Delhi.

and withdrawals at both the group and individual levels. Thus, all deposits in the group accounts can now be validated by a single biometric authentication by any mapped signatory, while withdrawals and internal lending are authenticated by the biometric of dual signatories. As a result, the transparency of operations is ensured through the provision of digitised acknowledgement receipts, banks are able to keep the clients' money disbursed in their accounts for a longer period, agents' earn more incremental revenue and SHG member incur lower transaction cost and are also able to build their credit history with the bank. A comparative picture of two pilots is given in Table 4.7.

A comparison of SHG members appointed as bank agents with other CSPs in both pilot area shows significant difference in performance. In Unnao, only 8% of accounts operated by Sakhis are dormant, while in case of other CSPs the figure is significantly high at 58%. Similarly in Indore, 46% of accounts operated by Bank Sakhis are active as against 7% in case of other CSPs. Detailed comparison of performance for Unnao is given in Annexure 4.3.

The focal point of this model are the SHG federations who are instrumental in identifying reliable candidates for the role of Bank Sakhi. Further, modifying the model depending upon geographic and socio-cultural contexts, offering a suite of demand-driven financial and non-financial services backed by an appropriate technology platform, regular trainings on financial concepts, usage of electronic platforms and proactive involvement of all stakeholders have contributed to the success of the pilot. In addition to generating income for the Bank Sakhis, the pilot also has significant value as it has empowered rural women to be agents of financial inclusion in their village, step out and visit bank branches, conduct awareness camps and also motivate other unbanked women to open bank accounts.

4.4.2 Entrepreneurship by SHGs in managing government programmes

Fifty case studies of ingenious and entrepreneurial ways in which individual SHGs have contracted, managed and implemented developmental initiatives of the State/Central Government have been documented by NABARD in '*SHGs: Paving Pathways to Possibilities*'.[19] This document is a compendium of decisive factors, constraints and opportunities, used by SHGs to beat their odds of poverty, indebtedness, social negligence and marginalised existence. The case studies illustrate how they have proven

Table 4.7 Comparison of the bank Sakhi pilot in Unnao and Indore

Parameters	Gramin Bank of Ayravat (GBA)	Narmada Jhabua Gramin Bank (NJGB)
Operations	Unnao, Uttar Pradesh	Indore, Madhya Pradesh
Launch date	May 2013	May 2014
Stakeholders	Bartronics—BC	Tata Consultancy Services (TSP)
	Bartronics—TSP	Network for Information and Computer Technology (NICT)—BC
	Rajiv Gandhi Mahila Vikas Pariyojna (RGMVP): (i) promoted SHGs and federations, (ii) appoint and manages bank Sakhis	Priya Sakhi Mahila Sangh (PSMS) in Indore, Aprajita Mahila Sangh (AMS) in Dewas—local district-level federations: (i) promoted SHGs and federations, (ii) appoint and manage bank Sakhis
Services provided to SHGs	• SHG can collect individual member savings in its account by fund transfer from member's individual account or cash deposit • Transfer funds from SHG to member account via dual authentication • Transfer funds from its savings bank account to cash credit loan account using dual authentication • Transfer funds from cash credit loan account to member account via dual authentication	
Other services	• Account opening, deposits, withdrawals, money transfer, recurring and fixed deposits, delivery of notices to loan defaulters, linking of Aadhaar with bank accounts, insurance and vehicle loans	
Progress (as on 31 March 2015)	• 50 Sakhis (48 active) operating in 174 villages; over 50% account holders are women (majority are first timers) • Opened 20,208 accounts; facilitated 265,335 cumulative transactions having cumulative value of ₹37,151,922	• 29 Sakhis (20 active) operating in 170 villages • Opened 7,628 accounts; facilitated 10,072 cumulative transactions having cumulative value of ₹8,038,077

Source: NABARD-GIZ. June 2015. *SHG Members as Bank Agents: Case Studies from Unnao, Uttar Pradesh.* New Delhi.

themselves to be more hard working, transparent, effective, efficient and dependable enterprises, in comparison to private contractors, for delivery of government's developmental programmes. In fact, the report says that government departments find SHGs a more convincing mechanism to translate policies into action plans.

4.4.3 Micro-insurance: NABARD religare pilot

The poor are most vulnerable to health hazards. Any saving-based group initiative can easily be derailed by an unfortunate and unforeseen health event that can permanently or temporarily debilitate a sole bread earner of a family of an SHG member. Inability of such member to meet his/her financial obligations towards the SHG has serious repercussion on financial sustainability of that entire group. Therefore, it is imperative to safeguard SHG members against such unanticipated health problems through micro-insurance. Micro-insurance as a component of financial inclusion has not been very successful so far because of absence of a suitable product and its delivery mix. NABARD has been in negotiation with various insurance service providers to customise their insurance products for SHG members. In 2014, NABARD in association with Religare Health Insurance Pvt Ltd. introduced an affordable and customised micro-insurance pilot scheme covering 1,000 SHG members and their families in Alwar District of Rajasthan through SHPA where NABARD will share part of the insurance premium for first two years (Box 4.4). Since launch of this initiative, the insurance company has settled eight claims.

Box 4.4 Features of NABARD–Religare micro-insurance pilot for SHG members

- Five members of the family including SHG member covered.
- Policy in the name of SHPA.
- Cashless hospitalisation treatment in network hospitals with sum insured up to ₹50,000.
- Annual premium ₹895 including taxes.
- Covers pre-existing diseases, in-patient services, accident and emergency services, cost of medicine and day care, maternity, one-day pre- and post-hospitalisation expenses related to hospitalisation.
- Premium recharge facility as the basic sum insured or on pro-rata basis for the rest of

the policy tenure in case limit of ₹50,000 is exhausted for a policy period.
- Covers death and permanent disability resulting out of an accident or injury.

Source: mCID, NABARD.

Though all these initiatives address critical issues of appropriate product for SHG members, these initiatives have also demonstrated the potential of SHGs using 'self-help' in creating social capital, environmental/natural capital, human capital and financial capital in rural India. However, all of these initiatives are still in pilot phase and their real impact can only be harnessed if these are scaled up. Typically pilots are more resource intensive and inability of making available commensurate resources in scale up phase leads to gradual weakening of such initiatives.

4.5 CLIENT-LEVEL OUTCOME: EVIDENCE ON SOCIAL EMPOWERMENT

The SHG programme is predicated on building synergy between banks, SHPAs and people's associations to build economic and social capital. However, considering the diversity of stakeholders involved in it and absence of any in-built parameters in the reporting format, the assessment of client-level outcome has remained reliant on one-off assessments. The digitisation project opens up possibilities of integrating client-level outcomes in the MIS, but as of now studies are the only sources of information on this aspect.

During last year, IFMR[20] conducted a study for NABARD in four districts of Tamil Nadu to assess the social and economic change in the lives of SHG members. The focus of the study was more in understanding the impact of SHGs in creating social capital, awareness on rights, and change in outlook towards social evils like dowry and participation in political process. To allow for the treatment effect, half of the selected SHGs were more than five years old and the vintage of the rest of the sample ranged between two to four years.

4.5.1 Social capital and economic development

The first part of NABARD-IFMR study delves into creation of social capital and access to networks. Responses of the members show that almost all

(97.5%) of the clients felt that their social networks had increased. Due to the increased interaction with bank officials, the members felt confident in meeting other officials such as government officials. Two-thirds (65.57%) of the respondents affirmed that they sought support from other SHG members. Pooling of savings was seen as representative of the trust the members (97%) had for each other and respondents (96%) felt that it instilled a sense of ownership. Majority of the respondents felt that obligation to pay for another member would not have an adverse effect on the group.

> ### Proxy indicators to measure empowerment of women
>
> - Creation of social capital and networks.
> - Capacity for personnel agency and voice in household decision making.
> - Knowledge of their rights.
> - Participation in community life and politics.

Economic development: The average monthly income of the respondents from primary and secondary sources was approximately ₹3,784. Most of the respondents affirmed the improvement in their lives due to access to credit via the SHG membership. This improvement in the economic status of respondent's post becoming members of SHG was substantiated by a paired t-test. The following table shows an upward movement of the SHG households across the economic classes.

> - Sixty-two per cent respondents indicated an improvement in their economic status.
> - Downward movement in economic position occurred due to death of primary bread winner or illness.

Change in economic status (% of members)

Economic status	Very poor	Poor	Low middle	Middle	Well-off
Before SHG	3.0	21.0	50.0	25.6	0.4
After SHG	0.0	5.0	23.0	68.0	4.0

4.5.2 Personal agency and respect from household and community

The participation of women in decision making was analysed against four decision points: routine household, education, career and marriage of children. In all the cases, majority of the respondents' families (80%) took a collaborative approach involving consultation with all family members.

Majority of the respondents stated that they were no longer hesitant to interact with officials and a smaller proportion participated in issues pertaining to infrastructure (67%) and corruption (61%). Individual stories reflected that the respondents are now able to demand their due from the government officials when it affects their livelihood or access to clean drinking water. Majority of the respondents felt that they were respected more by their families (95%) and communities (86%) after becoming SHG members.

4.5.3 Awareness of rights, outlook and action against social issues and political process

Respondents are well aware of their inheritance rights (>99.0%) as daughters, wives and mothers, and entitlements (widow pension: 98.0%, incentives for girl child: 97.7%, government insurance: 98.4%). 81% respondents reported that they voice their concerns against social issues, such as alcoholism and dowry, in the household.

On political process awareness and participation, the impact is not so pronounced as on other parameters. Though two-thirds of the respondents indicated that their awareness about the Panchayat had increased, only half of the respondents were aware of the name of the Panchayat member. Although 94.4% respondents acknowledged having voted in the elections, the participation in the panchayat (50%) or collectors meeting (35%) was low. Around 6% respondents had contested in an election, which they attributed to the position of their family in the political scenario.

Overall, the report presents a strong correlation between becoming members of the SHG and social and economic change. The report findings have a positive bias because of the geography and type of institutions included in the sample and cannot be generalised for the programme. Tamil Nadu has been a strong ground of SBLP with active involvement of the state through its Mahalir Thittam programme and accounts for nearly 15% share in number of SHGs in India. Further, SHGs chosen for study were nurtured by two prominent NGOs—Hand in Hand (HIH) and Integrated Village Development Project (IVDP). HiH has an integrated approach to poverty reduction by tackling social, economic and environmental factors through inter-linked interventions in microfinance focusing on job creation, education, health, livelihoods, information dissemination, empowerment and environmental management. IVDP has been working with SHGs since 1989 and has till date helped 171,380 SHG members avail loans totalling ₹3,384 crore. Its founder was awarded Magsaysay award in 2012. In absence of streamlined assessment of outcomes, it will be useful to have more such studies especially in areas other than southern region.

4.6 SUMMING UP

The SBLP is going through a mixed phase. The outreach and performance data show signs of weaknesses in the form of extreme regional concentration, dip in ratio of savings and credit-linked SHGs, less than adequate bank loans in many states and above all the steady decline of portfolio quality. Field realities show that the active involvement of state in many states and introduction of SGSY/NRLM at national level has led to watering down of SBLP's core principles of intensive social mobilisation efforts, savings-linked credit and absence of subsidies. Lack of synergy between NRLM and NABARD promoted SHGs is leading to confusion in the field as the promoting agency and not their characteristics identify SHGs. Deterioration of SHG quality and its impact on portfolio quality is adding to the conservatism of bankers. However, on the positive side, immense possibilities have opened up with the pilot project on digitisation.

Two issues need to be addressed by all stakeholders on a priority basis. First, the digitisation project needs to be scaled up in a time-bound manner. Coverage of SHGs under this project will address the problem of client indebtedness through credit bureau reporting, clean up data being reported at national level and increase the confidence of bankers. Other aspects relating to client-level outcomes can be added in the reporting format to have systematic tracking of client-level outcomes.

Second, the overlap of NRLM and NABARD supported SHGs needs to be harnessed for its possible synergies. The focus should remain on common set of SHGs, and the division, if any, should be in work area. SHGs require diverse support services like livelihood strengthening and market linkage for their products besides access to financial services. The existing approach focussing primarily on financial support to SHGs albeit through different modalities needs to change for harnessing the development potential of SHGs.

INTERVIEW WITH DR H.K. BHANWALA, CHAIRMAN, NABARD

Alok Misra: It is seen that the SHG-Bank Linkage Programme has plateaued after a period of rapid growth. From a high of 4.8 million SHGs credit linked in 2009, the figures for 2014 are 4.2 million. What are the main factors behind this?

Dr Bhanwala: It is true that the number of SHGs with outstanding loans sort of stagnated/declined during past few years and has again started picking up. It needs to be stressed that the slight dip came after a period of immense growth during 2006–10. The major reasons for the stagnation seem to be lower than expected expansion of SHG movement in northern and central states, sanitisation of data by banks to weed out duplications and saturation in southern states. The important point is that even in this period of deceleration, the amount of credit per SHG increased implying deepening of credit.

Alok Misra: NABARD did come out with V.2 of SBLP to revive the movement but nothing much seems to have changed at the field level. What are the key design and operational changes of V.2?

Dr Bhanwala: SHG-2 guidelines were issued by NABARD not per se to revive the movement but to address the shortcomings observed after prolonged implementation of SBLP movement. The key design and operational changes of SHG-V.2 are allowing voluntary savings, opening individual savings account, modification in credit product—cash credit/overdrafts for SHGs in place of term loans, enabling JLGs within SHGs, improving risk mitigation systems in the form of self-rating by SHGs and audit. These changes have had varying levels of impact. For example, as of now as per estimates nearly 80% of lending to SHGs is in cash credit mode. This itself has the potential to provide much needed flexibility to the group as well lowering the interest burden.

It is also pertinent that in past few years there have been various developments, viz. introduction of NRLM and PMJDY which have changed the ecosystem in which SHGs operate today.

Alok Misra: Are the challenges of SBLP different across regions? Do you feel the design aspect needs an overhaul as currently it is over-reliant on Self-help Promoting Institutions (SHPIs) and there are not enough quality SHPIs?

Dr Bhanwala: Yes. The challenges are different across regions as there are wide variations in the eco-systems. There are differences in terms of stage of economic development, socio-cultural milieu and geographic endowments. Despite being a national programme, NABARD always tries to integrate available local structures to adapt the programme to local context. To give you some of the examples of this approach, I will like to mention that 'Marup' in Manipur, 'Sanchoi' in Assam, and 'Dalbandhu' in Arunachal Pradesh have been dovetailed with the SHG programme and have shown good potential.

On the aspect of being over-reliant on SHPIs, first of all NABARD has extended support to many other organisations/individuals beyond NGOs as SHPIs. As of now, banks, farmers clubs, individual volunteers are also promoting SHGs as SHPIs. Additionally, NABARD is also thinking of other ways to meet the continuous capacity building and handholding of SHG members. Developing resource NGOs covering a wider geography in places where there is lack of quality SHPIs is one such example. Overall NABARD, as a learning organisation, realises the importance of working with regional variations and finding new ways to meet the capacity building needs of SHGs.

Alok Misra: What are your views on interest rate subvention being given by different state governments? Does it not vitiate the market in a deregulated pricing regime?

Dr Bhanwala: This is a very complex issue and it is difficult to give a categorical answer. While it is empirically proven that loan waivers and interest rate subsidy vitiate the credit market, the opinion on transparent interest rate subvention needs to be studied in detail. However, I see that in states where interest subvention is linked with on time payment and given directly to banks has, in fact, has improved recovery rates. You might argue that borrowers of other institutions like MFIs may feel discriminated, but one needs to understand that one programme or institution cannot meet the credit needs of all potential clients. The savings first approach of SBLP also implies that not all borrowers would prefer to associate with it.

Alok Misra: What are your views on rising NPL levels in SBLP (it has gone up to 20% in some states) from near perfect levels?

Dr Bhanwala: I agree that it is of some concern but the situation has improved over the last two years. The percentage of gross NPA had declined to 6.83 in 2013–14 from 7.08 during the previous year. There are multiple factors to it. On an analysis of gross NPA of few major banks in financing the SHGs across several states, during the last five years it is observed that NPAs have more to do with the states and the banks involved rather than the weaknesses in the programme. For example, Central Bank and Punjab National Bank have been successful to a certain extent in containing their gross NPA in Odisha and Madhya Pradesh, while others have not been so successful.

Studies conducted through National Institute of Bank Management (NIBM), Pune in Uttar Pradesh and NABARD Regional Office in Odisha reveal that subsidy under SGSY, lack of hand holding and monitoring, linking of groups without adequate quality, inadequate appraisal/credit rating and lack of training have affected the recovery.

Field-level interactions show that the banks over the years are facing problems of shortage of staff coupled with additional workload of national programmes; this has also played its part in weakening, monitoring and follow-up. NABARD is seized of the matter and will step up its efforts in sensitising banks and SHPIs on the need for constant follow-up and corrective actions.

Alok Misra: SBLP was predicated on encouraging thrift with savings as a key component of the programme. How do you see the recent policy shift focusing on PMJDY as the main savings mobilisation strategy? How will it interplay with SBLP at the ground level?

Dr Bhanwala: NABARD views the recent policy shift as an important development in tune with SHG-2 guidelines which also talked about individual accounts. Both programmes are in synergy and PMJDY accounts with their insurance and pension products will go a long way in providing financial and social security to SHG members. Besides that individual account is a necessary condition for SHG members to graduate from community banking to individual banking.

Alok Misra: NRLM approaches the issue of rural livelihood through the primary strategy of intervention through SHGs. At the ground level is this creating a disruption to the old groups? Has it helped the convergence and growth of the movement and what are the new challenges this programme is posing?

Dr Bhanwala: I feel there is enough room for both SBLP and NRLM to play their part in development of the poor and the excluded. There should not be any disruption at the field level and if any such instances come to our notice, we take it up at the highest level. I feel it will be unfortunate to see NRLM as competitor for SBLP and I believe there is a great scope to work together. My view is that financial inclusion and economic development in a vast country like India requires integration of multiple approaches, constant innovation and adaptability to changing circumstances. Taking this further, I feel we need to find ways for SBLP and NRLM to work together in this cause. One possibility relates to SBLP working on the financial inclusion side and NRLM complementing it with work on strengthening of members' livelihood. We are engaging continuously with MORD to evolve ways to build mutual strengths of NRLM and SBLP.

Alok Misra: What role do you see for NABARD in MFI sector especially given the fact that NABARD lending is an insignificant part of MFI's credit and reluctance of NABARD to take the regulatory role?

Dr Bhanwala: The challenge of reaching the BOP is so huge that a multi-pronged approach is required. The MFIs facilitate credit delivery in areas or to segments where the formal banking network is thin or banks are unwilling to finance due to high transaction costs or lower presence of SHGs, etc. Thus, NABARD views the role of MFIs in a symbiotic manner in the overall inclusion agenda. It appears that the Andhra Pradesh crisis followed by RBI regulations has had a positive effect on the MFIs and has led to 'responsible practices' by the sector.

Considering the high growth being seen by the sector, there is a huge requirement of funds by the MFIs. NABARD is already providing refinance to NBFC-MFIs and while looking to deepen that relationship, we are also looking at MFI sector as an opportunity where we could play a larger role in terms of providing direct finance.

Alok Misra: What are your views on MUDRA? How will it impact the working of NABARD?

Dr Bhanwala: The purpose behind MUDRA is to promote and develop small businesses and MSMEs, which play an important part in the economy. The lack of credit to this segment often referred to as the 'lost middle' has affected their growth and I hope MUDRA will evolve a 360° strategy for this segment. It is critical that the focus does not remain solely on credit as absence of a facilitating ecosystem in the form of credit registries and information gaps leading to deficient appraisal are more critical. NABARD has been supporting small business segment through refinance, promotional programmes as well as capacity building and will be happy to share our experience.

Alok Misra: Globally, the discourse has now moved from inclusive finance to responsible finance covering consumer protection, financial education and responsible strategy and governance. While MFIs have a defined framework like CPP, industry code of conduct and social performance pathway, not much beyond financial education has been done under SBLP. How does NABARD visualise integration of responsible finance principles in SBLP?

Dr Bhanwala: SHG-BLP movement is inherently based on responsible finance in which the clients, i.e., the SHG members become financially literate and manage their own finances. Constant hand holding by SHPIs takes care of their mentoring and financial awareness. Being bank-led, the issues of transparency, responsible pricing and grievance redressal are taken care of. On the aspect of appropriate products, NABARD is working on finding ways to introduce insurance and pension products. Health insurance pilot is running in Rajasthan and based on the learnings, it will be scaled up. We are also open to ideas on how to make the programme more suited to the needs of the clients.

Alok Misra: The problem of over-indebtedness is a key issue in terms of client protection. However, with SHG data not being part of Credit Bureau record, it is leading to moral hazard for other institutions like MFIs; are there any steps being taken by NABARD in this regard?

Dr Bhanwala: As a sequel to Aditya Puri Committee recommendations, the RBI has already decided to bring SHG data and its member-level information to the platform of the Credit Bureau. NABARD fully supports this initiative but it is a complex task on account of the informal nature of SHGs, group loans from banks and the extreme variance in maintaining their accounts. Appreciating these problems, the Department of Banking Regulation (DBR) is evolving a step by step roadmap for the process and different rounds of consultation with various stakeholders have been held.

NABARD on its own has initiated a pilot project (EShakti) for digitisation of SHGs, which is presently ongoing in two districts (Ramgarh and Dhule) in the country. This will facilitate creation of a platform for the banks to seek member-level information and upload on the Credit Bureau platform. The learnings from the pilot project will lay down a roadmap to broad base the project across the country.

ANNEXURES

ANNEXURE 4.1
Key differences in features of SBLP and NRLM

		NRLM	SHG-bank linkage
1.	Supporting agency	Ministry of Rural Development	NABARD
2.	Principal implementing agency	NRLM supported by State Rural Livelihood Mission (SRLM) being set up in states for implementation	Commercial banks, RRBs, cooperatives, SHPA which includes NGOs.
3.	Background	NRLM has replaced SGSY since 1 April 2013. It is the flagship programme of MORD, Govt. of India for promoting poverty reduction through building strong institutions of the poor, particularly women, and enabling these institutions to access a range of financial services and livelihoods services. NRLM is designed to be a highly intensive programme and focuses on intensive application of human and material resources in order to mobilise the poor into functionally effective community-owned institutions, promote their financial inclusion and strengthen their livelihoods.	The scheme is being implemented since 1992. After successful implementation of the Pilot Project, it was mainstreamed. It relies on formation and nurturing of groups by SHPAs and later linking them with banks for savings and credit.

(Continued)

(Continued)

	NRLM	SHG-bank linkage
4. Target area	6,000 blocks of 600 districts in the country. First phase: 150 districts	All India
5. How implemented	SHGs to be promoted by district units of SRLM with field staff, who in turn will nurture community resource persons (CRPs)	SHGs to be promoted by SHPAs
6. Objectives	1. Universal social mobilisation into the fold of SHG network followed by livelihood collectives 2. Infrastructure creation and marketing support 3. Skill and placement projects 4. Self employed entrepreneurship 5. Innovations	1. To provide access to banking services to the rural poor 2. To facilitate collateral free institutional loans to SHGs.
8. Grant support	1. No separate grant support for formation envisaged on a per SHG basis 2. Concept of revolving Fund and community investment fund (CIF) to federations	No grant envisaged for SHGs Up to a maximum of ₹10,000 per SHG for the SHPA
10. Default risk coverage	No such arrangement	No such arrangement
11. Interest rates	Interest rate @ 7% for loans up to ₹3 lakh. Further Interest subvention @ 3% for prompt repayment in 150 Category I districts.	Normal bank lending rate is applicable.
12. Operational structure for SHGs	SHGs formed to be federated to build higher tier community institutions. Further, promote specialised institutions like livelihoods collectives, producers' cooperatives/companies for livelihoods promotion	Relies on individual SHGs linked with banks through SHPAs; no concept of federations.

Source: By the author based on features of the schemes.

ANNEXURE 4.2

Position of non-performing assets of banks under SBLP—as on 31 March 2015

(Amount ₹ lakh)

Sr. No.	Region/state	Public sector commercial banks			Private sector commercial banks			Regional rural banks			Cooperative banks			Total		
		Loan amount OS against SHGs	Amount of gross NPAs against SHGs	NPA as %age to loan OS	Loan amount OS against SHGs	Amount of gross NPAs against SHGs	NPA as %age to loan OS	Loan amount OS against SHGs	Amount of gross NPAs against SHGs	NPA as %age to loan OS	Loan amount OS against SHGs	Amount of gross NPAs against SHGs	NPA as %age to loan OS	Loan amount OS against SHGs	Amount of gross NPAs against SHGs	NPA as %age to loan OS
Northern Region																
1.	Chandigarh	92.84	7.52	8.09	0.00		0.00	0.00		0.00	0.00	0.00	0.00	92.84	7.52	8.09
2.	Haryana	13,914.11	2,661.36	19.13	1,507.53	3.58	0.24	6,700.00	657.00	9.81	505.43	402.49	79.63	22,627.07	3,724.43	16.46
3.	Himachal Pradesh	4,493.49	499.52	11.12	162.95	0.00	0.00	2,171.00	337.00	15.52	4,445.63	926.25	20.84	11,273.07	1,762.77	15.64
4.	Jammu & Kashmir	446.95	45.23	10.12	674.49	3.16	0.00	0.00	0.00	0.00	0.00	0.00	0.00	1,121.44	48.39	4.31
5.	New Delhi	2,675.12	128.89	4.82	0.00	0.00	0.00	0.00		0.00	0.00	0.00	0.00	2,675.12	128.89	4.82
6.	Punjab	11,429.13	1,313.47	11.49	1,616.44	0.15	0.01	1,916.10	123.34	6.44	845.12	193.63	22.91	15,806.79	1,630.59	10.32
7.	Rajasthan	68,776.18	5,610.86	8.16	20,595.06	467.02	2.27	11,118.33	1,727.51	15.54	7,529.47	1,256.59	16.69	108,019.04	9,061.98	8.39
	Total	**101,827.83**	**10,268.49**	**10.08**	**24,556.47**	**473.91**	**1.93**	**21,905.43**	**2,844.85**	**12.99**	**13,325.65**	**2,778.96**	**20.85**	**161,615.38**	**16,364.57**	**10.13**
North-eastern Region																
1.	Assam	30,854.91	4,839.67	15.69	21.68	1.40	6.46	30,191.00	823.90	2.73	1,519.17	644.80	42.44	62,586.76	6,309.77	10.08
2.	Arunachal Pradesh	143.76	33.57	23.35	0.00		0.00	115.30	37.89	32.86	76.40	19.88	26.02	335.46	91.34	27.23
3.	Manipur	565.87	298.87	52.82	0.00		0.00	438.39	195.10	4,450.38	0.00	0.00	0.00	1,004.26	493.97	49.19
4.	Meghalaya	368.28	162.71	44.18	0.00	0.00	0.00	773.66	97.26	12.57	175.67	0.00	0.00	1,317.61	259.97	19.73
5.	Mizoram	112.75	23.44	20.79	0.00		0.00	1,260.00	103.12	0.00	34.68	0.00	0.00	1,407.43	126.56	8.99
6.	Nagaland	954.04	249.26	26.13	2.14	1.34	62.62	0.00	0.00	0.00	0.00	0.00	0.00	956.18	250.60	26.21

(Continued)

(Continued)

(Amount ₹ lakh)

Sr. No.	Region/state	Public sector commercial banks			Private sector commercial banks			Regional rural banks			Cooperative banks			Total		
		Loan amount OS against SHGs	Amount of gross NPAs against SHGs	NPA as %age to loan OS	Loan amount OS against SHGs	Amount of gross NPAs against SHGs	NPA as %age to loan OS	Loan amount OS against SHGs	Amount of gross NPAs against SHGs	NPA as %age to loan OS	Loan amount OS against SHGs	Amount of gross NPAs against SHGs	NPA as %age to loan OS	Loan amount OS against SHGs	Amount of gross NPAs against SHGs	NPA as %age to loan OS
7.	Sikkim	582.10	39.10	6.72	0.00	0.00	0.00	0.00		0.00	33.29	13.27	0.00	615.39	52.37	8.51
8.	Tripura	4,818.59	892.80	18.53	0.00	0.00	0.00	0.00		0.00	0.00	0.00	0.00	4,818.59	892.80	18.53
	Total	**38,400.31**	**6,539.42**	**17.03**	**23.82**	**2.74**	**11.50**	**32,778.35**	**1,257.27**	**3.84**	**1,839.21**	**0.00**	**0.00**	**73,041.69**	**8,477.38**	**11.61**
	Eastern Region															
1.	A & N Islands (UT)	75.67	6.30	8.33	0.00	0.00	0.00	0.00		0.00	519.04	53.21	10.25	594.71	59.51	10.01
2.	Bihar	52,460.18	6,340.82	12.09	7,894.35	0.00	0.00	42,321.16	789.53	1.87	0.00	0.00	0.00	102,675.69	7,130.35	6.94
3.	Jharkhand	35,926.57	3,872.46	10.78	8.63	0.00	0.00	6,471.37	3,452.90	53.36	43.69	2,307.00	0.00	42,450.26	9,632.36	22.69
4.	Odisha	81,530.88	16,861.92	20.68	21,566.62	4.12	0.02	76,845.96	12,730.20	16.57	13,689.00	0.00	0.00	193,632.46	29,596.24	15.28
5.	West Bengal	81,053.60	10,315.53	12.73	3,479.28	0.00	0.00	126,889.49	8,324.91	6.56	75,251.31	3,418.74	4.54	286,673.68	22,059.18	7.69
	Total	**251,046.90**	**37,397.04**	**14.90**	**32,948.88**	**4.12**	**0.01**	**252,527.98**	**25,297.54**	**10.02**	**89,503.04**	**5,778.95**	**6.46**	**626,026.80**	**68,477.65**	**10.94**
	Central Region															
1.	Chhattisgarh	10,211.02	1,525.74	14.94	619.91	11.07	1.79	12,146.00	1,107.00	9.11	731.86	141.32	19.31	23,708.79	2,785.13	11.75
2.	Madhya Pradesh	30,548.20	6,000.22	19.64	15,188.22	50.95	0.34	12,766.52	2,228.00	17.45	347.95	31.02	8.92	58,850.89	8,310.19	14.12
3.	Uttar Pradesh	69,799.00	11,042.56	15.82	19,258.65	0.00	0.00	68,031.19	18,824.38	27.67	78.32	65.04	83.04	157,167.16	29,931.98	19.04
4.	Uttarakhand	7,730.42	559.23	7.23	377.33	0.00	0.00	3,105.59	246.09	7.92	4,773.18	312.07	6.54	15,986.52	1,117.39	6.99
	Total	**118,288.64**	**19,127.75**	**16.17**	**35,444.11**	**0.00**	**0.00**	**96,049.30**	**22,405.47**	**23.33**	**5,931.31**	**549.45**	**9.26**	**255,713.36**	**42,082.67**	**16.46**

Western Region

1.	Goa	1,492.55	27.61	1.85	434.60	1.28	0.29	0.00	0.00	0.00	1,041.99	39.91	3.83	2,969.14	68.80	2.32
2.	Gujarat	28,243.06	1,325.57	4.69	14,061.78	12.53	0.09	386.02	4,978.38	7.75	1,583.13	305.58	19.30	48,866.35	2,029.70	4.15
3.	Maharashtra	62,051.67	9,360.36	15.08	55,129.71	32.02	0.06	2,404.36	27,014.52	8.90	13,360.38	3,420.79	25.60	157,556.28	15,217.53	9.66
	Total	**91,787.28**	**10,713.55**	**11.67**	**69,626.09**	**45.83**	**0.07**	**2,790.38**	**31,992.90**	**8.72**	**15,985.50**	**3,766.28**	**23.56**	**209,391.77**	**17,316.04**	**8.27**

Southern Region

1.	Andhra Pradesh	1,123,872.06	76,463.75	6.80	20.13	20.13	100.00	17,080.00	447,285.75	3.82	18,914.92	2,513.01	13.29	1,590,092.86	96,076.89	6.04
2.	Karnataka	401,673.93	8,204.91	2.04	58,247.02	163.24	0.28	25,077.52	98,855.14	25.37	70,155.42	3,316.47	4.73	628,931.51	36,762.14	5.85
3.	Kerala	163,608.77	9,418.92	5.76	22,540.73	184.98	0.82	786.00	22,411.00	3.51	25,589.10	2,453.23	9.59	234,149.60	12,843.13	5.49
4.	Lakshadweep	4.26	0.00	0.00	0.00	0.00	0.00	0.00	0.00	0.00	0.00	0.00	0.00	4.26	0.00	0.00
5.	Puducherry	4,938.97	881.25	17.84	0.00	0.00	0.00	57.82	1,518.77	3.81	674.30	0.00	0.00	7,132.04	939.07	13.17
6.	Tamil Nadu	345,351.52	45,525.61	13.18	174,508.62	3,412.18	1.96	2,857.60	41,383.07	6.91	76,869.72	5,591.04	7.27	638,112.93	57,386.43	8.99
7.	Telangana	507,121.86	18,876.57	3.72	0.00	0.00	0.00	6,099.51	228,246.00	2.67	12,589.87	891.78	7.08	747,957.73	25,867.86	3.46
	Total	**2,546,571.36**	**159,371.00**	**6.26**	**255,316.50**	**3,780.53**	**1.48**	**51,958.45**	**839,699.73**	**6.19**	**204,793.33**	**14,765.53**	**7.21**	**3,846,380.92**	**229,875.51**	**5.98**
	Grand Total	**3,147,922.32**	**243,417.25**	**7.73**	**417,915.87**	**4,369.15**	**1.05**	**106,553.96**	**1,274,953.69**	**8.36**	**331,378.04**	**28,317.12**	**8.55**	**5,172,169.92**	**382,593.82**	**7.40**

Source: mCID, NABARD.

ANNEXURE 4.3
Performance comparison between bank Sakhis and other CSPs of Gramin Bank of Aryavart, Uttar Pradesh: As on 31 March 2015

S. No	Parameters	Bank sakhis as CSP	CSP other than bank sakhis
1.	Average number of customers enrolled per CSP/Sakhi (cumulative since June2013)	449	393
2.	% of females enrolled to total enrolment since June 2013	42%	40%
3.	% of accounts dormant* as per GBA guidelines (as on 31.03.15)	7.88%	58%
4.	% of clients doing average of two or more transaction in last quarter (January to March 2015)	28%	3%
5.	Average no. of active** accounts per active Bank Sakhi/CSP in last quarter (January to March 2015)	190	54
6.	% of active** accounts (January to March 2015)	57%	7%
6.1.	Out of total accounts, % of accounts used by women	47%	41%
6.2.	Out of total accounts, % of accounts used by men	53%	59%
7.	% of clients doing zero transaction in last quarter (January to March 2015)	43%	93%
8.	% of deposit amount out of total transaction amount (cumulative till March 2015)	51.42%	36%
9.	% of deposit numbers out of total transaction numbers (cumulative till March 2015)	61.31%	56%
10.	Average quarterly balance per account in last quarter (January to March 2015)	271	78
11.	Average quarterly balance per active account in last quarter (January to March 2015)	397	188

Source: NABARD-GIZ. May 2015. *SHG Members as Bank Agents: Experiences from Two Pilot Projects in Uttar Pradesh and Madhya Pradesh.* New Delhi.
Notes: *An account is dormant if it has not been operated for more than 12 months.
**An account is active if a transaction has taken place in the account at least once in the last three months.

NOTES AND REFERENCES

1. Mysore Resettlement and Development Agency (MYRADA) in Karnataka and Professional Assistance for Development Action (PRADAN) in Rajasthan were the pioneers.
2. Thorat, Y.S.P. 2006. 'Microfinance in India: Sectoral Issues and challenges', in *Towards a Sustainable Microfinance Outreach in India: Experiences & Perspectives,* pp. 27–42. Mumbai: NABARD, German Technical Cooperation (GTZ), Swiss Agency for Development & Cooperation (SDC).
3. EDA Rural Systems Pvt Ltd. and APMAS. 2006. *Self Help Groups in India: A Study of the Lights and Shades.*
4. Asian Development Bank. 2005. *Microfinance Institutions* (Rural Finance Sector Restructuring and Development No. 3, Project No. 36343). Manila.
5. Ministry of Rural Development. 2009. *Report of the Committee on Credit Related Issues under SGSY.* New Delhi: Ministry of Rural Development, Government of India.
6. Aajeevika (NRLM). March 2015. *Mid-term Assessment Report.* National Mission Management Unit National Rural Livelihoods Mission, RL Division, Ministry of Rural Development Government of India.
7. The full text of the interview of NABARD Chairman Dr H.K. Bhanwala is given on page 86.
8. NRLM. *Framework for Implementation.* Ministry of Rural Development, Government of India.
9. Aajeevika (NRLM). March 2015. *Mid-term Assessment Report.* National Mission Management Unit National Rural Livelihoods Mission, RL Division, Ministry of Rural Development Government of India.
10. https://www.nabard.org/uploads/STMT%20IX.pdf (accessed on 8 October 2015).
11. APMAS. *Quality and Sustainability of Self Help Groups in Bihar and Odisha.* https://www.nabard.org/Publication/QualitySustainabilityofSHGsin-BiharandOdisaH.pdf (accessed on 8 October 2015).
12. GIZ-NABARD, 2013. Study on Satisfaction Level of SHGs on Financial Services and Demand for New Products and Services.

13. Shukla, Rajesh et al. 2011. *Assessing the Effectiveness of Small Borrowing in India*, NCAER.

14. IIM (Lucknow). November 2014. *Study of Transaction Cost: Perspectives of SHG and MFI Clients.* Mumbai: NABARD.

15. RBI. 'Report of the Committee to Recommend Data Format for Furnishing of Credit Information to Credit Information Companies'. https://rbi.org.in/scripts/PublicationReportDetails.aspx?UrlPage=&ID=763 (accessed 8 October 2015).

16. Ministry of Rural Development, Government of India. November, 2014. *Report of the Expert Group on Setting up a Developmental Financial Institution for Women SHGs.*

17. Based on telephone conversation with Mr Samaresh Parida, Lead Advisor of Digitisation Project.

18. NABARD-GIZ. May 2015. *SHG Members as Bank Agents: Experiences from Two Pilot Projects in Uttar Pradesh and Madhya Pradesh.* New Delhi; NABARD-GIZ. June 2015. *SHG Members as Bank Agents: Case Studies from Unnao, Uttar Pradesh.* New Delhi.

19. Case studies relate list of various entrepreneurial actives related to managing canteens, child welfare, cooking mid-day, stitching uniforms for schools, managing rural call centres, recycling of plastic waste, managing PDS, procurement of food grains, distribution of electricity bills, etc.

20. IFMR for NABARD. 2014. *SHGs as Agents of Change.* https://www.nabard.org/Publication/SHGasAgentsof-ChangeIFMRReportH.pdf (accessed on 10 October 2015).

Financial literacy of clients: Is it being integrated in service delivery?

Veena Yamini Annadanam

5.1 INTEGRATION OF FINANCIAL LITERACY AND FINANCIAL INCLUSION: INCREASED RELEVANCE IN INDIA

The inclusive finance space in India received a huge impetus last year (2014–15) with several innovative policies and programmes announced for furthering the financial inclusion agenda.[1] Some of the initiatives were: offering schemes to enable universal access of bank accounts (PMJDY), universal access of social security (PMSBY, PMJY, APY), policy recommendations to boost credit and insurance, and launch of MUDRA[2] Bank to facilitate last mile financing to small/business enterprises.

These initiatives provide policy push to encourage savings and insurance through PMJDY and social security schemes as well as push credit for businesses through MUDRA. On the other side, RBI's policy push towards setting up of differentiated banks (SFBs and PBs) will provide avenues for creating last mile institutional infrastructure for financial inclusion in the next 15–18 months. While these are tremendous efforts that can have significant outcomes in terms of making financial services accessible to all, especially to low-income households, these outcomes cannot be achieved if potential customers are not aware of the programmes and how to benefit from them.

Consider this: as on mid-September 2015, the three social security schemes[3] enrolled a staggering 115 million people![4] Within one year of introduction, the PMJDY scheme[5] reached to 184.7 million people who deposited a phenomenal 243,629.5 million rupees and engaged 12.6 million Bank Mitras

(business correspondents). Considering that these are self-contributory schemes, the long-term success of these schemes will be dependent on usage. Mere increasing of access and giving an array of products and services will not achieve the 'financial well-being' without the clients 'using the products'.

With increased access to diversity of financial service providers and more financial schemes and products, people are confronted with options they may not fully understand. When their existing knowledge and competencies are not applicable to an ever-changing financial landscape,[6] people are limited in their ability to act. So integration of financial literacy with inclusion efforts is even more relevant in India now than ever before.

The microfinance crisis in 2010 further accentuated the need for financial literacy as a part of consumer protection systems and the CoC. Knowledge and skills imparted to customers as a part of financial literacy are considered to help in suppliers maintaining transparency and full disclosure and for the customers to be aware of multiple borrowing that can lead to over-indebtedness.

5.2 WHAT IS FINANCIAL LITERACY?

There are different terminologies and definitions used to describe what financial literacy is. It is essential to understand what these are and their usage in the Indian context. Three terms—financial literacy, financial education and financial capability—are used interchangeably in the financial sector. There are several definitions for these three terms and each one of them differs with source and context. For the purpose of this report, the definition used

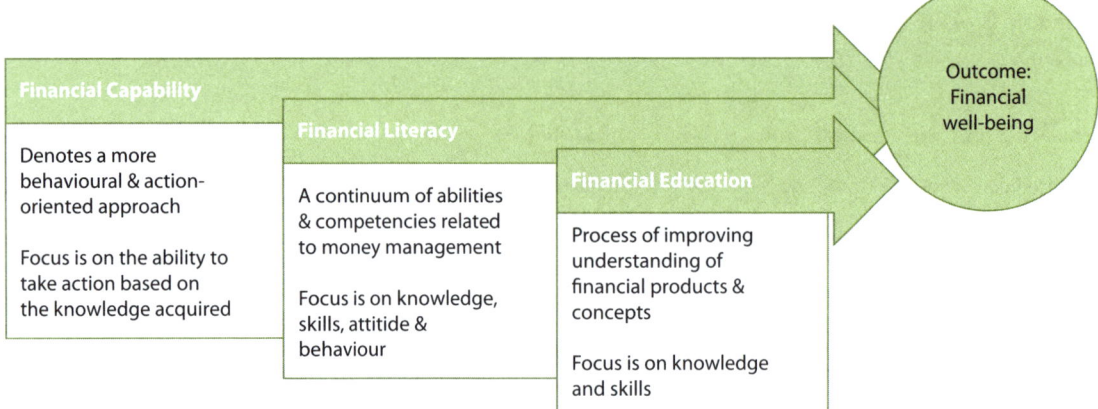

Figure 5.1 Interlinkages of various terminologies
Source: Author.

by the Organisation for Economic Co-operation and Development (OECD) along with the interpretations and explanations made by Microfinance Opportunities are adopted and referred to hereon.

Financial education is 'the process by which financial consumers/investors improve their understanding of financial products and concepts and, through information, instruction and/or objective advice, develop the skills and confidence to become more aware of financial risks and opportunities, to make informed choices, to know where to go for help, and to take other effective actions to improve their financial well-being' (OECD).

Financial literacy is defined as 'a combination of awareness, knowledge, skill, attitude and behaviour necessary to make sound financial decisions and ultimately achieve individual financial wellbeing' [(OECD/International Network on Financial Education (INFE)].

Financial capability is 'another term for financial literacy, used by some countries and organisations to denote a more behavioural and action-oriented approach' (The New Zealand Network for Financial Literacy).

From these definitions it can be derived that:

• Financial education focuses more on the learning process and thus is associated with the supply side, i.e., providers who play a major role in facilitating the process of understanding for the consumers.
• Financial literacy is associated more with the customer (demand side) and focuses on achieving a state of having knowledge, skills and attitude

to improve their financial well-being. Though it does not negate the role of providers who may facilitate the process.

• Financial capability is a mixed bag which combines and gives equal role to both the demand and supply side. It focuses on 'use factor'[7]—the ability and opportunity to use the knowledge and skills implied in financial literacy. Financial capability thus focuses on the ability to take action.

Though these terminologies are used interchangeably, they are distinct while having a common goal of 'financial well-being of customers' (Figure 5.1). To summarise, financial education is a tool to achieve financial literacy and more; financial literacy is a step towards achieving financial capability.

This report uses the term financial literacy, as regulators (RBI, SEBI, IRDA), self-regulatory organisations (MFIN, Sa-Dhan), donors and financial institutions in India use this term more often.

5.3 MAKING THE CASE FOR FINANCIAL LITERACY: DEMAND- AND SUPPLY-SIDE ISSUES

There are both supply-side and demand-side issues that challenge the financial inclusion agenda. Supply-side factors are: no banks or formal service providers in the vicinity, inappropriate or unsuitable products, complex processes, attitude of the bankers towards poor, etc. Some of the challenges on the demand side for financial inclusion are: low literacy levels, poverty, lack of awareness, limited and mostly irregular income and vulnerability to shocks. These clubbed with the geographical, socio-economic conditions of the vulnerable and low-income population adds to the challenge.

5.3.1 The need for financial literacy from a demand perspective

In the last few years, the focus has shifted from supply side of financial service delivery to demand side, that is, customers. The need to address demand-side issues got augmented mainly due to two factors: increased focus on financial inclusion (not just outreach, but also the usage) and increased attention on consumer protection issues.

Even the governments of developed economies, in G20 Summit agreements, have recognised financial inclusion and consumer protection as integral to achieving financial stability and integrity. Financial access has been highlighted as a 'key accelerator' to meet the millennium development goals (MDGs) (World Savings Bank Institute 2010).[8]

First and foremost, financial literacy plays a key role in accelerating the financial inclusion agenda, especially when financial inclusion focuses on not just increasing numbers or outreach of people accessing the service (i.e., quantity), but also about ensuring the usage of financial services and quality of products and delivery (i.e., quality). Three key dimensions[9] of financial inclusion are: (i) access to financial services, (ii) usage of services, and (iii) quality of products and delivery.

Financial literacy can influence two of these three dimensions (access to and usage of financial services) by making the clients more aware, building their skills and changing their attitude and behaviour towards accessing formal services. Financial literacy helps in:

1. increasing the awareness and understanding of options available for managing their money; dealing with formal financial services can help clients in making choices with their limited sources of money;

2. providing complete information on the products and making the product information simple to understand and easy to compare with other products; it will help clients make informed choices that work for them and in their context;

3. increasing knowledge and skills around financial services which can increase the confidence of clients to take calculated risks in accessing and using products.

Based on the key indicators shown in Chapter 1 (Table 1.1), it is evident that India has shown significant improvement in enhancing access, but the problem of exclusion is still huge and if access is juxtaposed with usage, it becomes more challenging. World Bank Global Findex 2014 Data for India shows that only 53.1% of the adults have access to bank accounts and only 14.4% have done any saving in the last one year. If the data for the poorest 40% is seen, it is only 43.9% of adults who have bank accounts. Only 7.7% have any borrowings from a financial institution in the last year. Even other financial services like insurance (with a penetration of 3.9% in 2013),[10] pension and remittances are much lower compared to the data from the South Asia.

These numbers of access and usage clearly indicate that the focus of financial inclusion going forward should be more on aiming to increase the usage, and financial literacy can potentially play a huge role.

While financial literacy addresses the demand-side issues of the financial inclusion, consumer protection addresses the supply-side issues. However, the supply side along with the regulator and other stakeholders has also a major role in increasing the trust in the formal financial sector, which is crucial for more people accessing and using the services. And this is where consumer protection comes into play.

As stated in Chapter 1 of this report, consumer protection and financial literacy are two of the three pillars (the third pillar being prudent regulation) of responsible finance and as such have considerable overlap and synergy between them.

Consumer protection[11] is about having in place mechanisms that service providers ought to follow to ensure that clients are not exploited in terms of unsuitable and complex products, multiple lending (and borrowing) leading to over-indebtedness, non-transparency or unscrupulous practices.

Financial literacy helps the agenda of consumer protection in several ways.

• It helps the consumers in understanding the products and services better. In the past few years, the landscape of financial sector in India has changed rapidly and this led to introduction of so many products and services some of which are complex. Such wider choice does not automatically translate to uptake of products or sustained usage unless consumers understand if and how these products can benefit them. Given that the usage of products is affected by information asymmetry and the transparency requirements under consumer protection standards, financial literacy can bridge this gap.

- Transparency principle requires that the existing and potential customers be provided with full information about products and services. While the onus of explaining the terms and conditions in a simple language or in a manner clients understand is on the supply side (or the financial service providers), however, if the clients are not able to understand the information being provided, the principle of transparency does not have much impact. Financial literacy thus can be the starting point in this journey.
- Financial literacy programmes with key messages around dangers of over-indebtedness can help in prevention of over-indebtedness, as lessons in financial planning, debt management, etc., are aimed at increasing awareness among clients about the risks of taking multiple loans which are beyond their repayment capacity.
- A financially aware client might be more vocal and access the complaint redressal mechanism that the supply side makes available for them. Thus, the consumer protection standards and effective financial literacy offer a level playing field for both the suppliers and consumers of financial services (Alliance of Financial Inclusion 2010)[12] by closing the gap of information asymmetry.

5.3.2 Supply-side imperatives for offering financial literacy

The supply-side imperatives for the financial service providers for offering financial literacy are driven mostly by: regulations or policy requirements, donor or investor driven mandates, global standards on responsible finance (be it client protection or social performance management), social responsibility and the business case that financial literacy offers to service providers.

Some of the policy guidelines that drive financial literacy programmes of formal financial institutions (banks, MFIs) are: inclusion of financial literacy in the financial inclusion strategy; setting up of financial literacy centres by the banks including RRBs and guidelines to NBFCs for providing full and complete information to clients on products and services.

The discourse on responsible finance clearly identifies financial capability as one of the main pillars of financial inclusion and stability. Financial capability is considered as an intervention aimed to build and enhance financial capability of clients of financial institutions who are the consumers of financial products and services.[13]

Consumer protection, another pillar of the responsible finance, is intricately linked to financial literacy. The global standards such as Client Protection Principles (as advocated by Smart Campaign) include a significant portion of guidelines on transparency (providing full and correct information to clients using language they understand) which are closely related to client education. In India, the industry CoC[14] provides that MFIs must have a dedicated process to raise clients' awareness of the options, choices and responsibilities vis-à-vis financial products and services available.

For many financial institutions and community-owned financial institutions, offering financial literacy is part of their social responsibility and for some, a part of their commitment to achieving better outcomes for their clients. In India, the only country with legislated CSR, financial literacy is one of the approved activities[15] under the Section VII of the Companies Act, 2013 (Box 5.1). In September 2014, a further notification was issued to all the public sector banks that the financial literacy activities

---

Box 5.1 Section 135 of the Companies Act mandating corporate social responsibility

The Section 135 of the Companies Act, 2013 mandates that every company having net worth of rupees five hundred crore or more, turnover of rupees one thousand crore or more or a net profit of rupees five crore or more during any financial year shall constitute a Corporate Social Responsibility Committee of the Board consisting of three or more directors, out of which at least one director shall be an independent director.

The Board of every eligible company shall ensure that the company spends, in every financial year, at least 2% of the average net profits of the company made during the three immediately preceding financial years, in pursuance of its CSR policy.

Seven broad areas are listed (which are supposed to be interpreted liberally):

1. Eradicating hunger, poverty and malnutrition, promoting health care, sanitation and safe drinking water.
2. Promotion of education, special education and vocational skills (financial literacy can fall under this by broad interpretation).
3. Gender equality, women empowerment, senior citizens and economically backward groups.
4. Protection of national heritage, art and culture.
5. Benefits to armed forces veterans and war widows.
6. Ensuring environmental sustainability, ecological balance, and wildlife and natural resources conservation.
7. Technology incubators within academic institutions.
8. Rural sports, Paralympic and Olympic sports.
9. PM National Relief Fund and any other funds setup by the Central Government for socio-economic development and welfare of SC/ST/OBC.
10. Rural Development projects.
11. Slum Development Projects.

Source: www.mca.gov.in

taken up under the PMJDY will be considered as CSR. Several banks in India have taken up financial literacy as a CSR activity and some microfinance institutions like Ujjivan, Utkarsh, Equitas, Janalakshmi have started to implement financial literacy under CSR though they have had these programmes started much before the new CSR clause in the Companies Act.

The 'social goal' emerges from the belief that financial literacy can lead to personal financial empowerment and improved money management in the formal financial system and results in improved welfare. Equipped with complete information and nuances of financial management, the poor are expected to save more, save more in safer options, access credit as per requirement (thus avoiding over-indebtedness), save for retirement, manage their expenses or cash flows better and access the investment opportunities that are suitable for them.

An example of such organisation is Grameen Koota Financial Services Pvt Ltd. (GKFSPL) whose mission is to enable economic and social change in the base of pyramid households. In line with this mission, it believes that women are the channel through which this change can be effected and therefore has started to work with women groups on issues of financial management. Recognising the critical role that relevant, contextual information plays in helping women take control over their lives, and in triggering overall positive development outcomes, Grameen Koota and Phicus Social Solutions created Jagriti, a financial literacy programme in 2011.[16]

The SHG movement, which has a strong social agenda of women empowerment encompasses financial literacy as a strategy for economic empowerment of women, along with focus on increasing the capabilities of the members on book keeping, maintaining accounts, financial management within the groups, etc.

There is a clear business case for financial institutions for investing in financial literacy—it potentially leads to increased product uptake and improved usage of products—both being outcomes of more aware clients. Financial institutions, be it commercial banks or microfinance institutions, support financial literacy either through direct implementation (through their staff) or through third parties, with the objective of increasing consumer activity with their organisations. Banks expect that financially literate clients may result into new accounts or increased account activity; microfinance institutions anticipate that clients may borrow more from them or repay on time as they are now familiar with the consequences of non-payment of credit (especially in countries where there is an active and functional credit bureau). This helps in building client loyalty with popular services. Some organisations club other social activities like health education, empowerment trainings, etc., with financial literacy.

5.4 EMERGENCE OF FINANCIAL LITERACY IN INDIAN FINANCIAL INCLUSION SPACE

Financial literacy within financial inclusion and microfinance space (catering to low income, poor and underserved clients) has been broadly driven by two sets of initiatives: (i) programmes of non-government organisations, community-based financial institutions and microfinance institutions supported through donor funding; and (ii) policy push by RBI directing banks to undertake financial literacy.

The evolution of financial literacy begins with SEWA Bank's pioneering work on financial literacy for its members in early 2000s. Since then till 2010, the growth of financial literacy in India has been slow, but steady. With the microfinance crisis in 2010, the focus on financial literacy has only increased.

Various initiatives of financial literacy can be broken down into three phases.

5.4.1 The beginnings: 2000–05

Given the history of several NGOs working in diversity of development areas in India, it is possible that there might have been few initiatives of financial literacy in some format. However, the notable programme on financial literacy was first initiated by SEWA Bank in June 2002 under the title 'Project Tomorrow' (Box 5.2).[17] This was a result of felt need from the field that the members need such an education to help them make better financial decisions.

Another organisation that played a significant role in promoting financial literacy in India is the Indian School of Microfinance for Women (ISMW) in Ahmedabad set up in June 2003. SEWA played an instrumental role in setting up ISMW with financial literacy as one of its key areas of focus.

Box 5.2 Project tomorrow by SEWA Bank

Project Tomorrow was started as a five-day financial literacy training programme. The content was divided into seven modules: introduction to financial planning, daily money management practices, planning for future events, savings and investment, borrowing and loan management, insurance and risk management, and making a financial plan. The programme used lectures with games, stories, role-plays and videos to teach these skills to its members. The programme was intended to help members escape cycles of poverty, make informed decisions about their finances, build their own future and live a secured life.

Source: Financial Education for SEWA Bank Members: A Facilitator's Guide. December 2013.

5.4.2 Build-up: 2005–10

During this period, financial literacy started getting traction for its potential role in financial inclusion and achieving financial well-being of the clients. Three key developments in this period helped in the build-up of financial literacy initiatives in India.

Since 2005, the RBI, as a part of its financial inclusion policy has given prominence to financial literacy by integrating it in its policy. Financial literacy had started to receive its due as a key element that addressed demand-side challenges of financial inclusion. Financial inclusion and financial literacy have come to be recognised as twin pillars in which financial literacy is expected to stimulate the demand side by creating awareness in people about what they can demand.[18]

In this period, further fillip was given to the financial literacy agenda with RBI's implementing a project titled 'Project Financial Literacy'[19] whose objective was to disseminate general banking concepts to target groups including schools and university students, women, the rural and urban poor, defense personnel and senior citizens.

Two working groups[20] recommended the importance of offering counselling to certain vulnerable groups. Based on the recommendations of working groups, and as announced in the Annual Policy Statement for the year 2007–08, Reserve Bank advised the Lead banks on 10 May 2007 to set up Financial Literacy and Credit Counselling Centres (FLCCs) on a pilot basis in any one district in the State/Union Territory coming under their jurisdiction and, based on the experience gained, the Lead Banks may set up couselling centres in other districts.

Subsequent to the implementation of pilot FLCC and lessons learnt from that, a model scheme for FLCCs was announced in February 2009 and FLCCs were scaled up.

Setting up of the Citi Centre for Financial Literacy (CCFL) in September 2005, CCFL was housed in the ISMW and was dedicated towards spreading financial literacy in India and elsewhere. The centre was started with the objective[21] of 'spreading of financial literacy amongst the poor, especially women by building their financial awareness, knowledge and skill to enable them to manage their finances and thereby making them financially self-reliant and provide them better and secured future'.

In October 2008, CCFL set up a network of partner organisations called 'National Alliance for Financial Literacy' (NAFiL) to significantly expand the reach of financial literacy across the country. NAFiL's first major goal was to reach one million poor women across the country by March 2010. To achieve this goal, a National Financial Literacy Drive involving partnerships with a range of stakeholders was taken up.

5.4.3 Take-off: 2010–15

Two factors led to take-off of financial literacy programmes among the microfinance institutions: (i) microfinance crisis in October 2010 and (ii) subsequent focal shift to consumer protection and CoC.

On the side of self-regulation, MFIN and Sa-Dhan, two industry associations for microfinance, have drafted and released a unified CoC in December 2011 (henceforth called 'Code of Conduct') that incorporated earlier versions of CoC developed by Sa-Dhan and MFIN; inputs from the CPP of SMART campaign and RBI's FPC for NBFCs. These guidelines that were mandatory for the associations' members to adhere to had included a significant component of client education. At the minimum level, MFIs are supposed to have a dedicated process to raise clients' awareness of the options, choices and responsibilities vis-à-vis financial products and services available. New clients must be informed about the MFIs' policies and procedures to help them understand their rights as borrowers; and awareness and understanding of key terms of products availed should be checked through regular monitoring.

In 2012, the RBI released its National Strategy for Financial Education (NSFE)[22] which was set to be implemented in a time frame of five years. NSFE was proposed to be implemented at various levels. It was first aimed to target the financially excluded population by providing basic financial education on fundamental aspects. Next, a sector-focused approach was taken up to target financially included customers. Four policy areas were identified: banking, the securities market, insurance and retirement planning. At the third level, consumers were to learn the features of various products available in the market.

In the same year, RBI issued a circular with modified model scheme for financial literacy counselling centres. This was done after reviewing the model scheme of FLCCs existing till then

and the evaluation of the scheme suggested limitations of the model scheme. Given the limitations and the need to scale up financial literacy efforts, RBI revised the model scheme and provided new guidelines and rechristened the centres as Financial Literacy Centres (FLCs). Lead banks were advised to set up and operate FLCs in each of the Lead District Manager (LDM) Offices and additional need based FLCs may be set up in other locations according to banks' discretion. In addition, the rural branches of all the scheduled commercial banks including RRBs were instructed to undertake financial literacy activities.

5.5 POLICIES AND PROGRAMMES OF REGULATORS AND SUPPORTING AGENCIES

5.5.1 The Reserve Bank of India

The policy push for financial literacy came in 2005 when RBI integrated financial literacy in the financial inclusion strategy. RBI's initiatives can be classified into two: (a) its direct interventions and (b) guidelines given to banks to push the implementation of financial literacy. Various guidelines and policy developments were discussed in the previous section, so this section discusses the direct interventions of RBI.

RBI's major direct initiative has taken shape in 2007 with its implementation of 'Project Financial Literacy'. The objective of the project was to disseminate information regarding the central bank and general banking concepts to various target groups, including school- and college-going children, women, rural and urban poor, defence personnel and senior citizens. To further boost the implementation, a multilingual website[23] in 13 Indian languages was launched in June 2007 keeping the common person as the target audience. Two animation characters— Money Kumar and Raju were created to create awareness about roles and functions of RBI and banking concepts, respectively.

RBI has created and made available materials on financial literacy keeping various target groups in focus, such as school children, youth and entrepreneurs. Financial literacy programmes have been launched in many states with the active involvement of the state government and the State Level Bankers' Committee (SLBC). These programmes include skits, road shows, exhibitions, workshops, seminars, and dissemination through radio and television. In several schools, essay competitions and quizzes for school children have been conducted.

RBI officials undertake visits to villages (called outreach programmes) across the country from time to time. During the outreach visits, messages on advantages of being linked to formal banking sector and functions and working of RBI are disseminated through lectures, skits, posters, short films, pamphlets, distribution of comic books on financial literacy (Raju and the Money Tree, Money Kumar, etc.), quiz competitions and essay competitions for school children, kiosk at the venue where besides providing information, notes and coins are exchanged.

5.5.2 Securities and Exchange Board of India (SEBI)[24]

SEBI has taken up several initiatives across the country to spread financial literacy. It has set up an independent public trust—the National Institute of Securities Markets (NISM) which works on financial literacy as one of the key areas. NISM has set up School for Investor Education and Financial Literacy (SIEFL) to enhance the levels of financial literacy in India.

SEBI launched a financial education drive through resource persons (RPs) in June 2010, where teachers and lecturers were trained and empanelled for conducting financial education workshops. The study material developed for these target groups is available in 10 vernacular languages. Refresher trainings are conducted from time to time and in 2013–14, these resource persons have conducted around 9,493 financial literacy workshops. SEBI invites students from schools, colleges and professional institutes who are interested to learn about SEBI and its role as a regulator of securities markets through a visit to SEBI. The programme was started in 2010.

SEBI collaborated with RBI and other financial services regulators to draft the NSFE under the aegis of Financial Stability and Development Council (FSDC). A special Institute called National Centre for Financial Education (NCFE) has been established under NISM with representatives from all financial sector regulators. A national-level exam for school students, National Financial Literacy Assessment Test (NFLAT) had been conducted by NCFE. The portal, www.ncfeindia.org, has been launched with information covering on various aspects of financial market including banking, pension, insurance and securities market and with inputs from various regulators including SEBI. The website is being updated with videos, audios and other materials.

5.5.3 Insurance Regulatory and Development Authority (IRDA)

IRDA has taken up financial literacy initiatives[25] since its inception and has adopted multi-pronged approach to enhance consumer awareness on insurance. It has both in-house programmes and external programmes in which it sponsored external entities. IRDA has taken a number of consumer education initiatives under the brand name Bima Bemisaal; it launched Hindi version of its consumer education website and introduced a games section 'Young Corner' targeting children to learn insurance in a playful manner. It conducts seminars and events that promote insurance education. It uses multimedia tools such as comic books, animation films which have been translated into 12 vernacular languages. It produced documentary film on various initiatives of IRDA towards protecting the interests of the policyholders. The visual education material was placed on Youtube site 'IRDA Connects' and a mobile website of IRDA was launched. IRDA published wall calendars and desk calendars with insurance messages carrying relevant pictures to depict the messages. IRDA published four handbooks, viz., *Role of Insurance Surveyors, Life Insurance Riders, Householders & Shopkeepers Insurance and Insurance Sector's Grievance Redressal Mechanism* for the benefit of policyholders. The insurance education material developed by IRDA is made available on consumer education website in easily downloadable form but the printed copies are also distributed through various channels such as financial literacy centres, consumer bodies, etc. IRDA sponsored a pan-India insurance awareness campaign through General Insurance Council, disseminating insurance education on common general insurance topics, viz., motor, health, rural and property insurance. In order to curb the menace of spurious callers, a print campaign was carried out cautioning general public against spurious callers and fictitious offers. IRDA is working towards campaign in the electronic media for wider reach amongst members of public. IRDA sponsors seminars conducted by consumer bodies and NGOs in rural, semi-urban areas. To promote academic research in the areas of insurance,

IRDA launched a research grant scheme promoting applied research in insurance with focus on policyholders' protection and insurance inclusion.

5.5.4 Pension Fund Regulatory and Development Authority (PFRDA)

PFRDA, since its inception, has been engaged in spreading social security messages to the public. PFRDA has developed frequently asked questions on pension-related topics available on its website. PFRDA's initiatives are more broad-based with direct mass publicity on New Pension Scheme (NPS)/ NPS Lite, both as individual model through Points of Presence (POP) and group models through aggregators. PFRDA is a member of the NAFiL.

5.5.5 Financial literacy activities of NABARD[26] in the last one year

NABARD has been actively pursuing the agenda of facilitating financial literacy towards the financial inclusion agenda mainly through various initiatives of RRBs and Cooperatives. As NABARD manages two dedicated funds:[27] (i) financial inclusion fund (FIF) and (ii) financial inclusion technology fund (FITF), it incorporates its financial literacy agenda through activities related to these funds.

1. NABARD continues to support cooperative banks and RRBs for setting up of FLCs from FIF: The scheme for supporting RRBs and cooperative banks for setting up of FLCs with an outlay up to ₹5 lakh per FLC under FIF has been continued for the last year. As on 31 March 2015, a total of 1,195 FLCs have been set up.

	No. of FLCs sanctioned	Amount sanctioned (in crores)	Amount disbursed (in crores)
RRBs	341	15.41	7.02
Cooperatives	854	41.05	13.64
Total	**1,195**	**56.46**	**20.66**

2. Printing and distribution of standardised financial literacy material prepared by RBI: With a view to facilitate the bank branches for creating financial literacy/awareness, support is available to the SLBCs of all the states for printing of the standardised financial literacy material. As on 31 March 2015, ₹20.29 crore has been sanctioned in 23 states against which an amount of ₹16.14 crore has been disbursed.

3. Financial Literacy Programme for Rural Adults—CSC e-Governance Services India Limited (CEGSIL): ₹47.30 lakh has been sanctioned to CEGSIL, a special purpose vehicle (SPV) promoted by the Department of Electronics and Information Technology, Government of India, for conducting financial literacy programmes in Chhattisgarh and Madhya Pradesh. The objective of the programme was to roll out financial literacy in a coordinated and phased manner through the CSC[28] village-level entrepreneurs (VLEs) in the above two states. The project has been completed and financial literacy training has been imparted to 10,000 persons in the rural areas of these states. A second project has been sanctioned to CEGSIL during the year for ₹3.77 crore to train one lakh rural adults across five states, viz., Bihar, Himachal Pradesh, Jharkhand, Rajasthan and Uttar Pradesh.

4. In addition to the above, NABARD has also extended support for organising financial literacy/awareness camps organised through District Development Managers and various partners, viz., government departments, All India Radio, FM radio channels, banks, NGOs, etc. The innovative/customised mode of awareness creation is by way of puppet shows, animated films, nukkad nataks, magic shows, jingles through regular and FM radio channels, display of posters on road transport vehicles, trains, text books, wall paintings, etc.

5. Assistance available to cooperative banks and RRBs:

   a. Organising financial literacy camps—maximum of ₹10,000 per programme.
   b. Setting up of financial literacy centres—maximum of ₹5 lakh per centre—RRBs may establish one FLC per district and cooperative banks may establish one FLC per block. This support is provided for the first year only.
   c. Mobile vans for demonstration of banking technology—₹10 lakh per van.
   d. All the above assistance is available to cooperative banks at 90% and to RRBs at 80% of the project cost.

6. Assistance available to all banks and NGOs:

   a. Organising financial literacy camps with grant support up to 60% of project cost subject to a maximum of ₹10,000 per camp for commercial banks.

b. Publicity material on financial literacy for commercial banks.

c. Organising financial literacy camps through NGOs with a maximum of ₹7,200 per programme.

5.5.6 SIDBI-PSIG interventions under financial literacy and women empowerment

Poorest State Inclusive Growth (PSIG) programme which is supported by SIDBI and DFID has developed the financial literacy concept as empowering strategy that can also address social empowerment issues. An integrated module of financial literacy and women empowerment was developed in close facilitation of SIDBI and DFID by the regional office. The module promotes women and men understanding of household relations and roles along with knowledge and skills to do financial planning, budgeting and savings. The modules not only aims to empower women with knowledge of financial products and services but help women and men analyse the unequal distribution of roles and responsibilities within household.

Based on the above facts and strategic directions laid down by the gender policy, the following initiatives were undertaken.

- **First pilot project on financial literacy and women empowerment in select 14 districts, Uttar Pradesh and Bihar**: The pilot project envisages Training of Trainers (ToT) approach for creating a cadre of 90 community resource persons on financial literacy and women empowerment and training of about 60,000 women clients of seven MFIs by these trained master trainers. The intent of the training is to provide a minimum 30 hours of training to the clients on financial literacy and social empowerment issues spread over a period of one year. The project is being implemented with the help of a resource organisation (ISMW) with support of seven MFIs and is designed to be conducted in three phases each followed by three days refresher trainings and then field trainings. The pilot has adopted a mobile-based open kit technology based MIS for monitoring and evaluation of trainings along with developing a gender-integrated financial literacy module for training master trainers. The project is being implemented now.

- **Second and third pilot project on financial literacy and women empowerment in Madhya Pradesh and Odisha:** The pilot aims to build a cadre of 36 and 65 community resource persons (master trainers) in the states of Madhya Pradesh and Odisha, respectively. The master trainers would be responsible for reaching out and training 30,000 and 50,000 female clients of select partner master trainers in Madhya Pradesh and Odisha. The implementing agencies have been contracted namely Hand in Hand for Madhya Pradesh and Accion for Odisha through technical bid process. The projects are in inception and strategy development stage.

5.6 CURRENT INITIATIVES ON FINANCIAL LITERACY IN INDIA

In the last 2–3 years, several entities have initiated financial literacy activities. Given the number of such initiatives being huge,[29] this report focuses on presenting general trends of various models that are being implemented and highlights specific cases where required.

In India, all the financial literacy efforts in the financial inclusion space can be categorised into those that are implemented by: (i) microfinance institutions, financial service providers who are in the group lending, individual lending or other forms of services; (ii) SHGs or SHPIs; and (iii) banks including RRBs and Cooperatives.

In addition to this, there are certain initiatives supported by technical assistance agencies or research organisations. There will be some overlaps of these initiatives with the above categories. Regulators, SROs and other development agencies play a role with their own guidelines and initiatives offering support to the agencies implementing programmes. This report briefly touches upon such policies, guidelines and initiatives.

5.6.1 Initiatives of microfinance institutions

Of the 28 MFIs that responded to a survey conducted for this report, 24 of them had some form of financial literacy awareness programmes implemented in their organisations. For a majority of these MFIs, the felt need from the field was the main reason for starting these programmes.

After the crisis in 2010, the financial literacy programmes among MFIs have increased. Though few organisations started some form of financial literacy prior to the crisis, clearly there is a marked change in the uptake after the crisis. The financial literacy initiatives of MFIs range from standalone approach to integrated service delivery approach implemented by the organisations themselves to outsourced to a third party or sister concern.

In any case, financial literacy programmes are viewed as non-financial services by MFIs and as such many are implemented as CSR. Though in such cases, there is some integration with respect to supervisory structures or common internal audit functions.

Some MFIs increasingly started to use MIS for tracking the programme outreach and challenges. Parinaam Foundation and MFIs supported by Accion are case in point. Monitoring and evaluation studies are taken up, though not much information is available generally in the public domain.

The GIZ-RFIP has supported financial literacy initiatives for business correspondents and one such 'Master Trainer Project'[30] was conceived as a public–private partnership between the RFIP and IFMR Rural Channels and Services (IRCS) the service provider, to develop an approach to integrate financial awareness-building interventions into the provider's operations and to pilot-test it in three regions of India. The education intervention was implemented by Kshetriya Grameen Financial Services (KGFS), a network of localised microfinance business units that are part of the IRCS legal entity. This programme was conducted in two phases with the second phase completed in September 2014. The actual training or financial awareness programmes were conducted by 'master trainers' who were the hand-picked staff from KGFS' branches. They conducted three types[31] of programmes: (i) wealth master programme, (ii) customer connect programme, and (iii) school programme. The 10 master trainers had a total of 4,250 interactions with wealth masters, conducted over 1,300 Customer Connect Programme sessions reaching out to 18,840 participants (with 99% women) and over 750 School Programmes reaching about 12,000 students. In total, the programmes reached about 35,000 people in the three KGFS locations of Uttarakhand, Odisha and Tamil Nadu.

A different approach adopted is that of Swadhar. Swadhaar FinAccess (SFA), a Mumbai-based non-profit section 25 company and a sister concern of Swadhar FinServe Pvt Ltd., an NBFC engaging in urban microfinance, has set up Financial Inclusion and Literacy Centres (FILCs) to promote financial literacy among its members and their communities. The objective of the FILCs is to provide training and access through a physical centre. SFA has 10 FILCs in Mumbai and Gujarat and has reached out to over 2 lakh people from low-income communities—women, men and youth—through financial education and product linkage activities. The approach is to maintain multiple touch points with the customer and hence SFA adopts both in-centre and community-based activities. Each FILC has a counsellor who is available at the FILC for counselling and information on financial matters to the walk-in members. SFA has a household membership fees that gives them access to ongoing interaction and counselling at the FILC by the member or the household. FILCs also have a set of trainers and mobilisers who visit the neighbouring slum communities and conduct financial literacy training. Financial Education for Youth (age group 18–22 years) is also one of the community-based activities. SFA has digitised the content of financial literacy modules to standardise the content and improve the effectiveness.

CASHPOR offers different programmes of financial literacy to its members: (i) it provides basic financial literacy to all the new incoming clients as a part of its five-day compulsory group training at the time of customer enrolment; (ii) it provides half-hour literacy programmes on microfinance products, savings, pension, insurance, remittance, credit through community facilitators at the time of centre meeting; (iii) and it offers a ten-day training on financial literacy and gender empowerment as a part of SIDBI-PSIG project. It is one of the organisations that has integrated financial literacy in its service delivery. While the gender empowerment training was funded by SIDBI-PSIG programme, for the other two models, internal funds of CASHPOR were mobilised and utilised. The half-hour literacy programme was a need-based programme aimed to stop multiple lending, ghost clients, helping the clients balance their finances, etc.

5.6.1.1 Status of implementation of financial literacy by MFIs and other organisations: Key findings and observations

- **Activities taken up and who implements them:** Training to new clients on organisation's products and processes to create transparency;

training on financial avenues and planning to all clients and business development programmes for entrepreneurs, especially in case of MFIs offering individual loans.

- **Target segments:** Majority of the MFIs focus on reaching out to women for the financial literacy programmes. Typically the MFIs reach out to both urban and rural areas. MFIs target their new clients with few topics (like organisation's product terms, rules of lending, ills of multiple borrowing, credit bureaus, etc.) and very few MFIs reach out the clients in older loan cycles with structured financial literacy programmes.

- **Communication techniques used:** This varies from initiative to initiative, but broadly the techniques used are: audio-visual tools like films, audio, radio, financial diaries, printed material, workshops, etc.

- **Content covered:** The scope of topics covered changes from initiative to initiative. Some of the MFIs that reach out to all client segments cover various topics according to the relevance of the content to the participants. For all new clients, basic financial literacy is provided around the group formation process, joint liability, multiple borrowing, product terms and conditions, and grievance redressal mechanism, if available, of the organisation. This is typically part of the CGT and GRT. For all clients, if the MFI is involved in financial literacy in traditional meaning of the term, content related to personal money management, savings, credit, household budget, investments, and financial planning are covered. Some organisations have started to discuss about newer government schemes on financial inclusion with clients.

- **Human resources, infrastructure and amenities:** Two main models of human resources are involved. One model in which the MFI staff themselves take up the training and in another separate project staff or NGO staff are used for delivering the training. With MFIs, not many have used the community-based model of creating local trainers. Generally, where the MFI staff themselves are involved in training, the scope of content tends to be limited to the organisation's products and processes.

- **Monitoring and evaluation:** Monitoring is done by the MFI supervisory structure if the programme is implemented in-house or is monitored by project staff if implemented by a third

party. Monitoring, though, is mostly restricted to reviewing the outreach numbers rather than the quality and outcomes of the programme. Some organisations have baseline and end line data collected to understand the project impact on the clients (Box 5.3). General practice is more towards conducting an end line study than baseline studies, thus posing challenges with data availability.

Box 5.3 Monitoring for effective programme implementation

Parinaam Foundation, a sister concern of Ujjivan Financial Services, runs a financial literacy programme for Ujjivan's customers. This programme is divided into two: (i) **Sankalp, a short film**, which creates awareness among members on the dangers of over-borrowing and ghost lending; and (ii) **Diksha training**, which aims to create awareness among the members on the need for financial planning; how to plan, monitor and track finances; saving; borrowing; and recap.

For both the programmes, Parinaam Foundation and Ujjivan have put in place monitoring mechanisms that use MIS. For Sankalp, MIS is maintained on the outreach or number of participants who attended each of the Sankalp screening. The branch managers compile the responses from the Q&A sessions after every screening and document the level of involvement displayed by customers which is reported to the financial literacy programme coordinators.

For Diksha, Parinaam has an MIS that tracks the progress of the programme progress and outcomes. Ujjivan/Parinaam's attendance tracking software, called the 'Seek tool' stores the baseline data. The baseline data is collected from the registration forms that CRSs fill with the participant profile, which basically contains the household income, expenses, the financial services being used, what the aspirations are, existing knowledge about the financial services, etc. Along with this data, every week the weekly attendance data of the trainees is entered. The tool prepares a trainer wise report, a weekly programme level report and a master schedule of all trainings, trainers' performance, material distributed to customers, etc.

In addition to the MIS that tracks the programme performance, many other processes have been put in place to track the programme progress. A hard copy register is maintained and customers sign it to mark their presence as well as receipt of materials given to them. A stock of materials is kept with the cashier at Ujjivan's branches and handed to the trainers against a written requisition based on the number of members in the current Diksha batch. Attendance registers and stock requisitions are tallied with the Seek tool by FLP coordinators during their supervisory visits.

Data entry is done at the branch. Coordinators/regional managers spot mistakes such as mismatches between material given and attendance for that day, and rectify the reports before the data is finalised and sent to the Chief Operation Officer (COO). Regional managers send a report every week to the COO, containing slot wise and branch wise attendance levels and listing the five best and worst performing branches under the programme. Branches with high dropout levels are also consulted and the reasons are discussed. When the COO sees attendance dipping consistently across two continuous modules, she contacts the CRSs in that branch and encourages them to improve performance.

The following parameters are considered as key metrics for monitoring:

- Certification of participants—all participants must attend all five sessions to be certified
- Opening of saving accounts
- Conversion to cashless transaction of their loan amount
- Conversion to individual lending from group lending
- Higher education scholarships disbursement for participants, which demonstrate that they are able to save for their children's education in the bank account.

Source: Interview with Parinaam Foundation and extracted from the case study written by M-CRIL for GIZ-IFC Financial Literacy Scoping Study (2013).

5.6.1.2 Challenges faced

- Integration of financial literacy with the service delivery has not been done widely as the MFIs do not see a business case in doing so and

the resources required (time and skills of the trainer required in the traditional methodology) are immense vis-à-vis the benefits. In few cases, where organisations have integrated financial literacy with service delivery, they were not able to scale up due to costs.

- Standardised modules are good for scaling up; however, they lack customisation which is required to provide relevance and context to clients. Whereas very broad and free-to-customise material requires high-quality trainers who are difficult to get by in local areas. A median approach is required for this (Box 5.4).
- Though it is experienced that financial education followed by relevant product delivery enables behaviour change, it runs the risk of mis-selling and in some cases even lack of appropriate products.

Box 5.4 Use of technology for delivery of financial literacy programmes

Use of innovative technologies, be it smart phones or tablets or media, is low in the field of financial literacy initiatives in India. However, increasingly digitisation of content is seen as a way forward to standardised the implementation of programmes and scale the programme. Organisations like Accion and Ujjivan are planning to digitise the content of their respective programmes.

There is one organisation which has started a pilot to this effect already. Swadhaar FinAccess (SFA) digitised the financial education modules, through the innovation grant received from Citi Foundation in July 2014. There are six modules in Hindi and Marathi which have been digitised and are being delivered through tablets within the community. The modules are interactive and engage the learners. SFA has recruited peer educators, who are women from the same community, as trainers. A pilot is being implemented in two locations in Mumbai.

With digitisation of content, SFA envisions two opportunities: (i) standardised content and interaction through the digital modules will maintain the quality of training and (ii) the trained trainers and mobilisers will be able to support increased number of peer educators.

Source: Swadhaar note on financial literacy using digital means.

- There is a duplication of efforts in content development—due to 'not invented here syndrome'. Even when at times it is the same donor supporting multiple ventures, there is funding provided for content development every time.
- There is limited motivation to take up financial literacy among the MFIs due to lack of buy-in and in some cases lack of relevance. In the survey conducted for this report, there were some organisations which did not take up financial literacy as there are no donor funds. Clearly, financial literacy is donor-driven in India than need-driven.
- Charging customers for financial literacy has not worked yet as the clients do not perceive a direct value in the same. Swadhar FinAccess charges ₹30 to ₹40 per client for using the FILC, but that is no way near the full cost recovery of the centres.

5.6.2 Initiatives of SHPIs/SHGs

SHGs movement is considered to be cornerstone for achieving women empowerment and financial inclusion. Several organisations that promoted SHGs including NGOs or banks taking up that role have recognised the importance of financial literacy in empowerment. Of the 28 organisations who were surveyed for this report, 6 of them were operating through SHG model of microfinance. The observations made in this section are a result of the data provided, interviews conducted with a few organisations working in the space and desk review.

Some of the financial literacy initiatives in the SHG space are as follows.

The APMAS is a member of the NAFiL engaged in campaigning on financial literacy and other international forums that focus on community-based microfinance. Being a resource organisation in the fields of capacity building and strengthening of community-based organisations (CBOs) including SHGs, it has taken up provision of financial literacy to SHGs and federations as a part of its pilot project on self-regulation. In the last two years, it provided Information Education and Communication material to MEPMA (Mission for Elimination of Poverty in Municipal Areas) activities including on financial literacy. As a part of its institutional capacity building, APMAS provided technical support in building the institutions of the poor by focusing on capacity building of the members of self-help organisations at various levels, developing resource pool for strengthening such institutions, imparting financial

literacy and facilitating policies related to financial management of the institutions, etc. It continues to provide capability building support to Mandal Samakhyas, village organisations and SHGs on various topics related to SHG management along with financial literacy.

Kudumbashree in Kerala introduced a financial literacy campaign to build knowledge about banking procedures, interest rates and awareness about various products and services through banks among the neighbourhood group (NHG) members. The first phase of the campaign was launched in 2010–11. It focused on Kudumbashree schemes related to microfinance, proper book keeping and banking procedures, services, etc. Presently, Kudumbashree is in the process of developing the second phase of its financial literacy campaign.

GIZ as a part of the NABARD-GIZ Rural Financial Institutions Programme worked on two major initiatives on financial literacy for SHGs. One, it developed a 'financial awareness and education toolkit for SHG members' called *Humaari Asha* and two, implemened a pilot with a new approach on 'financial capability of low-income households'. The first initiative is a toolkit (available in English and Hindi) that aims at increasing the financial awareness and education of the SHG members. The toolkit covers topics such as: savings, loans and other financial services, SHG Bank linkage and income-generating activities. The second initiative was implemented as a pilot with the Centre for Microfinance in Jaipur, which is a resource organisation for SHPIs. The pilot was designed based on a study conducted in GIZ through a tool used with 4,000 households across three federations. The idea was to develop a database on level of financial capability of households and use that information to develop the intervention. This research identified 13 abilities in four areas: generating, managing and using money; planning for the future; using financial services; and using social capital, assets and competencies (see Annexure 5.1). A baseline was conducted on the households using this framework to assess the level of financial capability of the target group before the invention and an endline assessment will be conducted to assess the change in financial capability. This approach gives importance to understanding the status on different parameters in order to customise and provide relevant financial counselling.

5.6.2.1 Status of implementation of financial literacy by and for SHGs: Key findings and observations

- **Activities taken up and who implements them:** Most of the initiatives take on master training approach with the local trainers or community facilitators provided with training to train the SHG members. The trainings are part of the SHG or federation-level meetings (Box 5.5).

Box 5.5 RGMVP financial literacy programme

Rajiv Gandhi Mahila Vikas Pariyojana (RGMVP) is a rights-based organisation that works for poverty reduction, women's empowerment and rural development in Uttar Pradesh in 275 blocks in 42 districts. RGMVP organises poor rural women into SHGs and offers various services to address issues of financial inclusion, healthcare, livelihoods, education and environment. Considering SHG bank linkage is the model adopted, financial literacy forms a vital part of RGMVP's activities. The financial literacy programmes are implemented directly by the organisation with an in-house team of community resource persons. External support is taken from partner organisations like SIDBI, NABARD, UNICEF, Bill and Melinda Gates Foundation. Till date 80% of the SHG members are covered under the financial literacy programme which is implemented phase-wise.

The topics covered by the financial literacy programme are: savings, loans and pension. The programme is structured to be a peer-to-peer learning through case studies, experience sharing by bank sakhis (experienced SHGs who have completed 2–3 loan cycle successfully). This is done through various means like SHG register, SHG flipbook and booklets with case studies.

RGMVP has an online monitoring system through which the management monitors the programme's progress in the field. The senior management tracks the programme implementation every month. Going forward, it is considering using mobile technology and mind mapping technology tools to encourage women to share the learnings in groups.

Source: Interview with RGMVP team, Rae Bariely.

- **Target segments:** Majority of the programmes are targeted at women from the SHGs and the messages are aimed at the household money management rather than individual financial planning.
- **Communication techniques used:** Booklets in local language, typically shared with the local trainers or community facilitators to aid them in providing training, posters and games.
- **Content covered:** The topics covered for SHGs training on financial literacy are almost similar to what MFIs offer to their members, but with some additional topics for specific case of SHGs like banking system, SHG-bank linkage, book keeping, and types of savings/deposit accounts, interest calculations, cash book maintenance and maintenance of other registers.
- **Human resources, infrastructure and amenities:** In most of the initiatives, the community facilitators are used to provide training to SHG members. No specific infrastructure or amenities are created, but the existing meeting places of SHG or federations are used for trainings.
- **Monitoring and evaluation:** Monitoring is done by supervisory structures in place that monitors the SHG trainings.

5.6.2.2 Challenges faced

- Quality of local trainers is an issue for many of the initiatives. While the tools and material created are useful and appreciated, lack of good-quality trainers, especially in rural areas is a huge challenge. There is a correlation between level of knowledge and skills of trainers, and are directly linked to trainee results.
- Some SHPIs conduct day-long training to save on time which may not be effective due to fatigue among the group members. And along with the longer training hours, sometimes the trainers go from one module to another in a standard way without understanding the level at which the SHG members are.
- In general, it is observed that while the SHG members may show improved knowledge on financial literacy aspects, their knowledge and skills on procedural aspects of groups like attendance, record keeping, etc., have not improved due to extraneous factors.
- As with the programmes implemented by other models, sustainability of financial literacy initiatives

in absence of any external donor or funding support is a limitation.

5.6.3 Initiatives of banks including RRBs and cooperatives

A large portion of the banks' financial literacy programme is implemented through the FLCs approach—especially by the public sector banks and RRBs.

State Bank of India for instance has set up FLCs in line with the RBI guidelines. Its FLCs will impart financial literacy in the form of simple messages like 'why save', 'why save early in your life', 'why save with banks', 'why borrow from banks', 'why borrow as far as possible for income generating activities', 'why repay in time', 'why insure yourself', 'why save for your retirement', etc. Apart from providing financial literacy at the centres, the FLCs are also conducting camps in villages, seminars and workshops to create awareness among the people. As on March 2014, 203 financial literacy centres were run by SBI across various locations with a total outreach of around 785,188 people.[32]

Union Bank of India provides support to setting up and running of the village knowledge centres (VKCs) in rural areas. To further spread financial literacy in rural areas, Union Bank of India plans to open 24 FLCs across its 14 lead districts to begin with to fulfil its mandate of financial literacy and counselling of the unreached and unbanked sector. As per recent guidelines of RBI, all the rural branches are conducting one financial literacy camp once in a month in their command area for appraising the villagers about the various products of bank. Currently Union Bank of India has 26 FLCs.[33]

Some of the private banks like ICICI Bank, Citi Bank, Axis Bank, etc., have taken up financial literacy under their CSR initiatives. Although none of the banks yet spent 2% of the average net profit of the previous three years on CSR;[34] beginnings have been made to work on CSR more intently. Axis Bank Foundation (ABF), ICICI Bank and HDFC bank were some of the private banks that have invested in financial literacy activities under CSR.

5.6.3.1 Status of implementation of FLCs: Key findings and observations[35]

- **Activities take up:** As mandated by the RBI guidelines, the FLCs undertake a number of activities throughout the year to create awareness

and to link the excluded segment to the banking system (Box 5.6). All FLCs are required to conduct at least one financial literacy camp in a month and conduct three-stage modular sessions with the same set of beneficiaries over three months. Emphasis on activities like conducting mega camps, sessions with Gram Sabha, mini camps, camps through business correspondent

---

Box 5.6 Financial literacy in Uttar Bihar Gramin Bank (UBGB)

UBGB follows a unique model in terms of financial literacy. Since March 2013, the bank has established 18 financial literacy centres, which are operational one per district for all districts in its command area. The financial counsellor of UBGB is a serving officer of the bank in middle management grade scale II or III. The financial counsellor is provided with a furnished office cum residence, a vehicle, Laptop computer, LCD projector, financial literacy material, etc. He is also vested with the authority to oversee and supervise the activities of business correspondents and the other branches in the district. Hierarchically his position is second in rank in the region (next to the regional manager). All financial counsellors under UBGB are given a customised, week-long training at BIRD, Lucknow. In 2013–14, the FLCs specifically concentrated on conducting mega financial literacy camps attracting around 2,000 people per camp on an average (in some camps the attendance was as high as 7,000 also). Nukar Nataks by professional troupe also turned out to be crowd puller. In 2013–14, the FLCs conducted 1,928 financial literacy camp (including village level and mega) with a total attendance of around 465,753 people. In 2014–15, FLCs concentrated on large number of small village camps within the command area of brick and mortar branches and BCs. Each of these camps were attended by around 40–50 people. The bank organised around 2,118 camps in 2014–15 attracting 263,518 audience. The bank also uses the business correspondents to further increase the outreach of financial literacy initiatives. Special efforts have been made to train the BCAs on the same.

Source: Case of UBGB, Muzaffarpur HO.

agents (BCAs), etc., is currently being pursued with a vision to create financial awareness for masses. Of all the activities, camps (whether at village level, block/district level) seem to be more prevalent followed by debt counselling/ counselling of walk-in clients. In a number of instances, the FLCs also take support from voluntary organisations, NGOs in mobilising the people, to achieve greater outreach. In some places, financial awareness for school students is also undertaken by FLCs. Wall painting, setting up of galleries, etc., were initiated through FLCs in two school per FLCs in Bihar. Though the initiative is at nurturing stage, negotiations with school officials and government department is currently undergoing.

- **Communication techniques used:** The most commonly used communication method is lecture by financial counsellor and other resource persons in camps. However, some FLCs are using more diverse tools such as mobile/mini vans, nukkad nataks, magic shows/puppet shows and videos (RBI and PMJDY) and presentations using projectors.

- **Content covered:** Typically six themes are covered during the financial literacy camps: savings, credit, banking services, insurance, remittance, and pension. While discussing these themes, respective government programmes under each theme are covered. For instance, kisan credit cards are discussed under credit theme; PMJDY under banking services theme and so on.

- **Human resources, infrastructure and amenities:** Usually there is one financial counsellor for one FLC who is responsible for the overall working and activities of that particular centre. The financial counsellor is often a retired banker of scale II and above with experience of handling credit and having worked in rural/semi-urban area. The counsellor is appointed on contract basis for a period of one year, subject to satisfactory performance which shall be evaluated by competent authority. The financial counsellor's purview of work spans across conducting of outdoor camps, overseeing activity of BCA, dealing with indoor customers, database maintenance, attend district- and block-level banker's meeting and monthly submission of progress reports. He is also responsible for arranging visits by higher bank officials from NABARD, RBI, etc. Special trainings are provided to the financial counsellor with an objective to develop professional skills, updating on the financial inclusion initiatives and updating the skills.

The FLCs are usually set up in rural, semi-urban and urban area, and the office premise is situated in places like LDM office, office sharing with Rural Self Employment Training Institutes (RSETI), regional office or independent spaces on rent. The basic infrastructure varies across FLCs of different banks. It was found in a number of centres that the movement of the financial literacy counsellor to the field becomes an issue in the absence of provision of vehicles. Generally, the counsellor has to use own vehicle or depend on public transport or they could coordinate with LDM, Regional Manager or RSETI for travel. The FLC is generally equipped with signage, stationery, furniture (which includes chair and table), printed material, almirah, etc. The availability of infrastructure which includes laptop, computer system, camera, projectors, mic and genset and other fixed asset varies across banks. However, the FLCs have provision to hire items on rent for financial literacy camp which includes projector, laptop, tents, etc.

The budget of FLCs varies across states and banks. The major chunk of the total budget is allocated to HR (which includes salary, mobile expenses travel and halt allowance). Other items include expenses for organising camps, office rent, budget for printing material, stationary, etc.

- **Monitoring and evaluation:** FLCs maintain book-keeping methods to gauge month-wise progress. The registers maintained at FLC include Programme Implementation and Management Committee meeting register, outdoor camp register (which includes details of people attending the camp), customer visit register (in which the details of customer, query and follow-ups are recorded), expenditure register, tour register, etc. These registers are provided during external audits to monitor the progress made during the month/quarter and are also used to plan activities for the next phase. To further ensure support of the top management of the bank in the financial inclusion process and to ensure accountability of the senior functionaries of the bank, one or one annual review meetings are also conducted at the bank level.

5.6.3.2 Challenges faced

- Low literacy level among the client populations works as a major hindrance in advancing the financial literacy initiative. Given limited exposure and knowledge, the clients are often reluctant to participate in the activities and programmes. Initial mobilisation and sensitisation activities are a huge challenge for the FLCs across the states.
- The awareness camps are conducted mainly in sub-service area of the host bank. Banks do not commonly seek support from the existing FLCs of other banks which ultimately restricts the potential outreach of the financial literacy initiative.
- BCAs are considered to be an important mechanism to mobilise the community. The base branch and financial counsellor mainly use the BCAs for community mobilisation and follow-ups; the remuneration for this activity is negligible. Monetary support could be provided for this service.
- In several places there is a lack of adequate infrastructure facilities available for the FLCs to function. The FLC are often run in bank's premise (like LDM office and Regional office). There is no separate premise available where they can make new initiatives.
- Several FLCs faced problems from the local moneylenders as well. The local lenders having an existence in the villages often misguide the clients and create problems in the operations of the FLCs.

5.7 MOVING AHEAD WITH FINANCIAL LITERACY

Though a long way to go, the key to build sustainable financial literacy programmes is developing a more holistic approach in designing and delivering financial literacy programmes. The shift should be from tokenism to outcome-oriented programmes; from standalone interventions to result-oriented integrated models; and from intuitive or subjective decisions to data-driven decisions for programme implementation.

Across all the models and initiatives discussed in the previous sections, there are similar strategies and solutions to be implemented to make financial literacy more entrenched in the systems.

First, for making the shift as discussed earlier, it is very important to build the business case for financial literacy programmes which can bring in buy-in among the financial service providers. An industry-wide study should be undertaken across various models and initiatives to prove the business case for financial literacy—that there is a correlation between financial awareness and product uptake and usage. This should be driven by data and not anecdotal evidence alone. Carrying out any such study would have to be a concerted effort of different stakeholders involved—be in MFIs or SHGs or bank-driven financial inclusion programmes. SROs like MFIN and Sa-Dhan, SHPIs and support agencies can play a key role here. They can facilitate an industry-wide study, across various models and initiatives, about the business case of financial literacy. If the links between financial awareness and product uptake and usage can be proven, it will motivate more organisations to start investing in financial literacy instead of relying on donor funds or subsidy.

Data-driven analysis will not only help in making business case for financial literacy, but they will also improve the programme effectiveness and outcomes. SROs have a significant role for measurement of the outcomes of the initiatives. These organisations should start capturing the numbers around outreach and impact—something similar to what they are doing now with credit bureaus. One of the organisations that has attempted this is Parinaam Foundation in India which continuously collects data as a part of the monitoring and evaluation (see Box 5.7 to understand Parinaam's evaluation exercises) of the programme and the data collected from time to time is used to pivot the programme for better results.

Box 5.7 Evaluation of financial literacy programmes: A case of Parinaam

To understand how customers' financial behaviour has changed, an evaluation matrix for Diksha, starting with a baseline survey of pre-programme financial literacy levels is maintained. To complete the evaluation, surveys are conducted at intervals of 1 (dipstick), 3 (midline) and 6 (endline) months to analyse the impact of the project and the change in behaviour and knowledge of Ujjivan customers.

Parinaam has created 'Success Parameters' on which Diksha's achievement is measured. These goals are realistically low and were set using Parinaam's initial efforts in financial literacy. The surveys are supplemented by a coordinator's report based on the use of the financial diaries. These reports track whether customers are maintaining their cash-flows, are demanding more information on interest rates, EMIs, tenure on their loans prior to taking them and repayment frequencies, and also ensure that the savings accounts are being utilised to save regularly.

Source: Extracted from the case study written by M-CRIL for GIZ-IFC Financial Literacy Scoping Study (2013).

More resources (be it financial or human) should be invested in motivating the service providers about the importance of financial literacy for their clients and how it makes a business case for them. SROs can play a role in encouraging compliance related to their members adhering to the CoC guidelines on client education and this should be done stringently. It is these organisations that should ensure that their clients have adequate knowledge about their products—the principle being that clients should be given all information that enables them take informed choices.

Financial service providers should re-look at the content of financial literacy. With so many changes in the financial sector—mobile banking, small finance banks, payment banks, new government schemes, Mudra Bank, etc., content of financial literacy has to change. The same messages about personal finances in the traditional manner will not work. The content developed and delivered should be relevant to the context of clients and the stage of the sector. Programmes should be made relevant to the audience—for this it is important to understand the financial behaviours of the target audience.

Holistic approach of financial literacy should be advocated for and adopted by financial service provides. The holistic approach to financial literacy includes: integrating business literacy for helping women to expand business or start new business or enterprises and integrating other key messages on health or gender or life skills (depending on the target population) along with the financial literacy programmes. Few organisations have either been doing this for a long time or have started recently based on the need felt in the field (refer to Box 5.8 for the cases of Mann Deshi Foundation and Sahayog).

Box 5.8 Business literacy training programmes: A step towards holistic approach

Mann Deshi Foundation works for the empowerment of female entrepreneurs in areas ranging from management to accessing markets. Mann Deshi Business School (MDBS) for Rural Women is a programme of the Mann Deshi Foundation that provides training in technical, financial and marketing skills to women with no formal education and to girls who have dropped out of high school, allowing them to start and improve their own small enterprises. MDBS helps to make microfinance available to all women by providing not just business capital but also skills, knowledge and motivation. With the support of Mann Deshi Mahila Ltd. Bank, the business school guarantees suitable loan options to its graduates for seed capital to start micro-enterprises. Most courses are offered in a classroom setting, although some classes are also offered in few villages through the Mobile Business School. A business school was set up in Satara in September 2010 and in Hubli in May 2010. The courses are designed to provide the skills needed to start and run a successful enterprise in the local market. The levels of the courses range from basic to advanced, to meet the varied needs and skill levels of women. Courses last between two and eight weeks, and are offered on at least a two-year rotation, ensuring that the market will be able to absorb new graduates.*

Sahayog Microfinance, an MFI, operating in Madhya Pradesh, Gujarat and Maharashtra has started business literacy training programmes on a pilot basis for its members as an extension of its existing financial literacy programme. From the interactions with clients, Sahayog realised that their members have a fair understanding of the importance of savings, managing money and saving rates, but what they need is visioning of their businesses, the financial future of their families, basics of business and planning, book keeping and how to link with a bank for loans.

Based on this understanding, Sahayog started its 'Badhat business literacy training programme' for its members with both classroom training and follow-up components. The classroom training focuses on topics like the importance of dreaming or visioning, setting goals for the next 3 to 5 years, basic book keeping, components of business and documentation required for business loan. The follow-up consists of gathering data about their current practices, offering need-based mentoring, and handholding to connect them to banks.[†]

Notes: *Extracted from the Financial Literacy Scoping Study Part 2 conducted by M-CRIL for IFC-GIZ.
[†]https://prezi.com/mooev10c5ajl/badhat-sahayog/

There should be continued efforts to address the scalability and sustainability challenges of the financial literacy programmes. Regulators like RBI, MUDRA Bank, IRDA and others should continue to play a major role in driving the financial literacy agenda. Given that financial literacy is a public good, the government should provide some resources for the objective.

There should be a convergence of efforts and resources of all the regulators in the direction of achieving financial literacy goals. The regulators, especially RBI, can instruct or authorise some agencies that can develop a certification programme for all resource persons to ensure quality of trainers. There is a need for convergence beyond only financial services regulators. The Government of India is setting up common service centres across the country and the same can be used along with the FLCs to propogate financial literacy.

One of the stakeholders who get less attention is the trainers and other human resources involved in the programmes. There should be considerable investment that should go into identification, training and remuneration of good quality trainers and coordinators who can drive the programmes in the field effectively. Some of the challenges identified in the previous sections, especially those related to remuneration and additional resources (at the FLCs) and quality of trainers, should get addressed with some funding support.

Implementation of FLCs still has many challenges, and there are gaps in implementation on the ground. There needs to be a discourse from the RBI, followed up by a stringent monitoring and evaluation of the programme. Especially on FLCs, overall there is need for standardisation of resources allocated by banks for FLCs, including HR, infrastructure such as separate office, equipments (projector, computer, etc.), vehicle and petrol expenses, that are required for delivery of financial literacy with desired effectiveness and scale. Accordingly, standard rating system for performance assessment of FLCs should be developed, which will enable recognition of good performance of FLCs. This is important also for motivation of well performing financial literacy counsellors, since they are mostly persons from outside of banking structures.

Banks and FLCs should move beyond conducting mainly camps as they are only effective to create initial sensitisation. After that follow-up is required, especially by encouraging and requiring the financial counsellors to go to the communities for counselling and not just focus on walk-in clients. The FILC model of Swadhar is a good example to follow. Mobile vans, community radio and other multimedia should be used by FLCs.

The financial institutions should integrate financial literacy in their service delivery instead of designing them to be standalone projects which may not be sustainable in the long term. Integration with service delivery will also help in scaling up the projects. Invest in high-quality local trainers. Though technology will play a major role, that cannot substitute for good trainers or good (read relevant) programme.

Experience to date shows that understanding what the clients' context is or their existing abilities (similar to what GIZ has done with CMF in Jaipur) is valuable and organisations should be willing to invest time and resources in that while the programme is being designed. Find teachable moments to impart relevant information. This has the potential to trigger action from the participants. Also, clients have to be taken through different levels of financial literacy depending on the stage they are in. One-size-fits-all approach to content or delivery does not work.

It will be useful to explore alternative forms of financial education. In classroom training methodology, women or participants tend to forget the content. Though videos and games help in reinforcement, it is important to explore more methodologies which can provide repeated dialogue or interaction, which can give confidence to use grievance redressal mechansims or take action.

Sustainability is an issue in scaling up financial literacy. Hence, new sources of funds such as CSR funds of banks that are eligible should be tapped.

Financial literacy should be a process and not just an event or activity. And as such donors or funding agencies should acknowledge and encourage for due processes to be followed and not just focus on the outreach which can help improve sustainability of the programmes.

5.8 CONCLUSION

The focus on financial literacy is here to stay. Though it is not the only solution for all problems associated with financial inclusion, it is a very important demand-side intervention which requires concerted efforts of various stakeholders. In India, with a changing financial landscape and ambitious goals of financial inclusion, efforts of financial literacy have gained more significance and relevance now. However, implementation of financial literacy should be accompanied by a strong ecosystem to deliver services and as such ideas (innovations), people (human resources) and technology (use of mobile phones and social media) should be invested in.

The role of technology, especially mobile phones, should be tapped to make the financial literacy programmes reach to more people. Though sustainability should be a long-term goal, in the short and medium term, there should be continuous donor/funding support from supporting agencies. This is where agencies like SIDBI, NABARD, SROs (partly funded from the membership fees) come into picture. Also, the latest CSR guidelines can be tapped for more support. There are instances of programmes in health, women empowerment, life skills for youth, etc., including financial literacy as one of the components, and this will only increase going forward.

ANNEXURE 5.1
Financial capability index: A framework to understand 'how rural low-income households perceive financial capability'[36]

As a part of GIZ-RFIP project, a local financial capability study was undertaken by GIZ in India with an objective to understand the financial behaviour of low-income people by looking at their own perceptions as users of money and financial services. The study which was conducted in Odisha, Uttarakhand, Rajasthan and Karnataka resulted in identifying 13 abilities (categorised under four areas) that the research participants deemed necessary in order to manage money and use financial services effectively. The approach used in this study has been inspired and guided by the financial capability index (FCI) methodology developed by Microfinance Opportunities (MFO).

The FCI can be used as: *An assessment tool* to measure financial capability across a population to identify priority target groups for a financial education programme, *a design tool* to prioritise content areas for a financial education programme (e.g., saving, budgeting, debt management), and *an evaluation tool* to measure changes in the financial capability of target groups over time in order to help assess effectiveness of an intervention. The four thematic areas and 13 capabilities are as follows.

Thematic areas	Generating, managing and using money	Planning for the future	Using financial services	Using social capital, assets and competencies
What is it about?	How households: generate income, handle money and spend money	How households: invest and plan for the future	How households: use loans, save, use bank accounts and insurance	How people interact within the family and community, households use assets; and gain knowledge and skills
Abilities	1. Ability to generate sufficient income 2. Ability to spend money responsibly/wisely 3. Ability to handle money on a daily basis	4. Ability to plan for the future 5. Ability to invest	6. Ability to use bank accounts 7. Ability to use loans 8. Ability to save 9. Ability to use insurance	10. Ability to coordinate within the family 11. Ability to participate in the community life 12. Ability to use assets 13. Ability to gain knowledge and skills

NOTES AND REFERENCES

1. For more details of the policies and programmes, refer to Chapter 1 of this report.
2. Micro Units Development & Refinance Agency Limited set up as a subsidiary of SIDBI, MUDRA Bank is expected to be responsible for regulating and refinancing all microfinance institutions which are in the business of lending to micro/small business entities engaged in manufacturing, trading and service activities. The bank would partner with state-/regional-level coordinators to provide finance to last mile financier of small/micro business enterprises.
3. Known as Jan Suraksha Schemes—these consist of Pradhan Mantri Jeevan Bima Yojana (PMJY), Pradhan Mantri Suraksha Yojana (PMSY) and Atal Pension Yojana (APY).
4. http://www.jansuraksha.gov.in/Files/Reports/23.09.2015.pdf (accessed on 12 October 2015).
5. http://www.pmjdy.gov.in/Default.aspx (accessed on 12 October 2015).
6. Financial literacy varies significantly among the poor, especially in relation to a financial landscape that is changing rapidly as seen in section 5.1. Even studies conducted through the financial diaries approach have demonstrated that most poor people are good financial managers in familiar environments where a majority of financial transactions occur either informally or involve money stored at home.
7. Cohen, Monique and Candance Nelson. 2011. *Financial Literacy: A Step for Clients towards Financial Inclusion.* 2011 Global Microcredit Summit Commissioned Workshop Paper, 14–17 November 2011, Valladolid, Spain.
8. World Savings Banks Institute. 2010. *Financial Inclusion: How Do We Make It Happen?* http://www.microfinancegateway.org/sites/default/files/mfg-en-paper-financial-inclusion-how-do-we-make-it-happen-oct-2010.pdf (accessed on 3 November 2015).
9. The G20 basic set of financial inclusion indicators.
10. http://timesofindia.indiatimes.com/business/india-business/Insurance-penetration-in-India-at-3-9-per-cent-below-world-average/articleshow/46518607.cms (accessed on 12 October 2015).
11. The seven client protection principles are: appropriate product design and delivery, prevention of over-indebtedness, transparency, responsible pricing, fair and respectful treatment of clients, privacy of client data and mechanisms for complaint resolution.
12. Alliance for Financial Inclusion. 2010. *Policy Note Consumer Protection Leveling the Playing Field in Financial Inclusion.* http://www.afi-global.org/sites/default/files/publications/afi_policynote_consumer-protection_en128.pdf (accessed 3 November 2015).
13. https://responsiblefinanceforum.org/about/the-three-pillars/ (accessed on 12 October 2015).
14. Code of conduct for microfinance institutions in India.
15. Refer to the latest circular General Circular No. 21/2014 of the Ministry of Corporate Affairs.
16. Can Information Provision Trigger Positive Developmental Outcomes? A Study of an Information Dissemination Tool in a Multi-state Micro Finance Organisation in India.
17. *Financial Education for SEWA Bank Members: A Facilitator's Guide.* December 2013. http://www.coady.stfx.ca/tinroom/assets/file/SEWA_Financial_Literacy_Manual.pdf (accessed on 13 October 2015).

18. Financial Inclusion & Financial Literacy: BI OECD SEMINAR—Roundtable on the updates on Financial education and Inclusion programmes in India, 2011. Speech by Dr Deepali Pant Joshi. http://www.oecd.org/finance/financial-education/48303408.pdf (accessed on 13 October 2015).

19. https://rbi.org.in/FinancialEducation/Home.aspx (accessed on 13 October 2015).

20. A Working Group constituted by Reserve Bank to suggest measures for assisting distressed farmers (Chairman: Shri S.S. Johl) had also suggested that financial and livelihood counselling are important for increasing viability of credit. Another working group to examine the procedures and processes of agricultural loans (Chairman: Shri C.P. Swarnakar), appointed by Reserve Bank, had recommended in its report (April 2007) that banks should actively consider opening of counselling centres, either individually or with pooled resources, for credit and technological counselling. This would make the farmers aware of their rights and responsibilities to a great extent.

21. www.ismw.org.in (accessed on 13 October 2015).

22. Advancing National Strategies for Financial Education: A Joint Publication by Russia's G20 Presidency and the OECD. http://www.oecd.org/finance/financial-education/G20_OECD_NSFinancialEducation.pdf (accessed on 13 October 2015).

23. https://rbi.org.in/FinancialEducation/Home.aspx (accessed on 13 October 2015).

24. Sourced from SEBI's website and its annual reports.

25. IRDA. 2015. *Annual Report 2013–14.* https://www.irda.gov.in/ADMINCMS/cms/frmGeneral_NoYearList.aspx?DF=AR&mid=11.1 (accessed on 13 October 2015).

26. Information provided by NABARD on its financial inclusion activities.

27. FIF for meeting the cost of developmental and promotional interventions and FITF for meeting the cost of technology adoption for financial inclusion.

28. Common Service Centres (CSCs) are established as per the National e-Governance Plan launched by Government of India in 2006. They already have existing infrastructure including ICT enabled kiosks and CSCs are already into financial inclusion as BCs/BCAs.

29. An M-CRIL study for IFC and GIZ titled 'Financial Awareness Scoping Initiative' from August 2012 identifies 63 institutions across India that were involved in various types of financial literacy programmes in India.

30. Internal Impact Assessment study of the programme.

31. Wealth Master Programme: Master trainers identified and trained 'Wealth Masters' who were experienced villagers who could act as local champions to encourage participation in the financial education programmes; Customer Connect Programme (CCP): Master trainers conducted programmes in IRCS' villages of operation to both customers and potential customers in groups of 10 to 25 largely made up of women; and School Programme (SP): Master trainers conducted programmes for children at school to instil financial awareness and to indirectly influence their parents.

32. http://www.sbi.co.in/portal/web/agriculture-banking/financial-inclusion (accessed on 14 October 2015).

33. http://www.unionbankofindia.co.in/RABD_Finance_FLCC.aspx (accessed on 14 October 2015).

34. NGOBOX. 2015. *CSR in Banking Sector in India: An Analysis of Data-sheet of Projects and Partners in FY 2014–15.* www.ngobox.org (accessed on 14 October 2015).

35. Extracted from the dipstick study on FLCs Status, Constraints and Way Forward in Four States of Bihar, Uttar Pradesh, Madhya Pradesh and Odisha conducted by Access Assist in 2015 as part of Poorest States Inclusive Growth (PSIG) programme.

36. Bickel, Jonna, and Thomas Mehwald. 2014. *An Exploration in How Rural Low-Income Households Perceive Financial Capability. GIZ-Nabard Rural Financial Institutions Programme.* New Delhi: GIZ-Rural Financial Institutions Programme.

Strengthening responsible finance for the excluded

The landscape of financial services for the excluded and the poor has witnessed enormous changes in the past year. While existing arrangements in the form of MFIs and SBLP continued their journey towards being more 'responsible lenders', new arrangements in the form of MUDRA Bank, SFBs, PMJDY and its umbrella schemes of insurance and pension have come into existence. These new institutional and policy arrangements are designed to ensure universal financial inclusion and fulfilling the promise of 'funding the unfunded'. The institutional arrangements for financial inclusion of the poor in its true sense are seeing a Hegelian 'synthesis' moment. The policy stance in India after independence started with using existing financial institutions (cooperatives and banks) in extending rural finance to the poor based on the premise that poverty is mainly rural. The suboptimal achievements of this approach became evident by 1990, and it was realised that the formal sector banks may not be the best channel for last mile delivery of financial services. The alternative strategy of microfinance and specialised institutions for rural outreach (RRBs) heralded the next phase, where the role of banks shifted more towards wholesale lending from last mile delivery. The current synthesis phase riding on past experiences and technological advances is seeing a blend of the two past approaches. Banks are extending their outreach under PMJDY, riding primarily on the back of BCs, and MFIs are getting converted as banks—both universal and SFBs. While these changes will have an impact in future, currently the microfinance models (MFIs as well as SBLP) continue to dominate poverty lending.

How this blended strategy impacts financial inclusion of the excluded and the poor is a thing of future, but the new institutional arrangements have the potential to induce momentous changes to the future of financial inclusion landscape. As these, especially SFBs, overlap with microfinance, and will impact current state of microfinance in India, it is useful to examine them, as also suggest measures to ensure that they remain true to the spirit of 'responsible finance'. This concluding chapter analyses the key new initiatives (SFBs and MUDRA) from this perspective, identifies possible issues in their future journey, and suggests measures to ensure they remain on course for making inclusion of all a reality. The journey of MFIs and SBLP towards responsible finance has been detailed in previous chapters, and building on that theme, *this chapter presents future actions for policy formulation, and for institutions to strengthen their mission of responsible finance.*

6.1 SFBs: MORPHED MFIs OR MAINSTREAM BANKING?

6.1.1 RRBs: Initial SFBs and their gradual drift

The idea of SFB catering to the excluded sections of the society is not new. Though the draft guidelines on SFBs released by the RBI on 17 July 2014[1] traced the origin of the concept to Narasimham Committee (1995)[2] and Rajan Committee (2009),[3] it can be said to have originated with the advent of RRBs in 1975. RRBs were intended to marry the financial management practices of commercial banks and local touch of cooperatives to serve the rural poor. Commercial banks sponsored RRBs to provide the financial and managerial strength, while local recruitment was supposed to provide the local touch. Their financial inclusion focus was ensured through specifying that their loans should be exclusively for the 'target group', defined as small and marginal farmers, landless labourers, rural artisans and other weaker sections of the society.

However, the problems started quite early, with infirmities in lending process leading to unviable operations. The initial diagnosis was that they should be allowed to lend to other than the assigned target group, to cross subsidise, and as a result initially RRBs were allowed to lend 60% of their incremental lending to non-target group. Later, further diluting the specific population focus, the guidelines require RRBs to follow priority sector guidelines applicable to commercial banks with two caveats. First, they have a higher quota for priority sector loans (60% of outstanding advances). Second, RRBs need to have at least 15% of the total advances for the weaker sections of the society.[4] Operationally, the extension of salaries applicable in their sponsor banks to RRB staff and extension of recruitment catchment area to state hiked their operating costs as also led to losing of the local touch.

Various committees deliberated the complexity of issues facing RRBs, even as the relaxation of lending norms did not help the cause of viability. Their weak financial condition required financial support as part of comprehensive restructuring programme. The first process started in 1994 continued until 1999–2000, and covered 187 RRBs with aggregate financial support of ₹2,188 crore from shareholders. The Vyas committee,[5] while reviewing the performance of RRBs noted that though 156 out of 196 reported operational profit during 2002–03, 57% of total income came from interest on investments, as against 37% from lending operations. It observed that the turnaround is based on treasury operations rather than lending operations, which was the main

purpose for their establishment. The committee recommended merger of RRBs to improve their viability, and to de-risk them from the formerly limited area of operation to a district. The consolidation process was initiated in the year 2005 as an off-shoot of the Vyas Committee recommendations. The first phase of amalgamation was initiated sponsor bank-wise within a state in 2005, and the second phase was across the sponsor banks within a state in 2012. As a result, in place of 196 RRBs, there were 64 RRBs as on 31 March 2013.[6] In between, based on the recommendations of the Chakrabarty Committee (2010), 37 RRBs have been provided further recapitalisation support of ₹2,015 crore.

While riding on the two doses of recapitalisation, economies of scale through larger operational area and dilution of the lending restrictions, the profitability position of the RRBs has improved over the years (as on 31 March 2013, 63 out of 64 RRBs reported profits), their performance in lending to the excluded merits attention. The performance of RRBs over the years in terms of number of rural branches, lending performance under small borrowal accounts[7] and priority sector is presented in Table 6.1.

The indicators shows that *while RRBs have gone much beyond the minimum stipulated for priority sector lending, their loan sizes have moved upwards.* Loan accounts below ₹25,000, which can be compared with MFI loans, fell from 50% in 2010 to 32% in 2014. The share of these loans in total portfolio was a mere 6.8% in 2014. The drift towards higher-sized loans, seen with higher compliance under priority sector loans, shows that 'activity' inclusion is not sufficient for covering the excluded. On similar yardstick, as expected, commercial banks perform worse than RRBs. Loans below ₹25,000 accounted

Table 6.1 Performance of RRBs over the years (2010–14)

	2009–10	2010–11	2011–12	2012–13	2013–14
No. of rural branches	11,629	11,778	12,263	12,850	13,609
No of loan accounts					
No. of loan accounts with loan amounts less than ₹25,000 in million (% to total accounts)	9.42 (50.54)	9.88 (49.28)	9.33 (44.99)	7.77 (38.32)	6.89 (32.07)
No. of loan accounts with loan amounts ₹25,000 to ₹200,000 in million (% to total accounts)	8.59 (46.15)	9.34 (46.5)	10.29 (49.63)	10.95 (53.98)	12.60 (59)
Priority sector advances as % to total advances	82.2	83.5	80	86	

Source: Trend and Progress of Banking in India, Banking & Statistical Returns.

for 23.5% of total accounts and 0.5% of portfolio share in case of commercial banks in 2014. Over the years if this trend continues, RRBs loan book will start resembling that of commercial banks.

6.1.2 The idea of SFB is born

Rajan Committee[8] first broached the idea of SFBs in 2009. It cited the need to move away from 'bank-led, public sector dominated, mandate ridden … strategy for inclusion' to entrusting the task to motivated financiers with low cost structure who see the poor as profitable business. It recommended entry of well governed, private and deposit-taking institutions termed as 'small finance banks'. It sought to lower their geographical risk through higher capital adequacy, restrictions on related party transactions and lower exposure norms. The recommended SFBs (sometimes referred as small banks) were to have geographical limits but no cap on loan size was recommended. Alluding perhaps to RRBs, the committee observed that the past experiments in small banks have not been a success on account of excessive political interference, weak governance and inability of the regulator to take prompt remedial actions. The key success features of SFBs were listed as local, low cost, private and decentralised decision making.

The idea was again revived in the discussion paper on Indian banking released by the RBI in 2013.[9] The paper noted that while the past experience in the form of RRBs, Local Area Bank (LAB) and Urban Cooperative Bank (UCB) had not been favourable, there was a case for small banks, as global experience suggested that small banks had the potential to facilitate financial inclusion. The discussion paper suggested overcoming risks inherent in the business model of small banks through calibrating prudential regulations, faster resolution of deposit insurance claims, freedom to decide interest rates and reliance on technology to lower costs. More importantly, based on global experience of higher cases of failure of small banks, it cautioned that introduction of local banks would require greater tolerance of failures from the political economy.

Both Rajan Committee and the RBI discussion paper used the terms 'small finance banks' and 'small banks' interchangeably. However, while no loan size restriction was suggested but since both reports talked about area limitation, it can be inferred that 'small' was used to signify limited area of operation.

Subsequent to this, RBI released draft guidelines for licensing of SFBs in July 2014,[10] and based on comments from the public and stakeholders, released the final set of guidelines in November 2014,[11] inviting applications from the prospective applicants. Table 6.2 summarises the key aspects of draft and final guidelines relating to financial inclusion.

The focus of these guidelines was on NBFC-MFIs as not only NBFC-MFIs were listed as eligible applicants but concessions in the form of promoter's initial equity contribution were considered for them. The key difference between the draft guidelines and final set of guidelines related to doing away with any area limitation. 'Smallness' in the final set of guidelines only related to having 50% of loans below ₹25 lakh. The regulatory intent in converting NBFC-MFIs as SFBs was validated with the issue of licenses on 16th September 2015[12]—8 out of 10 selected institutions were NBFC-MFIs.

Table 6.2 Draft and final guidelines for licensing of SFBs

	Draft guidelines	Final guidelines
Objectives	(i) Provision of savings vehicles to underserved and unserved sections of the population, (ii) supply of credit to small business units, small farmers, micro and small industries, and other unorganised sector entities	Same
Operational model	High technology, low cost	Same
Area of operation	Restricted to contiguous districts in a homogenous cluster of States/Union Territories so that the bank has the 'local feel'	No area restriction
Minimum paid up capital	₹100 crore	Same
Loan conditions	At least 50% of its loan portfolio should constitute loans and advances of size up to ₹25 lakh	Same, with the following added: 75% of its Adjusted Net Bank Credit (ANBC) to the sectors eligible for classification as priority sector lending (PSL) by the Reserve Bank.
Maximum loan size	15% of capital funds	10% of capital funds

Source: Prepared by the Author based on RBI guidelines.

While the real intent of this move will be seen in years to come, it seems the action stems more from limiting microfinance sector risks and regulatory comfort with 'banks' rather than furthering the cause of financial inclusion of the poor and the excluded.

However, if the transformed NBFC-MFIs stick to their current clientele, the impact of this on the responsible finance agenda of the microfinance sector will be enormous. In terms of size impact, if the portfolio of Bandhan, which has already commenced operations as a universal bank, and the eight NBFC-MFIs who have received SFB license is removed from the total portfolio of NBFC-MFIs as on 31 March 2015, the total loan book shrinks by half. Thus half of the sector has moved to operating as banks!

6.1.3 Positive impact of SFBs on financial inclusion agenda

The final guidelines learning from past experience of RRBs and LABs avoid any area limitation for the operations of SFBs. *This move will not only allow multistate NBFC-MFIs to build on their existing operations, but also mitigate the concentration risk.* As observed by Rajan Committee, private ownership takes away the risk of capture of political economy and weak governance. The transformation as SFBs will help NBFC-MFIs move away from their sole dependence on debt funds from banks, which in past cases of unfavourable events led to huge liquidity crises. *The ability to mobilise deposits from public will not only lower the cost of funds but also better their liquidity position and asset-liability match.*

Lowering of cost of funds should lead to lower interest rate for clients, and also achieve the political economy objective. *Microfinance in its true sense can take place with SFBs. Continued insistence on bankled model has reduced NBFC-MFIs product offering to only credit.* The SFBs can offer full range of services directly—savings, loans and remittances, and continue to offer third-party insurance and pension products to complete the product suite. As the SFBs will not have the restrictions of loan size and tenure, or classification between production and consumption loans, they can offer various products according to the needs of clients.

The customer seems to win with lower interest rate on loans and the complete range of financial services

from one source. Coverage of deposits with SFBs under deposit protection scheme of Deposit Insurance and Credit Guarantee Corporation (DICGC) is beneficial to clients and takes away the security risks, which they face currently. The higher level of regulation due to their new identity as banks, mobilising public deposits adds to the systemic stability side of responsible finance framework. *The concern expressed with regard to high growth, and the need for patient capital that is comfortable with lower returns, has also been possibly met with this move.* The profitability ratios for banks in India are much lower than MFIs, and if SFBs follow that trend, investors wanting annual return of ~20% will have to exit. Overall, if the SFBs stick to the population segment they serve now as NBFC-MFIs, it will be a win-win situation for all stakeholders.

6.1.4 What are the pitfalls? Will it lead to drift?

Along with the win-win paradigm, there are possible risks. The NBFC-MFIs granted in-principle approval for transforming as SFB currently serve rural households with annual income of less than ₹60,000, and urban households with annual income of less than ₹120,000.[13] These income levels are marginally above the national poverty line suggested by Rangarajan Committee in July 2015.[14] On the other hand, the loan size in the sector is low at ₹16,327. The existing loan portfolios of these NBFC-MFIs can said to be truly poverty lending in terms of household income classification.

The SFB guidelines will allow the transformed NBFC-MFIs not to be limited by the household income criteria. The limitation that 50% of loan book should be of loans below ₹25 lakh seems to be too liberal. Even if the loan sizes go to 25% of the cap of ₹25 lakh, the nature and profile of operations will change from microfinance for the excluded to enterprise financing. Going further, the guidelines permit them to lend without any limit for remaining 50% of the loan book subject to capital exposure norm. This has the potential to lead to drift of these transformed NBFC-MFIs from their existing segment. *The history of RRBs shows that in pursuit of viability, their loan sizes have moved upwards, and commercial banks' loan sizes also prove a similar point.* Despite numerous policy directives to lend to weaker sections, loans below ₹25,000 constitute mere 0.5% of their portfolio, and the share of small borrowal accounts is 8.5%.

Against this, the share of loans above ₹100 crore is a high 32.8%. It is seen the world over that in pursuit of viability based on higher productivity, loan sizes tend to move upwards. As discussed in Chapter 3, MFIs are also going through a similar phase of increasing loan sizes within the prescribed cap. After decades of public policy push for poverty lending, the performance analysis of scheduled commercial banks shows that the operational dynamics and ethos of banks are not suited for poverty lending. Lending small amounts without the assurance of collateral requires deep understanding of client's household dynamics, frequent last mile contact and regular collection of low value repayments. Yet, with the new liberal loan book regime, to expect the transformed NBFC-MFIs to stick to their existing segment seems against available experience.

It is nobody's case to argue that inclusion of the segment requiring higher loan sizes is less important, but the point is that it should not come at the cost of poorer sections of the society. The financial access divide is more pronounced at the bottom of the population pyramid (AIDIS 2002 shows that 8.7% rural households with asset holding of less than ₹60,000 had access to institutional credit as against 26.7% for households having assets of ₹0.8 million and above).

The performance analysis of RRBs also shows that activity-based inclusion through priority sector guidelines does not provide protection against dilution of poverty focus in lending. The other factor that adds to the possibility of upward drift is the regulatory concern on safety of public deposits. As SFBs will largely fund their loan assets through public deposits, it seems doubtful that the RBI will allow public deposits to be deployed in unsecured small loans beyond a limit. Hopefully, the transformed NBFC-MFIs will resist the opportunity to drift upwards in their outreach, continuing to serve the similar segment of clients. RBI will put in place some adequate mechanism to ensure this. While this is only a hope, on the ground, the move seems to be aimed more at financial deepening than retaining the poverty focus of microfinance.

Considering a positive scenario, wherein the transformed NBFC-MFIs remain committed to serving the same client base, gives rise to the apprehension of unequal competition for other players. The operational areas of NBFC-MFIs, which will

transform as SFBs, and the other NBFC-MFIs overlap, and cater to same/similar clients. SFBs in future should be able to offer diverse financial services at a much lower cost, while NBFC-MFIs will continue to be credit only organisations, and their lending rates will be higher. This will possibly lead to unequal competition as clients will prefer to choose SFBs over NBFC-MFIs. Faced with this competition, NBFC-MFIs can lose existing clients, and clients not able to switch to SFBs may feel discriminated. The Rajan Committee said,

> With the creation of a small bank category, that operate at a local level—MFIs, community based organisations etc. would have the choice of deciding their institutional structures. Those that will like to remain purely credit-based institutions can chose to remain as NBFCs—as most MFIs today are, or Section 25 companies.

The question is not of choice as most of the NBFC-MFIs had applied for SFB license and it is pragmatic that all could not be considered for approval, but nonetheless it is likely to create conditions loaded against NBFC-MFIs. Regulation seems to have missed this crucial aspect, and if this happens, the only hope for remaining NBFC-MFIs will be to wait for next round of licensing.

Both possibilities of SFB's future direction—upward drift or sticking to the same segment—have implications for financial inclusion of the excluded, and need to be carefully considered. As NBFC-MFIs transform as SFBs, the policy should ensure that they do not start mirroring existing banks. For this, it is suggested that the *performance metrics of SFBs should incorporate best practices in social performance of MFIs.* The key aspects, which should form part of performance, relate to poverty outreach, client protection principles and social goals in business planning. Ignoring these aspects and focusing only on higher target under priority sector lending has the potential to cause 'mission drift'.

6.2 MUDRA: FUNDING THE UNFUNDED OR SUBSTITUTING EXISTING ARRANGEMENTS?

Before the discussions could settle on the discussion paper on banking brought out by RBI, the Union Finance Minister in his annual budget speech of 2014 announced the setting up of MUDRA Bank.

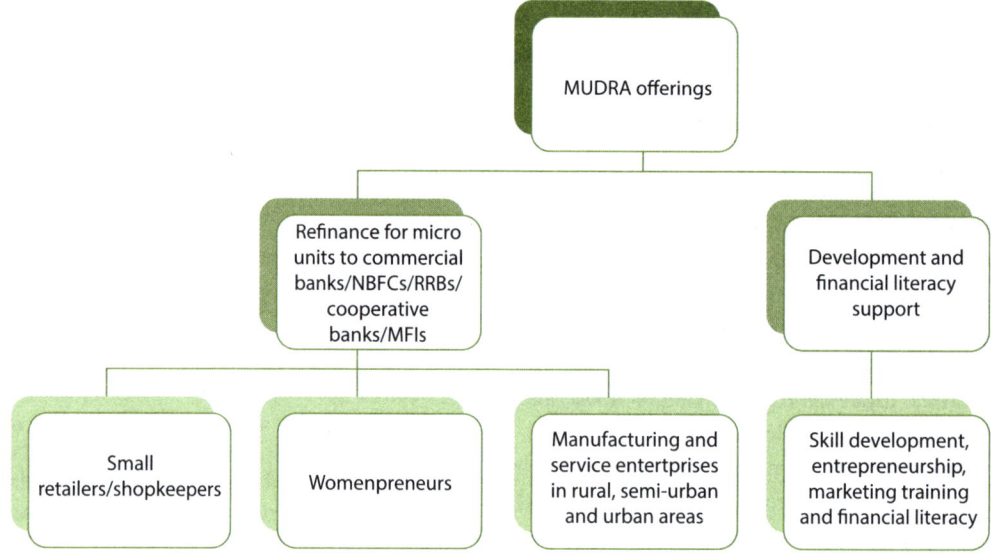

Figure 6.1 Functions of MUDRA

Source: Website of MUDRA http://www.mudra.org.in/offerings.php

The budget speech also described the proposed functions by saying:

> While large corporate and business entities have a role to play, this has to be complemented by informal sector enterprises which generate maximum employment. There are some 5.77 crore small business units, mostly individual proprietorship, which run small manufacturing, trading or service businesses. 62% of these are owned by SC/ST/OBC. These bottom-of-the-pyramid, hard-working entrepreneurs find it difficult, if not impossible, to access formal systems of credit. I, therefore, propose to create a Micro Units Development Refinance Agency (MUDRA) Bank, with a corpus of ₹20,000 crore, and credit guarantee corpus of ₹3,000 crore. MUDRA Bank will refinance Micro-Finance Institutions through a Pradhan Mantri Mudra Yojana. In lending, priority will be given to SC/ST enterprises. Just as we are banking the un-banked, we are also funding the un-funded.

The budget speech made it look like another financing agency for the MFIs with focus on micro-enterprises and SC/ST clients. The press release of 1 March 2015 expanded the scope of the MUDRA Bank. According to the press release, MUDRA Bank will cover SBLP as well as MFIs organised as NBFCs and NGOs. Significantly, it added other critical aspects to its work area namely (i) regulation, (ii) accreditation/rating, (iii) laying down responsible finance practices, (iv) technology solutions and (v) credit guarantee scheme.

The way MUDRA has evolved since its establishment shows that it has added various functions ranging from refinance to capacity building (Figure 6.1).

Even within funding, it started with MFIs but now covers the entire spectrum of banking including commercial banks. As of now, MUDRA has three products—Shishu that refinances loan sizes up to ₹50,000; Kishor covering loans from ₹50,000 to ₹5 lakh; and Tarun covering loans from ₹5 lakh to ₹10 lakh. The refinance assistance to various agencies is provided at differential rates (Table 6.3).

By end of September 2015, MUDRA had sanctioned around ₹50 crore to three commercial bank and ₹475 crore to 14 NBFC-MFIs.

Development and financial literacy have been added to its functions and it is learnt that MUDRA might have supervisory and regulatory functions as well. The lack of clarity in functions is evident as while regulation is still at concept stage, the MUDRA website lists—supervision of MFIs and accreditation/rating of MFIs as part of its roles and responsibilities.[15]

Table 6.3 MUDRA refinance: Rates of interest

Agency	Refinance rate
Commercial banks	Cost of funds + 0.75%
NBFCs/NBFC-MFIs	10–12.25% based on rating/grading
Cooperatives and RRBs	Cost of funds + 0.75%

Financial literacy function has not seen any action till date and though the concept of regulation is still evolving, it is obvious that the only regulatory space to be filled in by MUDRA is regulation of NGO-MFIs.

6.2.1 What should MUDRA do to promote responsible finance for the poor

The existing refinance schemes of MUDRA give an impression that on the credit side, it is aimed more at the space beyond MFIs, as MFIs loan size do not go beyond ₹50,000. Thus, the loan sizes of MFIs fit only under one product—Shishu, which covers loans up to ₹50,000. However, the pattern of assistance gives a different picture, as NBFC-MFIs have accounted for the lion's share of MUDRA refinance. It is not clear as to whether it is due to SIDBI's comfort based on past experience with MFIs or just an initial step, which will get broad based as it expands. *The rationale for MUDRA on the funding side appears weak. Commercial banks, including RRBs, have no shortage of funds, and the problem in financing the micro-enterprise segment, which requires loans up to ₹10 lakh, lies somewhere else.* This space of enterprise financing has been challenging to banks on account of information asymmetry—lack of reliable information, business diversity and often lack of traditional collateral. This is reflected in the progress under Prime Minister Mudra Yojana (PMMY) consisting of all three schemes—Shishu, Kishore and Tarun. As on 21 September 2015, scheduled commercial banks have disbursed ₹23,504 crore (34.75 million loan accounts[16]) under PMYY, while MUDRA's support is negligible at ₹50 crore. In the case of NBFC-MFIs, the product fit with MUDRA refinance window is narrow on account of their existing loan size and with the formation of Bandhan as full scale bank and other eight MFIs as SFBs, the remaining NBFC-MFIs will have a surfeit of funds. Bandhan and these eight SFB in-principle approval holder MFIs account for 50% of market share, and in near future they will not be eligible to borrow from other banks. Devoid of this market, banks have to restrict themselves to the remaining MFIs to meet part of their priority sector targets.

Further, the funding corpus of MUDRA comes out of priority sector shortfall of commercial banks, hitherto deposited with Rural Infrastructure Development Fund (RIDF) with NABARD. RIDF corpus has been around ₹20,000 crore annually, and it forms mere 1% of the total annual target of priority sector credit. RIDF is mainly used for creating infrastructure in the form of roads, warehouses and bridges in rural areas. It is difficult to rationalise taking away this corpus from the much-needed work of building rural infrastructure and channelling it to institutions, which do not have shortage of funds. The only advantage of MUDRA refinancing MFIs is that it can lower interest rates, as its refinance is cheaper than other source of funds.

MUDRA can serve the cause of funding the unfunded better, if its focus shifts from credit, to building a supportive ecosystem through its work in regulation, credit guarantee mechanism and financial education. The problems of NGO-MFIs have been discussed in Chapters 2 and 3. While over the years, their market share has gone down to less than 10%, their contribution in serving the poor and the excluded should not be left to wither away. At present, bankers do not seem to have confidence in funding them and the rejection of the draft microfinance bill in 2014 has further accentuated their predicament. Starved of funding and devoid of being covered under any national regulatory framework, NGO-MFIs face an uncertain future. Wilting under the situation, quite a few have started moving over to being banking correspondents. MUDRA can fill this regulatory vacuum by being the regulator for NGO-MFIs, which in turn will inspire the confidence of bankers. If the RBI considers NGOs as not the right legal form for financial intermediation, MUDRA should work on providing a framework for their graduation to NBFCs.

It is heartening to note that MUDRA Bank also lists evolving rating norms for MFIs, as also the principles of responsible finance. By doing so, it will fill another critical void in the sector. The rating of MFIs in India has been left to mainstream rating agencies with focus on financials, and does not reflect the international best practices. Specialised microfinance rating agencies work on a globally accepted rating framework, which accords due importance to field verification, client protection issues and other aspects of responsible finance, like poverty outreach and staff welfare. If MUDRA can take the lead in this space, it will pave the way for more responsible microfinance.

The critical role of financial education in ensuring demand driven financial services, and responsible behaviour of customers can hardly be overemphasised.

As brought out in Chapter 5, despite many isolated/institution specific initiatives and a few sector-level initiatives like Financial Literacy and Counselling Centres (FLCC), integration of financial education in service delivery is yet to happen. MFIs operating under margin cap find it hard to spend a large chunk of their budget on financial education, and banks generally do not have the mindset to impart financial education to the poor. MUDRA's undivided attention and financial support can go a long way ensuring that financial education goes hand in hand with service delivery. In the absence of robust and timely financial literacy inputs, the huge numbers generated under PMJDY and its associated schemes of insurance and pension will cease to translate into meaningful financial inclusion of the excluded. According to the progress report on PMJDY website, by 16th September 2015, a total of 18.34 crore accounts have been opened, of which 42% are zero balance accounts.[17] MicroSave's study of PMJDY found that 86% of account holders mentioned this being their first account. The high number of first-time account holders, seen with nearly half of the accounts having zero balance point to an urgent need for financial education of the newly included. *World Bank's Global Financial Development Report 2014* aptly sums up the point by saying 'the objective should not be financial inclusion for inclusion's sake. For example, creating millions of bank accounts that end up lying dormant has little impact'.

6.3 MICROFINANCE (MFIs AND SBLP): POLICY AND OPERATIONAL IMPERATIVES

Microfinance in the form of MFIs and SBLP has a combined outreach of around 90 million loan clients—this excludes SHGs with only savings. The enormity of their contribution in ensuring financial inclusion of the excluded becomes more evident when compared with similar segment outreach of banks. After years of policy push, the number of loan accounts with credit facility less than ₹25,000 (which is comparable with microfinance) for all scheduled commercial banks is 32.56 million.[18] If the accounts are equated with clients, it shows that bank's outreach is one-third of microfinance outreach. The advantage of microfinance over similar-sized lending by banks goes beyond outreach, and includes their constant touch with clients, smaller loan repayment frequency, doorstep delivery and collection. The poverty outreach of microfinance programmes is also higher than the banks.[19] In this context, it is imperative that microfinance policy and operations build on the gains made so far in ensuring universal financial inclusion of the excluded. The review of both MFIs and SBLP in previous chapters shows that the journey of both strands of microfinance towards responsible finance needs to be further strengthened. This requires action on both policy and operational fronts.

MFIs are going through a very challenging time. On one hand, the regulations are being gradually eased to allow them more operational flexibility, while on the other they have to gear up to face the competition from SFBs in near future. The analysis of the current phase of growth shows that risks similar to past are emerging again. These challenges can be met by being more 'client-centric' and retaining the edge through deeper relationship with the client. This is an opportune time to move from seeing responsible finance from a compliance angle and integrating it in the institutional DNA. Policy measures also need to support their move by placing higher emphasis on double bottom line performance.

The SBLP movement has also come a long way from the pilot project in 1992. Over the years, signs of weaknesses in the form of stagnant growth, rising NPAs, lack of product innovation and varying forms of account keeping have come to the fore. NABARD as the promoter of SBLP needs to take immediate steps on few critical areas, like the quality of SHPAs and computerisation of SHG records, to ensure that the slippage seen in past few years is arrested. Simultaneously, it needs to work on ways to revitalise the movement through design changes.

6.3.1 Policy issues to promote responsible microfinance

6.3.1.1 Reporting on responsible finance parameters (MFIs and SBLP)

At present, the data reported across both channels is mainly operational and financial. MFIN and Sa-Dhan report data for their member MFIs on operational aspects, like number of clients served, loan portfolio, number of branches and number of staff, as well as financial performance ratios. MFIN has gone a step ahead and started reporting more granular data for operational areas in terms of state, as well as reporting it quarterly. However, despite being a double bottom line industry, no data on key social aspects like social goals, poverty outreach, policy on balancing financial and social performance, client-level outcomes and product diversity is captured. In the absence of sector-level data, it becomes difficult to assess the double bottom line performance of MFIs, and the wider community does not see much of the good work being done by the sector. Reporting by individual institutions does not have the credibility that comes with reporting by industry association. As discussed in Chapter 3, despite the impressive work done by the MFIs, voices of criticism keep coming in the news. *Credible reporting, by industry associations, of social performance data will go a long way in spreading the social performance of MFIs. This has become doable, as the industry has been able to evolve globally accepted social performance metrics.* However, to be credible, it also needs to be checked by external agencies. Self-reported data on social aspects is better than no data, but leaves a lot of questions on validity. MFIN has started to move in this direction by seeking to empanel agencies to verify its members' compliance on UCoC. It will be useful to agree on a common set of social data protocol, and tag checks on it along with assessment of UCoC. By doing so, external assessments can provide comprehensive and validated data on compliance in addition to other aspects of social performance.

The reporting performance of SBLP on social parameters is non-existent, and even under operational information lags far behind MFIs, much of it is explained by the informal nature of SHGs, operational flexibility to groups and the diverse range of stakeholders. As the digitisation programme is being piloted and likely to be scaled up soon, the reporting parameters can be added now. Being a pan India programme based on common mission and objectives, SBLP reporting on social goals has to be different than MFIs. Industry experts believe that the key things which need to be captured are poverty outreach and client-level outcomes. To keep it simple in line with the nature of the programme, SBLP can start with recording PPI scores of each group member to reflect the poverty outreach. The analysis of PPI scores over time will provide a reasonably accurate picture of client-level outcome. SBLP also needs to report more granular data on group-level savings and loan proportion, range of

loans within a group to see if equity is being maintained, subsidy provided, if any, the loan tenure and the nature of facility—cash credit or term loan. The data being reported as of now is limited to state and bank level, and broadly consists of savings and credit linked SHGs, savings and loan outstanding amount and NPAs. This level of reporting misses a lot of detail, which if captured, could shed light on the performance of SBLP and help in revitalising the programme.

6.3.1.2 Credit bureau: Need to integrate CIBIL and microfinance bureaus (MFIs and SBLP)

Protecting vulnerable clients from over-indebtedness is one of the key principles of responsible finance. RBI regulations for NBFC-MFIs accord a central place to this by prescribing loan size, the number of MFIs that can lend to one client, repayment tenure, and mandatory check of credit bureau record. MFIs have adopted mandatory credit bureau checks. But as discussed in Chapter 3, the current practice of client data being in silos across the microfinance focused credit bureaus (Equifax and CRIF High Mark) and credit bureau being used by banks [Credit Information Bureau (India) Limited (CIBIL)] poses risks to banks as well as MFIs. Lending by banks under small borrowal accounts category is to a segment, which overlaps with the microfinance institution's clientele. Puri Committee (2013) constituted by the RBI to look into credit information services has rightly recommended integration of reporting formats across institutions to harmonise data being reported to credit bureaus. It has suggested use of CIBIL format for consumer and commercial segment, and use of High Mark format for MFI segment. Not much progress has been made since then. As such besides uniform reporting by all financial institutions, *it is necessary that both segment credit bureaus integrate their data to provide a holistic view of client's credit history.* As discussed in Chapter 3, customer identification is a key challenge in lending to low-income clients, who often lack proper identification documents. The progress in the issue of Aadhaar and adoption of Aadhaar by MFIN is a positive step, and banks also need to follow a similar strategy.

For MFIs, an even bigger risk is the non-availability of SHG data in credit bureau. The concept of SHGs was based on tracking of loans at group level, and allowing groups the flexibility to manage their internal dynamics. However, the nearly complete overlap of SHG clients with MFI clients necessitates that microfinance bureaus capture individual member record of SHGs. In the absence of this, the responsibility of both SHG programme and MFIs towards preventing over-indebtedness of their clients is severely compromised. It is heartening that during this year a pilot has been started by NABARD to digitise the SHG records, including individual member details in two districts. The Puri Committee had also observed that banks must furnish member-wise information within a period of 18 months to CICs. However, as discussed in Chapter 4, the task of capturing nearly 60 million member-level records is humongous, and has to face the additional hurdles of sifting through different formats of accounting, missing records in many cases and tracking defunct groups. The task is enormous but needs to be accorded priority by NABARD, banks and RBI, so that it is completed in a time bound manner.

6.3.1.3 Requirement of domestic patient capital to temper growth (MFIs)

The MFI sector is going through a surge, recording 60% annual growth in 2014–15, and its associated risks in terms of saturated markets, multiple loans and incidences of distress have been discussed in Chapter 3. The situation seems quite similar to pre-2010, with renewed interest of investors and lenders. Sector experts believe that the return expectations of private equity investors necessitate MFIs to take the high growth path. It also leads to expanding their operations in areas with existing high levels of microfinance activity, as these areas provide ready markets. In this situation, leaving the blame at the door of MFIs is not fair, and policy has to take major part of the blame. Even after two decades or so, there are no substantial sources of publicly owned domestic debt. NABARD's Microfinance Development Equity Fund (MFDEF) has been closed. The activities financed under MFDEF are being covered under FIF, and the commitments as on 31 March 2013 have been taken over by FIF during the year 2013–14. Even before being merged with FIF, the support from it was a small proportion of sector's need.[20] SIDBI is the only existing source of publicly owned domestic equity for MFIs. The IMEF was set up in 2011–12 with SIDBI by the Government of India, with the primary objective of providing equity and quasi-equity to smaller MFIs. As at end of March 2015, SIDBI has committed an amount

of ₹162.25 crore to 56 MFIs under the scheme. NABARD's MFDEF was also aimed at smaller MFIs. As against this, the NBFC-MFIs had a portfolio of ₹40,138 crore as on 31 March 2015. Assuming a conservative debt to equity ratio of 1:5, the equity requirement of the sector is of the order of ₹8,000 crore. The figure will come down substantially with the graduation of Bandhan as a universal bank and eight MFIs as SFBs, but will still be around ₹3,500 crore. *The concern of stakeholders and policymakers on high growth needs to be backed by providing sources of patient capital.* Adequate provision of patient capital can temper the growth processes, and avoid the ills of fast paced growth.

The role of banks in fuelling growth is also significant. Bank's debt funding to NBFC-MFIs grew by 86% during 2014–15 touching a high of ₹27,682 crore. Two major issues need action on the side of bankers. First, their lending decisions should not be solely based on financial ratings but strive to use double bottom line rating of microfinance rating agencies. Other mainstream rating agencies should also use this double bottom line rating framework, while assessing MFIs. The distinction between performance parameters of microfinance and mainstream financial intermediation is quite clear, and the assessment framework of MFIs needs to capture that distinction. Developing rating norms for microfinance is one of the stated objectives of MUDRA. It will be a great service to the cause of responsible microfinance if MUDRA can work on moving the sector away from pure financial ratings. Second, the movement of MFIs towards responsible microfinance needs to be supported by banks through incentives like reduction in interest rates. At present, banks do not distinguish between institutions focused on balancing social and financial performance, and institutions driven solely by financial performance. *While the lending decisions of banks depend on financial performance and compliance with guidelines, there is hardly any difference in interest rates charged to different MFIs.* For facilitating responsible microfinance, this needs to change, and banks need to take responsibility.

6.3.1.4 Time to reduce burden of multiple assessments (MFIs)

After 2010, as the microfinance industry has been subjected to a greater degree of regulation, it has also been burdened by the load of multiple assessments and ratings. A typical microfinance institution has to undergo (i) bank loan ratings from RBI accredited rating agencies, (ii) securitisation ratings, in case of securitisation deals, (iii) non-convertible debenture (NCD) ratings, (iv) microfinance institutional rating (MIR) from M-CRIL or microfinance gradings from other raters for institutional performance assessment, (v) social rating in case social investors demand it or if the institution wants to measure its social performance, (vi) CoC assessment and (vii) CPP certification.

These are onerous requirements, and consume both time and resources of MFIs. Further, in absence of public disclosure of various reports, it induces institutions to choose the most favourable assessment, and constrains investors/lenders in their due diligence. A broad typological analysis of these different assessments shows that they fall under two categories—instrument ratings (NCD and securitisation) and institutional assessments. While instrument ratings need to be there as they look at underlying risk of specific instruments/deals, there is an urgent need to harmonise various other assessments/ratings. This issue was covered in *Social Performance Report 2012*, wherein it was suggested that there is an urgent need to collate all narrow focussed assessments under one comprehensive framework like MIR. The comprehensiveness of MIR framework has been discussed in Chapter 3 Section 3.5. Though MIR is a global microfinance rating framework covering both financial and social aspects, it can be made to accommodate country-specific issues like CoC and RBI guidelines. *It is high time that stakeholders work on harmonising various types of institutional rating/assessments to a single offering.* As shown in Chapter 2, different codes have significant overlap and can easily be incorporated in a single assessment. Though some loss of granular information, of narrow focussed assessments like CPP, is bound to be there in an omnibus product, the gains for the sector will be immense.

6.3.1.5 RBI needs to lift the last barrier to product innovation (MFIs)

The first set of RBI guidelines issued for MFIs in December 2011 had two elements, which affected the terms and conditions associated with MFI loans. The loan size was restricted to ₹35,000 in the first cycle and ₹50,000 in the subsequent cycles. Additionally, it stipulated that tenure of the loan should not be less than 24 months for loan amount in excess of ₹15,000. In July 2015, RBI has revised the annual

household income limit for eligible microfinance clients, and hiked the loan ceilings to ₹60,000 and ₹100,000 for the first and subsequent cycles, respectively. It has also reduced the proportion of loans to be used solely for productive purposes to 50%. These are welcome changes, and will allow MFIs to expand their outreach, deepen their credit penetration and meet a wider range of client credit needs. However, the loan tenure restriction has not been changed. *This implies that all loans above ₹15,000 need to have minimum loan tenure of 24 months. While this stipulation did stifle demand-driven loans under earlier set of guidelines, the raising of household income criteria has made it even more obsolete.* The prime rationale of this stipulation seems to be not to burden the clients with higher loan repayments. This was critiqued earlier on the ground that regulation should focus on transparency of communication, and the choice of loan tenure should be left to the borrower. Many urban clients engaged in trade want higher loan sizes but shorter repayment tenure based on their turnover. Similarly, agriculture clients want loans linked to their cropping cycle in place of loan amount. In the absence of an enabling provision under the regulation, to meet the demand of clients, few MFIs have started the practice of offering accelerated payments. It implies that though the loan tenure is of 24 months, nearly 80% of loan is collected in the first year, and the client can take another loan as a top up. With the raising of annual household income limit to ₹1 lakh and ₹1.6 lakh in rural and urban areas, respectively, the concern of repayment burden has also been taken away. RBI needs to consider this aspect, and leave the choice of repayment tenure to the borrower. This will enable product innovations in tune with the cash flow of clients.

6.3.1.6 Convergence between NRLM and SBLP to improve quality of SHG-bank linkage programme

The big issue facing the SHG movement relates to the overlap between NRLM and other SHG programme like NABARD supported SHGs. The basic difference between these two is the concept of federations and interest and capital support under NRLM. Under the NABARD supported SHGs, SHGs are not federated, and bank linkage for savings and credit is devoid of any subsidy. While these are design issues, the more pressing concern is that in the field, new structures are being formed under NRLM in place of strengthening the existing SHGs. Availability of capital support to SHGs covered under NRLM adds to the feeling of being left out for other SHGs. As both programmes envisage working with SHGs, it is imperative that this overlap should result in synergy rather than disruption. SBLP supports SHPAs in nurturing groups and linking them with banks and has experience and history to do this, while as the name suggests, NRLM's strength derives from its focus on strengthening livelihood of SHG members. Financial inclusion is the first step in economic development and its potential can be realised through building livelihood of persons provided financial access. *The national-level policy needs to consider functional specialty of both these programmes and carve distinct roles for them in working with SHGs.* This aspect of working out synergy between NRLM and NABARD supported SHGs needs to be accorded utmost priority. At present, efforts are being duplicated and service delivery is contingent on the type of SHG one belongs to.

If synergy is worked out and SHGs are not only linked with banks but also provided livelihood support and market linkages, it will lead to improvement of SHGs quality and prudent use of loan amount. The dip in portfolio quality being seen now can only be arrested by higher level of capacity building of SHGs and this in turn will lead to increased confidence of banks in funding SHGs. At present, other than southern region, the finance being extended to SHGs is not adequate for productive investments.

6.3.2 Operational issues for MFIs: Going beyond 'no harm' to 'doing good'

Indian MFIs have come a long way since 2010, becoming more client-centric and meeting the long list of norms prescribed by the industry and regulation. Historically, Indian MFIs have the best performance in efficiency, measured by cost per borrower and rates of interest (Table 6.4). These strong metrics have been bolstered by positive changes in governance and client protection post 2010.

However, as discussed in Chapter 2, microfinance institutions have a social mission, and need to move to effective social performance to ensure that they positively impact the lives of clients. The framework of social performance as captured in USSPM and discussed in Chapter 2 has three broad dimensions (Figure 6.2).

The major changes post 2010 have taken place under client protection dimension, as that has

Table 6.4 Cost per microfinance borrower in India and other regions

Country/Region	Cost per Borrower
India	$14
Africa	$146
East Asia and Pacific	$68
Latin America	$239
Global	$89

Source: M-CRIL Microfinance Review 2014.

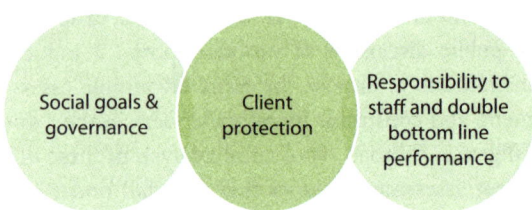

Figure 6.2 Social performance dimensions
Source: Author.

been the thrust of regulation. On the remaining two dimensions, despite some progress, the sector has remained fixated more on meeting compliance- related restrictions. *The tendency to focus on compliance not only impedes full realisation of social performance potential, but also affects progress on other fronts.* For example, unbridled growth in saturated markets leads to debt stress for clients, and erodes the efficacy of compliance with norms on multiple loans and permissible indebtedness. Based on the review of the sector on USSPM framework, quite a few areas emerge requiring action from MFIs. Proactive action on these areas will help the sector be more client-centric and be in a better shape to face the future competition.

6.3.2.1 Social goals and governance: Going beyond good governance

The microfinance sector by and large has adopted good governance practices, and this is reflected in board composition, public disclosure of information, subcommittees of the board and monitoring of regulatory provisions. However, improved governance performance does not extend to social performance. Barring a few institutions, the practice of identifying SMART social goals according to the institutional mission, and incorporating achievement of such goals in business planning has not received the desired attention. Both governance and management structures have a tendency to correlate corporate social responsibility with social goals. Tracking of socio-economic indicators related to client well-being is often not done systematically, and even when done, is not used for designing business strategy.

Considering the developmental mandate of microfinance, it is critical that governance and management structures are sensitised with the core principles of social performance. This will help enlarge the focus from corporate governance to include social governance. This is what distinguishes microfinance institutions from mainstream financial institutions, as its objectives do not end with providing financial access, but extend to making a positive impact in the lives of clients. The sector has to go beyond offering outreach, gender and one-off social initiatives as examples of social performance. In the absence of a systematic approach towards social performance, the efforts of MFIs often do not give corresponding benefits to their clients. For effective social governance, institutions should set social goals related to one's mission and objectives. Identified social goals should be specific, measurable and embody the essence of positive changes the institution seeks to achieve in lives of its clients. Embedding social goals in business practices will ensure that financial services go hand in hand with intended social goals and cover the entire client base. Clarity on this aspect and setting measurable targets will help institutions monitor achievement, as well as report the progress for other stakeholders. Availability of concrete data on social and economic indicators has the potential to reveal whether the desired client-level outcomes are being achieved, and if not, force a rethink of the service delivery model. This needs to come through strategic changes at institutional level, and cannot be induced by external guidelines.

The microfinance sector needs to work on an urgent basis on this aspect, and the role of industry associations is critical in helping institutions achieve this. It is empirically proven that according primacy to achieving and monitoring social outcomes is highly valued by clients, and provides comparative advantage to the institution. Giving importance to social goals will help MFIs retain their competitive edge in a crowded market, as also enable them to achieve their double bottom line mission.

6.3.2.2 Need for product diversity and robust measures to prevent client distress

Learning from the earlier events, and aided by regulation, MFIs have achieved significant progress under transparency in communication with clients, establishing grievance redressal systems and lowering rates of interest. It is not out of place to say that the efforts in this direction have gone beyond the minimum requirements by following best practices. Regulation has played a critical part in ensuring standards under these parameters, and the progress achieved justifies the attention paid to client protection by the regulation. The progress on these aspects has however not extended beyond adhering to external guidelines on the critical aspect of preventing over-indebtedness. Similarly, *the aspirational aspect of offering diversity of products and services suited to client needs has lagged behind—possibly in the rush for growth.*

On the prevention of over-indebtedness, the sector has generally limited its practices to mandatory credit bureau checks, and on following the guidelines on multiple loans and loan size. As delineated in Chapter 3, this approach is fraught with risks, as the credit bureau data, besides not covering all channels, is also not foolproof. The risk is aggravated by the current market strategy of increasing loan portfolio through higher depth rather than expanding outreach. Other than the macro analysis of credit bureau coverage and operational strategy, empirical proof about the inadequacy of current approach comes from recent events of client unrest in several parts of the country. As loan sizes are likely to further go up with recent increase in permissible loan size, *the sector needs to graduate to integrating robust cash flow analysis, and putting in place realistic debt threshold guidelines.* This calls for investment in staff capacity and training, as the skills required to do cash flow analysis, in absence of any formal records with clients, are entirely different from relying on group guarantee as the fall back mechanism. Situations such as overstretched clients, juggling loan instalments beyond their capacity, sooner or later results in events like those seen this year in Madhya Pradesh and Uttar Pradesh. The sector has to demonstrate proactive action on this front, as these events have the possibility of spreading and causing irreparable damage. At the cost of repetition, *it is worth mentioning that credit bureau check and group guarantee can at best be additional cushions, but cannot replace diligent cash flow analysis.*

Closely related to over-indebtedness is the issue of near absence of loan reschedulement policies in the sector. The near zero delinquency rate reported by the sector sits oddly with pockets of saturated markets, multiple loans, increasing loan size, higher repayment amounts with increase in repayment frequency, absence of cash flow analysis, and fluctuating incomes of poor clients. Sector experts have been pointing to this anomaly for long. Interactions with clients and field officers bring out a picture, which differs from the stated policy of not insisting on zero delinquency. The sector cannot afford to ignore this aspect anymore. *Robust cash flow analysis has to be backed with policies for accommodating clients in case of genuine repayment problem.*

Product diversity in the sector has remained limited to individual business loans, emergency loans, WASH loans and micro-housing. Accounting for a low share in loan portfolio reduces the impact of limited scale of innovations. However, the processes have seen a major shift on account of growth and efficiency imperatives. Much of the sector is moving towards fortnightly/monthly repayments to increase productivity, and adoption of technology in disbursement and collection has seen a marked positive shift. However, this traction is not seen on product diversity, and the sector continues to rely on group loans as its growth strategy. As responsive and client centric institutions, MFIs need to offer loan products based on specific livelihoods and its associated cash flow. To do this requires seeking client feedback, designing livelihood-based products, piloting them, and then scaling up. Near absence of such an approach is attributable to the fact that it can slow down growth in the short term. This is the right time to go beyond the standard group loans; profitability is well and truly back, and the recent changes in guidelines, relating to loan size and loan use, have addressed the concerns of the sector. Hopefully, the only remaining regulatory barrier, stipulating loan sizes above ₹15,000 to have two-year repayment period, will be eased soon. In the absence of any noticeable distinction of products between MFIs, there is hardly any comparative advantage for an institution over others. Along with offering diverse products matching needs of clients, *MFIs also need to question whether the shift in repayment frequency has happened because of client needs, or on account of productivity considerations.*

On deposits, while the policy stand is clear in not allowing any institution other than banks to mobilise deposits, it was hoped that allowing NBFC-MFIs to act as banking correspondent will change things. However, NBFC-MFIs have not taken up offering savings services as BC. Though providing deposit services as BC may not be financially attractive for MFIs, it benefits clients immensely by having access to both credit and savings from one provider. The high level of exclusion, and low usage of existing bank accounts by the poor, is primarily on account of absence of regular touch with the service provider. MFIs with their doorstep model are ideally suited to bridge this gap. NGO-MFIs have taken a lead in this area, and provide deposit services as BC to 1.8 million clients as on 31 March 2015.[21] The predominant market share of NBFC-MFIs entails that the majority of microfinance clients do not have access to a unified source of deposit and credit services. Some NBFC-MFIs, besides concerns of financial viability have also reported reluctance of banks to engage NBFC-MFIs as BC. While the issue of financial viability needs to be viewed by MFIs from the perspective of benefit to clients, acceptance of partial cross-subsidisation across other services, dialogue with banks to address their passivity and the reported reluctance towards engagement of NBFC-MFIs has to be taken up by MFIN. Offering holistic inclusion through both deposit and credit services will make NBFC-MFIs more client-centric, and plug the long-standing gap in one legged microfinance in India.

6.3.2.3 Investing in staff and balancing growth

Responsibility to staff particularly field staff needs attention on multiple counts. The sector needs to balance the focus between responsibility to clients and responsibility to staff. It is a cliché to say that institutions need motivated and trained staff to deliver financial service in a responsible manner. Field staff pressured on account of productivity targets or to maintain zero delinquency is more likely to short circuit processes as well as deviate from norms of appropriate behaviour with clients. Microfinance is a field-based activity and no amount of technology can take away the importance of the need to build last mile contact with clients, which can only be achieved by field officers. The trend in the sector shows a few areas of concern; *high staff attrition, field staff remuneration veering towards minimum required under law, increasing productivity and lack of gender balance being the key issues. All these are interlinked issues and feed into a vicious cycle as also have the potential to lead to inappropriate behaviour with clients.* Tough working conditions in field coupled with depressed salary and increasing workload on account of rising productivity lead to higher attrition. Higher attrition causes institutions to spend more on continuous staff recruitment and training and thereby not only increasing the cost but also limiting the scope of increase in wages. *Productivity levels have seen a significant increase, and the sector needs to ponder and evolve benchmarks relative to operational model and area.* The boundaries of productivity measured as clients/ portfolio per loan officer are being overstretched and need to be rationalised. Investment in staff capacity also needs to be stepped up to address the issue of staff attrition as well as meet the challenges of the future. The product diversity being handled by the field staff has increased over last five years and will further increase as MFIs get ready to face competition from SFBs and banks downscaling through BCs. The margin cap limitation is often cited as the limiting factor in increasing remuneration or investing more in capacity building. MFIs need to find creative ways to work around this by looking at possible options like having a look at the possibility of having a less layered but more skilled staff hierarchy in place of the current elaborate staff hierarchical structure or accepting short-term reduction in profitability in pursuit of long-term sustainability.

The cardinal principle of double bottom line microfinance is balancing financial and social objectives and having controlled growth. The sector is back on high growth path and seen with market saturation in certain pockets and recent events of client distress in various parts of the country, it raises questions on controlled and balanced growth. To be responsible, the sector needs to go beyond reliance on credit bureau checks especially in saturated markets, compete on product differentiation rather than offering similar products to same set of clients and expand in underserved areas. The focus on social performance needs to be integrated in core business rather than be limited to compliance with RBI and industry code. Equal focus on social performance will require clear defining of social goals,

monitoring progress on them, product innovations to meet client needs, financial education of clients, investing in staff capacity building and integrating social performance metrics in performance evaluation of staff.

6.4 CONCLUDING NOTES

The report looked at the two main channels catering exclusively to the poor and financially excluded (MFIs and SBLP), and the two emerging institutions MUDRA and SFBs that have the potential of making significant contribution in this sector. Significant progress has been made by both MFIs and SBLP by bringing nearly 100 million clients to the fold of financial inclusion. In the course of their journey of providing financial access, several issues have emerged across both channels, which reduce their effectiveness and client centricity. The policy and operational action points detailed in this chapter have been made with a view to strengthen their client centricity as well as to ensure that they continue to grow sustainably. The suggestions made for future agenda of MUDRA and SFBs are also in the same spirit.

The link between inclusive growth and depth of financial access has been referred to in the first chapter. Faced with rising levels of inequality and the huge gap in financial access in the country, it is critical that the strength of all channels—MFIs, SBLP, Banks, SFBs, BCs—is harnessed to achieve meaningful financial inclusion. Meaningful financial inclusion of the poor and excluded requires financial education, provision of need based financial services efficiently and transparently, keeping clients at the centre of operational design and avoiding chasing of numbers over effective usage of services. It is hoped that action on suggestions made in the report will lead to a more client- centric service delivery system and thereby contribute to the inclusive growth of the country.

NOTES AND REFERENCES

1. https://rbi.org.in/scripts/bs_viewcontent.aspx?Id= 2856 (accessed on 14 October 2015).
2. Committee on Banking Sector Reforms (Chairman: Shri M. Narasimham) 1998.
3. Committee on Financial Sector Reforms (Chairman: Dr Raghuram G. Rajan) 2009.
4. https://www.rbi.org.in/scripts/BS_ViewMasCirculardetails.aspx?id=8194 (accessed on 14 October 2015).

5. Vyas, V.S. 2004. *Report of the Advisory Committee on Flow of Credit to Agriculture and Related Activities.* Mumbai: RBI.

6. https://www.nabard.org/English/rrbs.aspx (accessed on 14 October 2015).

7. RBI classifies loans below ₹200,000 as small borrowal accounts.

8. Planning Commission, Government of India. 2009. *A Hundred Small Steps: Report of the Committee on Financial Sector Reforms.* New Delhi: SAGE Publications.

9. Reserve Bank of India. August 2013. *Banking Structure in India: The Way Forward, Discussion Paper.* https://rbi.org.in/scripts/PublicationReportDetails.aspx?UrlPage=&ID=713 (accessed on 14 October 2015).

10. https://rbi.org.in/Scripts/BS_PressReleaseDisplay.aspx?prid=31646 (accessed on 14 October 2015).

11. https://rbi.org.in/Scripts/BS_PressReleaseDisplay.aspx?prid=32614 (accessed on 14 October 2015).

12. https://rbi.org.in/Scripts/BS_PressReleaseDisplay.aspx?prid=35010 (accessed on 14 October 2015).

13. The upward revision done in July 2015 has still not changed the client profile of MFIs and will happen over time.

14. Per capita expenditure less than ₹32 in rural areas and ₹47 in urban areas.

15. http://www.mudra.org.in/objectives.php (accessed on 14 October 2015).

16. http://www.mudra.org.in/pmmy-report.php (accessed on 14 October 2015).

17. http://pmjdy.gov.in/account-statistics-country.aspx

18. As on 31 March 2014, Source, Banking & Statistical Returns, RBI.

19. NCAER.

20. During 2012–13, ₹107.78 crores were sanctioned under MFDEF. https://www.nabard.org/Publication/AR%202012-13%20E%20fullrr.pdf (accessed on 15 October 2015).

21. Bharat Microfinance Report 2015.

About the Author

Alok Misra is the CEO of Micro-Credit Rating International Limited (M-CRIL), a global microfinance rating agency. He has 23 years of professional experience in rural development, rural finance/microfinance and research at both policy and implementation level. Prior to M-CRIL, he worked with the National Bank for Agriculture and Rural Development (NABARD). He was part of a multi-institutional task force responsible for setting up India's first online commodities exchange. He has undertaken professional work across 22 countries in Asia, Africa, CIS and the Pacific. He is a Fellow in financial inclusion from Tufts University, Massachusetts, and holds a doctorate in Development Studies from Victoria University and a Masters in Development Management from the Asian Institute of Management, Manila.